THE HOUSE IN EAST AND SOUTHEAST ASIA

**Scandinavian Institute of Asian Studies
Monograph Series**

Architecture and Archaeology
No. 12 Sten Nilsson: The New Capitals of India, Pakistan and Bangladesh
   A study in their historical and social setting
No. 46 D. P. Agrawal: The Archaeology of India
   A summary and survey of Indian pre-history

SCANDINAVIAN INSTITUTE OF ASIAN STUDIES
MONOGRAPH SERIES   NO. 30

The House in East and Southeast Asia

Anthropological and Architectural Aspects

Editors
K. G. Izikowitz, P. Sørensen

Curzon Press

Scandinavian Institute of Asian Studies
Kejsergade 2, DK-1155 Copenhagen K

First published 1982
Curzon Press Ltd: London and Malmö

© Scandinavian Institute of Asian Studies 1982

ISBN 0 7007 0104 4
ISSN 0069 1712

Sole distributors in India:
India Book House : Bombay and branches

Printed in Great Britain by
Nene Litho, Earls Barton, Northants
Bound by Weatherby Woolnough, Wellingborough, Northants

CONTENTS

	PAGE
List of Contributors	vii
FOREWORD Per Sørensen	ix
INTRODUCTION K. G. Izikowitz	1
A BRIEF SURVEY OF EAST AND SOUTHEAST ASIAN PREHISTORIC HOUSES Per Sørensen	7
THE FIRST EXCAVATED PREHISTORIC HOUSE SITE IN SOUTHEAST ASIA Merete Aagaard Henriksen	17
THE TRADITION OF CHINESE BUILDING Else Glahn	25
THE HOUSE OF SWIDDEN FARMERS AS A SPECIAL OBJECT FOR ETHNOLOGICAL STUDY Lucien Bernot	35
THE TWO-DOOR HOUSE: THE INTHA EXAMPLE FROM BURMA Lucien Bernot	41
THE LAO HOUSE: VIENTIANE AND LOUANG PRABANG Sophie Charpentier	49
THE SPATIAL ORGANIZATION OF THE LAO HOUSE Pierre Clément	62
THE LAO HOUSE AMONG THE THAI HOUSES: A COMPARATIVE SURVEY AND A PRELIMINARY CLASSIFICATION Pierre Clément	71
TWO HOUSES IN THAILAND Jørgen Rahbek Thomsen	81
A SOCIO-ARCHITECTURAL CASE STUDY IN NORTH THAILAND Hans Haagensen	103
THE INFLUENCE OF THE SPIRIT WORLD ON THE HABITATION OF THE LAO SONG DAM, THAILAND Lise Rishøj Pedersen	115
THE GROUP OF PEOPLE LIVING IN A HOUSE Wil Lundström	129
HABITATION AMONG THE YAKAN, A MUSLIM PEOPLE IN THE SOUTHERN PHILIPPINES Inger Wulff	137
CERTAIN ASPECTS OF HOUSING IN NEPAL Camille Milliet-Mondon	151

HOUSING IN THE UPPER KALI-GANDAKI VALLEY:
ITS ADAPTATION TO THE ENVIRONMENT
Camille Milliet-Mondon 168

THE ORGANIZATION OF SPACE IN A TIBETAN REFUGEE
SETTLEMENT
Claes Corlin 173

THE HOUSE IN MADAGASCAR
Otto Chr. Dahl 181

THE ZAFIMANIRY HOUSE: A WITNESS OF THE TRADITIONAL
HOUSES OF THE HIGHLANDS OF MADAGASCAR
Daniel Coulaud 188

CONTRIBUTORS

Professor, Dr. Lucien Bernot
   Ecole Prâtique des Hautes Etudes, Paris, France

Dr. Sophie Charpentier, Architecte
   Ecole des Hautes Etudes en Sciences Sociales, Paris, France

Dr. Pierre Clément, Architecte
   Ecole des Hautes Etudes en Sciences Sociales, Paris, France

Fil. dr. Claes Corlin
   Institute of Social Anthropology, University of Gothenburg, Sweden

Dr. Daniel Coulaud
   50 Ave. Jean Beaudoin, 45430 Checy, France

Dr. philos, Otto Chr. Dahl
   Rogalandsgaten 1A, N-4000 Stavanger, Norway

Else Glahn, M.A.
   East Asian Institute, University of Aarhus, Denmark

Hans Haagensen, Architect, m.a.a.
   Royal Academy of Fine Arts, Department of Town Planning, Copenhagen, Denmark

Merete Aagaard Henriksen, exam. art.
   East Asian Institute, University of Copenhagen, Denmark

Emeritus Professor, Dr. K. G. Izikowitz
   Erik Dahlbergsgatan 10, S-41126 Gothenburg, Sweden

Fil. dr. Wil Lundström
   Institute of Social Anthropology, University of Gothenburg, Sweden

Mme Camille Milliet-Mondon
   Ecole des Hautes Etudes en Sciences Sociales, Paris, France

Curator Lise Rishøj Pedersen, M.Sc.
   The National Museum, Copenhagen, Denmark

Per Sørensen, M.A.
   Scandinavian Institute of Asian Studies, Copenhagen, Denmark

Jørgen Rahbek Thomsen, Architect, m.a.a.
   School of Architecture, Aarhus, Denmark

Curator Inger Wulff, M.Sc.
   The National Museum, Copenhagen, Denmark

ACKNOWLEDGEMENTS

All drawings and photographs are by the authors concerned,
unless otherwise stated

The final editorial revision of this work was undertaken by
Mr. Frede Højgaard

Foreword

Besides supporting symposia and conferences proposed and organized by other Nordic institutions, the Scandinavian Institute of Asian Studies (SIAS) has itself from time to time organized different kinds of scientific gatherings. The Inaugural Lectures (Readings on Asian Topics. Monograph Series, No. 1), illustrate SIAS' areas of interest, both in time and space, from West to East Asia, from Central Asia to the Indo-Pacific Archipelago, from prehistory to the present — in short, the humanistic and social science fields of research.

This monograph contains most of the papers presented at a colloquium in Gothenburg in 1975 with the theme: The House in East and Southeast Asia—anthropological and architectural aspects. This colloquium was proposed by Professor K. G. Izikowitz while he was still a representative of Sweden on the Governing Board of SIAS, partly because the institute had co-sponsored architectural investigations in North Thailand at its field station in Lampang, and partly because of his co-operation of many years with Professor Elias Cornell of the Chalmers Technical High School, Department of Architecture in Gothenburg, where the students, as a part of their training, were requested to build miniature houses, bridges, etc. from many different places and cultures of the world. It is a great pleasure for SIAS to acknowledge all the help and support given by Professor Izikowitz during the planning, organizing and conducting of the colloquium, and to Professor Cornell for housing, and for putting his department's facilities at our disposal where the visible results of his cooperation with Professor Izikowitz were on view.

Most of the papers presented are based on field research conducted during the last decade. The Himalayan papers bring in a touch of Central Asia, and the 'excursion to Madagascar' once more shows the cultural relations existing between this island and Southeast Asia, but also stresses one of the shortcomings of the colloquium—the lack of information on Ceylon and India. The need for this becomes even more felt as no less than nine of the papers presented are focussed upon mainland Southeast Asia, particularly Burma, Laos and Thailand. It would have been interesting to compare this evidence with that from the western side of the Bay of Bengal since other cultural connections are known to exist between these two areas. However, this meeting was a beginning, a presentation of studies on a topic in an areal frame, a blend of ideas and concepts between anthropologists and architects which was very fruitful. We hope that such efforts may be continued with the inclusion of further aspects, because it is essential to bear in mind that a house is not just a building, but also a home.

Per Sørensen

Introduction

The house is a central part of every society. As a point of departure for many different activities of its residents, it seems to me that the house must be very important to observe and study—not only for itself but in its social context as well. There is plenty of material concerning the habitation in many kinds of field reports and ethnographical works from various parts of the world. Most of this material, however, reports primarily investigations of buildings and the people using them, and until now no real effort has been made to systematize and coordinate all data. At the present state of research it is of course impossible to try a kind of general synthesis. As a beginning we therefore have to concentrate on rather limited areas. Fortunately there have been anthropologists and architects—many of whom are both—who have brought back new material and documents of considerable value. Some come from the Nordic countries and some from France. The Danes and Swedes, for example, have done important field-work in Thailand, Indonesia and Nepal, and the French not only in Nepal but also in Laos, Madagascar and Burma. Some of the French have produced very important monographs on their research of which the biggest part is as yet unpublished but available as mimeographed manuscripts.[1]

For this reason the Scandinavian Institute of Asian Studies (SIAS) brought this small group together for a colloquium, which was held in Gothenburg June 11-13, 1975, so that its members could discuss their different materials and consolidate them. I sincerely hope that such meetings will continue not only with those present at this colloquium, but with new members interested in these questions, and that in a not too distant future it will be possible to make a kind of inventory for at least the regions involved. We are very grateful indeed to SIAS for the interest in and support for this small meeting.

Fortunately all papers but one given in Gothenburg are included in this book. Maybe this approach can be continued, not only with material from Southeast Asia, but from other parts of the world as well. The material of course should not be limited to houses and buildings, but should include information on the villages, towns or other kinds of settlements as a whole. The excellent drawings of the Danish architects and their maps of some villages in Nepal already provide a good starting point.[2]

At the end of the last century some human geographers were interested in a comparative study of different village forms. I am afraid that nobody has seriously pursued this worthwhile idea further.

Many years ago when doing field-work in Laos I became interested in questions about houses. I then tried to make as exact drawings as possible of the buildings I saw in the Lamet villages, but I am afraid they were not good enough. This kind of research is more complicated than can easily be imagined, because there are so many different social factors involved.

Later on Professor Elias Cornell at the Department of Architecture of the Chalmers' Technical Institute in Gothenburg started a model-building project which served as an introduction to the architecture curriculum. He then asked me to try to look out for good material in the museums and in the literature, good drawings and pictures which could be used by the students when building their models. At that time I happened to be a director of the Ethnographical Museum in Gothenburg, and as I had an excellent library at my disposal and good contacts with different museums, I thought it would be very easy to find some good material. I must confess, however, that it was a hard job to find appropriate drawings and pictures which could be used by the students. Anyhow, due to great efforts over several years the result can now be seen in the Chalmers' Technical Institute in its excellent model room which gives the students a good idea about buildings from many countries and from different epochs. This collection was of course a marvellous basis for the colloquium, and as a matter of course the Department of Architecture was used for the meeting.

Most of the contributions to this colloquium deal with dwelling-houses, and we can consider them to be a kind of artificial interface or perhaps better a physical envelope around the group living in the house. We thus have to do with this envelope on the one hand and with the dwelling group on the other.

The envelope-house has some sort of structure and is built of material found in the neighbourhood. The framework is mostly made of a solid material and it must be resistant to the climate and to attacks of insects, as for example ants. This framework is the most important part to manufacture, and when a new house must be built or the village must be moved, the old material is used insofar as possible for the framework. For the walls and the floor split bamboo may be excellent because, if it is not too tightly plaited, it is easy to clean. In pile buildings in particular cleaning is easy: the dust is simply swept down between the bamboo strips. In some regions stamped earth is used for the floor, and the walls are sometimes made of wooden planks. In Madagascar the houses are mostly made of wood and so constructed that they can easily be dismantled and thus moved. The roofs of such houses are usually made of various kinds of leaves or grass. In Nepal, on the other hand, different kinds of materials are used, such as stone slabs.

Before a house can be built it must be planned according to certain principles which vary in different societies but which are based on an old tradition. Even if the bamboo walls are later replaced, for example by wooden planks and the roof materials by corrugated tin, the old plan is retained.[3]

In most of the papers presented to the colloquium the plans of the different houses are dealt with in some detail. They show, whatever their differences, that there is always some special kind of arrangement where the bunks and sleeping places are to be found and where the kitchen and the hearth are situated. In some cases, as among the Lao, there may be a special house for the stove and often this part is joined to the dwelling. There are different sections for men and women and a special space used by guests. There may be different entrances for men and women and even for the living people in contrast to the dead who have to leave the house through a special opening. The stores are sometimes placed inside the house, sometimes outside, e.g. in a separate building or granary in the outskirts of the village, so that the rice may be protected against fire in case the village should burn. Among the Thai the rice receptacles must be situated at a higher level than the living space of the ordinary people in order to show respect for the rice spirit or goddess.[4]

There are many important things in a house plan, and even if we know the principles of different kinds of arrangements, I think we could go much further in trying to comprehend these principles. To be able to do that we have to investigate their connections with the society concerned. The whole plan and the use and form of different details of a house very often have to do with special beliefs and norms. In some of the papers presented mention is made of the fact that some of the pillars and poles of the framework or some corners inside the house are very sacred. That is why a stranger cannot move about freely. Everything is regulated by rule and etiquette, and most things have their special place.

The erection of a new house is often associated with certain rites and ceremonies. An important thing is to find the right place for a house. Its position has to do with the 'ritual topography' and the beliefs about this. One must pay respect to the different spirits in the place and these spirits must be able to pass freely or else they may cause misfortune to befall the family involved. Lise Rishøj Pedersen gives us an excellent example of this among the Lao Song Dam in southern Thailand.[5] It reminds me of the practice of geomantics in China. In order to find the proper place for a new building one has to ask a person or a specialist who knows the abode of the spirits and the rituals appropriate to them. Generally the house is built by the ordinary members of the society, but in the case of China which used to have a highly organized bureaucracy the construction activity was managed by experts. There were bureaucrats and professional people who had the right knowledge about how to build a house. Here we find documents and books about this matter dating a long way back in history. Else Glahn describes this in a very interesting way,[6] and everybody must admire the very intricate construction of the Chinese roof. I have seen a similar construction in North Vietnam, and there is no doubt that they have learned it from the Chinese.

The house is not a purely technical or physical object, but made by human beings for human beings. Unfortunately the human beings are often forgotten in this connection. The social context is always important to consider. The form of the dwelling cannot be understood only by a consideration of the technique and the material used. It is first of all necessary to be aware of how the principles of the local group are applied, and which kinds of work are performed by this group, and in which roles. And only when we have acquired this knowledge will it be possible to understand the form of this envelope surrounding the group and how it is planned.

Mostly this group is called a household, but during recent years scholars have begun to be sceptical about the use of this concept,[7] and personally I prefer to call it a dwelling group. In every case it is necessary to mention which individuals are included in this group and what their mutual relationships are. According to which principles have they been recruited? In most cases we have to do with some kind of kinship group. This seems to be the case in the limited geographical area treated here. In this case we have, however, to differentiate the dwelling group from such other groups as, for example, age-groups found among the Naga where the bachelors live in the men's house, something seen in other ethnic groups as well. Among the Buddhists the young men often live for some time in the monastery. Some old men remain there for the rest of their lives. In some societies, the bachelors start travelling or migrating to distant places for some time in order to get a job. In olden times the reason was head-hunting. Sometimes they will be absent from their villages for years.

As I said, it is necessary to consider the kind of production of the group. Those cultivating rice in swiddens and even other agriculturalists stay during the cultivation and especially at harvest time in special huts in the fields, these being often located far from the village and in need of protection against wild animals.

As some members of the group are often absent for a long time due to wanderings or for some other reason, the house or the dwelling group remains a station or meeting place with a relatively permanent character, a place to which these members always return. This is a fixed point, and I am sure that even nomadic people have such places, one or several, between which they oscillate.

In her paper about the house-group in Minahassa, Celebes,[8] Wil Lundström analyses the group itself and its rights and duties. She includes a description of the role which the guest must play in order to gain acceptance, and of the rules governing the part of the house in which he can stay. The right to the hearth seems to be very essential. It is of course not always possible to admit guests into the house as, according to Bernot,[9] it is neither a guest house nor a place for work. Many peoples have a special house for the guests and in the Lao villages there is often a *sala*— mostly a meeting place for Buddhistic preaching—which is used as a guest house. The non-Buddhistic Black Tai in upper Tonkin receive the guests on the covered veranda, situated at one of the gables of the bigger house. How to behave as a guest in a dwelling house demands knowledge of the norms and rules. Sophie Charpentier mentions that the Lao houses have a special scheme for the movements in the house, like some kind of 'choreography'. Those who have visited Japan know perhaps how important it is for a visitor to know the etiquette of the movements when introduced in a house. It is very formal indeed. Unfortunately such things are far too little studied; they have undoubtedly some connection not only with the customs in general but also with the beliefs and the cosmology of the society concerned.

In a way a house may be considered as a microcosm, where every part of the building has its meaning and can be regarded as a symbol of something; this is what Corlin does in his paper.[10] Some of these symbols have to do with the social position and status of the owner, and this can even be expressed in the entire form and size of the structure, and in the decoration. Other symbols refer to the beliefs of the members, regarding, for example, ancestor worship or similar things. Part of the house must always be ritually purified. Many of the papers presented stress this point of view, and Dahl especially mentions that the house among the Zafimaniry of Madagascar can be considered as an astrological calendar.

In this connection I can recommend two papers outside this colloquium which from a methodological point of view seem to be very useful and elucidating. First, there is the interesting paper by Pierre Bourdieu about the Berber house in Morocco, which provides an excellent model for the carrying out of symbol analyses. It was first published in the *Melanges* for Levi-Strauss and later on translated into English and republished in Mary Douglas' *Rules and Meanings*.[11] Secondly, there is a similar study about the Thai in north-east Thailand by S. J. Tambiah in the same volume. Both refer to symbol analyses of the houses. I sincerely hope that there will be more such studies.

INTRODUCTION

Nowadays there is a rapid social change going on in most countries. How does this influence the form and use of the houses? Is there a tendency to keep the traditional style while using new materials? Several of the papers of this colloquium indicate that this is so. Beside the ordinary dwellings, there will be new kinds of structure in the towns, buildings for which the use is outside the traditional life in these societies. Here new problems come up for the architects and for those who are going to plan the houses. How much of the old style is it necessary to preserve? In any case these new structures must be adapted to the new society and to the new way of life. I suppose that there are many such problems to be solved by the architects, whether they are born in the country or come from places outside it. It might be that some anthropologists who have been working on architecture and are trained to analyse different societies will be able to help.

In this little book we have tried to describe the ordinary residences that are more or less a part of the micro-society. Until now these aspects have been observed and investigated very inadequately. In general it seems that the more conspicuous public buildings such as temples, monasteries, and palaces have been the objects for research because they tend to be more ornate and perhaps from the aesthetic point of view are more striking. They belong, however, to the macro-society, and it has not been our intention to treat this type of buildings here. In this connection I will only remark that many of these public buildings use the same traditional principles and constructions as do the ordinary houses, even if their framework is translated into stone or some other kind of time-resisting material. To limit oneself only to the study of objects which are aesthetically attractive must be dangerous. In order to understand the public buildings I am sure that we must in most cases return to the ordinary dwelling-houses. It is in the villages that we can find the tradition in a purer form, and it is here that we can learn something about the thoughts, ways and ideas of the builders. It is a mistake to sneer at simple structures.

I must repeat that all the varied activities and roles of the members of the dwelling group are projected in the house. And thus a study of the ordinary house gives us the key to an understanding of many of the important aspects of a given society. Therefore it would be very appropriate to undertake a field study to investigate the different houses in a society along with the dwelling groups which use them as a permanent base, in order to increase the understanding of the society as a whole.

This little colloquium may be considered as a starting point for future investigations. I am convinced that just as kinship analysis or research concerning the economic life or any other single aspect of a given society can give us some valuable information about how the society is functioning and expressing itself, so can the study of the house.

In the long run it is of course not enough to limit ourselves to the part of Asia treated here. Later on we must include other regions of the world in order to establish a basis for comparative studies. At some point in the future we could perhaps discover the principles which constitute the basis for all this variation. If this beginning can stimulate a continuation of the research into the principles of architecture, I believe that this will be a great advancement.

K. G. Izikowitz

Notes and references

1. Charpentier, Sophie et Clément, Pierre, *L'habitation Lao—dans les régions de Vientiane et de Louang-Prabang.* Tome I-II. 1974-75. Mimeographed.
2. Landsby i Nepal (Village in Nepal). *Arkitekten*, no.5, 1969. (By a group of Danish architects in collaboration with Werner Jacobsen.)
3. See e.g. Lucien Bernot's paper, p.35.
4. Lene Rishøj Pedersen's paper, p.128.
5. Ibid., pp.115 ff.
6. Else Glahn's paper, pp.25 ff.
7. See Wil Lunström's paper, p.129 ff.
8. Ibid.
9. Lucien Bernot's paper, p.35 ff.
10. pp.173 ff.
11. P. Bourdieu, The Berber House, p.98 ff. S. J. Tambiah, Classification of animals in Thailand. p.127 (both in Mary Douglas, ed., *Rules and Meanings. The Anthropology of Everyday Knowledge.* Penguin Education. Harmondsworth 1973).

A Brief Survey of East and Southeast Asian Prehistoric Houses

Per Sørensen

The Igloo is a very good example of man's ability to adapt himself to prevailing climatic conditions. Similarly, the Yurt easily packed and moved along, reflects a type of housing highly specialized and extremely well suited to the subsistence and way of living of a certain population. Other examples may well be found to illustrate man's way of housing in relation to factors such as ecology, economic or social background or acquired social level and position. However, both globally and locally examples may be found, which seem to be contrary to all logic or in direct contradiction to the above-mentioned examples.

One such case is that of the house of the Lao Song Dam people, described below by Lise Rishøj Pedersen. The Lao Song Dam, ultimately to be traced to North Vietnam, were moved about 200 years ago from the Vientiane region in Laos and resettled in Peninsular Thailand. Throughout the many years they have maintained their traditional house type, which is built on piles and has rounded gables and a steep heavy thatched roof reaching to the floor. Such a construction is well suited indeed for climates cooler than those prevailing around the Gulf of Thailand, and it is not surprising that it is also found to exist, for example, in Nagaland, as pointed out by Merete Aagaard Henriksen in the following paper. The Lao Song Dam themselves admit that these houses are actually too warm to live in, and yet they are now only reluctantly giving up the building and use of them "due to lack of the special kind of grass required for thatching". However, it seems more likely that for reasons of group identification, ancestor worship or other religious practices this conservative group retains a less functional but traditional house type. This example is put at the beginning of the present brief survey of East and Southeast Asian prehistoric houses, partly because it brings into focus some of the problems with which we are faced when it comes to interpretation of the scanty and unevenly distributed material at our disposal, namely the role of traditionalism, partly because of the discovery of a prehistoric house ground in the same area apparently of a house of similar type.[1] The latter immediately raises the following problems:
a) Did cooler climatic conditions exist in the area at the time of settling (estimated at 1300-1100 B.C.)?
b) Does the presence of this specific kind of house within a cultural context, clearly pointing to a relationship to the Ban Kao culture,[2] express a physical and cultural relationship to the Thai tribes culture in general?

The problem is fascinating, but cannot be solved right away.

Our knowledge of prehistoric houses from East and Southeast Asia is based on two sources of information:
a) Evidence from observations during the process of excavation (of both regular house or hut foundations). This may be found in the form of discolourings of the soil, either such regular ones as those caused by rotted poles, or the deep discolourings of a more extensive area. The latter develops particularly where the ground under a house with an elevated living floor is kept wet from water dripping regularly

from above, or a combination of the two as exemplified by the Nong Chae Sao house ground.

b) Pictures of houses. These may be either sculptured in the round as the house on one of the drums from Shih-chai-shan, Yünnan,[3] or models of houses to serve some purpose, as the small bronze coffin from Ta-p'o-na, Yünnan,[4] or the funerary house models from the Han Dynasty, not to forget the Haniwa models from Japan, both of which are made of clay. However, the pictures may be incised or engraved on objects of metal (bronze) or clay[5] as well, thus adding to the list of information in general. But from a prehistoric point of view the latter are chronologically so late that they cannot be taken into consideration within the scope of this paper.

While foundations of houses or huts of different kinds elsewhere in the world are now known from sporadic evidence, at least from Mid-Palaeolithic times (400,000 years ago at Terra Amata in South France), none have been discovered so far from the region to be dealt with here. So Early Palaeolithic evidence from North Thailand points to man's living in the open,[6] perhaps protected from sun and rain by a kind of simple shelter or wind-screen, while the Chou-k'ou-tien evidence points to settlement in caves during cool and arid climates as well as during periods of more humid warm climates.[7]

Habitations in caves and rock-shelters have probably also been motivated by annual or climatic migratory cycles of the game to be hunted, and have thus resulted in periodic changes in the place of settling. However, as far as Southeast Asia is concerned, the natural environment may then, as now, have offered, in addition, a wide selection of edible wild plants and berries, and probably also a sufficient number of shellfish and fresh-water fish in the rivers to allow a semi-permanent subsistence and habitation pattern to develop. This may have ultimately given rise to some kind of horticulture, the prehistoric evidence of which has perhaps been discovered, although proof of full domestication of wild plants yet remains to be indisputably established.[8] However, at this time, the Palaeolithic had already come to an end, and the Mesolithic/Epi-Palaeolithic cultures like the so-called Hoabinhian are found to have existed in Southeast Asia, with evidence of habitation both in caves and in the open.[9] So for Southeast Asia, as for East Asia, the settling in proper houses or huts arranged in villages is chronologically a late phenomenon compared to the time span of man in general, appearing after 10,000 B.C., and generally first with the advent of the more sedentary way of life associated with semi or full farming.

In China the earliest farming society remains the so-called Yang Shao culture in the 'nuclear' area around the Huang Ho. Here at the Pan P'o site near Sian in Shensi a whole Neolithic village has been found and excavated.[10] The finds seem to represent the oldest phase of the culture so far recorded, recently C-14 dated to the fifth millenium B.C.[11] At the site, remains of 47 houses representing five different types were excavated.[12] Fortunately, sufficient details were preserved to allow fairly reliable reconstructions of the houses. Stratigraphical evidence points to their falling in two different periods, 22 from the earliest period and 24 and a 'long house' to the later period. The 'long house' was approximately 20 m by 12.5 m, oriented N–S and divided into compartments by partition walls. The other houses are rather similar in both periods, either square and approximately 15 m^2 or circular with a diameter of 5–6 m. They are all semi-subterranean, in the early period generally with a shallow circular fireplace and a smooth floor, while those of the second period tend to be oblong with a deep circular to gourd-shaped fireplace. Walls are low and of wattle-and-daub. The roof is supported by wooden poles which rest upon a flat stone, a feature to become so typical of later Chinese architecture. The upper structure of the houses is often tent-like, a feature perhaps reminiscent of a former, less sedentary life style. The subterranean element points towards an origin in cooler climatic areas, or at least suggests an influence from local climatic conditions. This supposition actually gets some support from the pollen diagrams, as the presence of certain grasses indicates a somewhat cool and dry climate. On the other hand this is peculiar, as the scanty evidence from elsewhere in Asia and the fauna points to hypsothermal climatic conditions following the glaciations of the Late Pleistocene.[13] The cool and dry climate may, of course, have been a local phenomenon caused by the deforestation of the area by the early farmers, but anyway it was not much different from that prevailing in the area nowadays.

The Yang Shao culture undergoes a chrono-cultural development as exemplified in the Miao-ti-K'ou I to II stages,[14] into the Lungshan culture as seen in the nearby San-li-ch'iao site I-II. During the Miao-ti-K'ou phase II, the culture spreads to various parts of China, and there—adapting to local ecological possibilities—develops local groups which, in turn, further develop into local Lungshanoid groups.[15]. How does this affect the house types?

Within the 'nuclear' area itself, the semi-subterranean square or round houses and the 'communal' long houses recur at many sites together. The same holds good within the Shensi Lungshan, for example, at K'o-hsing-chuang, as well as the Honan Lungshan, where round houses at Hou-kang have the floors plastered with white limy clay. At other places it has been observed with increasing frequency that floors and/or walls were hardened by fire. And at the 'classical' Lungshan culture site of Ch'eng-tzu-yai in Shantung the village is fortified by a wall made in Hang-t'u technique: layers of earth compacted by a stick, usually used in connection with wall building and for platforms of houses to be raised over the surrounding ground, e.g. the palaces at Anyang.[16] In Chekiang, south of Yangtze Kiang, the Liangchu culture—another local Lungshan group—has the houses built on flat ground. They are usually square to rectangular, 4 by 4 m or 4 by 5m, most likely with a gabled roof over the wattle-and-daub walls, but in mountainous Yünnan further south semi-subterranean houses were excavated on the slopes of the Tien-tsang mountain. Many other examples can be found without any fixed pattern of housing. Yet one thing remains clear: the use of semi-subterranean houses appears to be a very strong and probably age-old traditional element which moves along with the culture even into areas where it appears out of ecological, environmental or climatic context. At the same time, we can observe construction elements like Hang-t'u foundations for big houses, and the base stones for wooden pillars and poles, the fire-hardened floor and the white-washing of walls to enter, develop and to remain as basics in Chinese traditional architecture. Several of these details may be seen already on pictures incised on bronzes dating from the late Chou dynasty.[17]

When we turn from China towards Japan, it is interesting to obsserve how many similarities to China actually exist despite the cultural differences. Here huts are

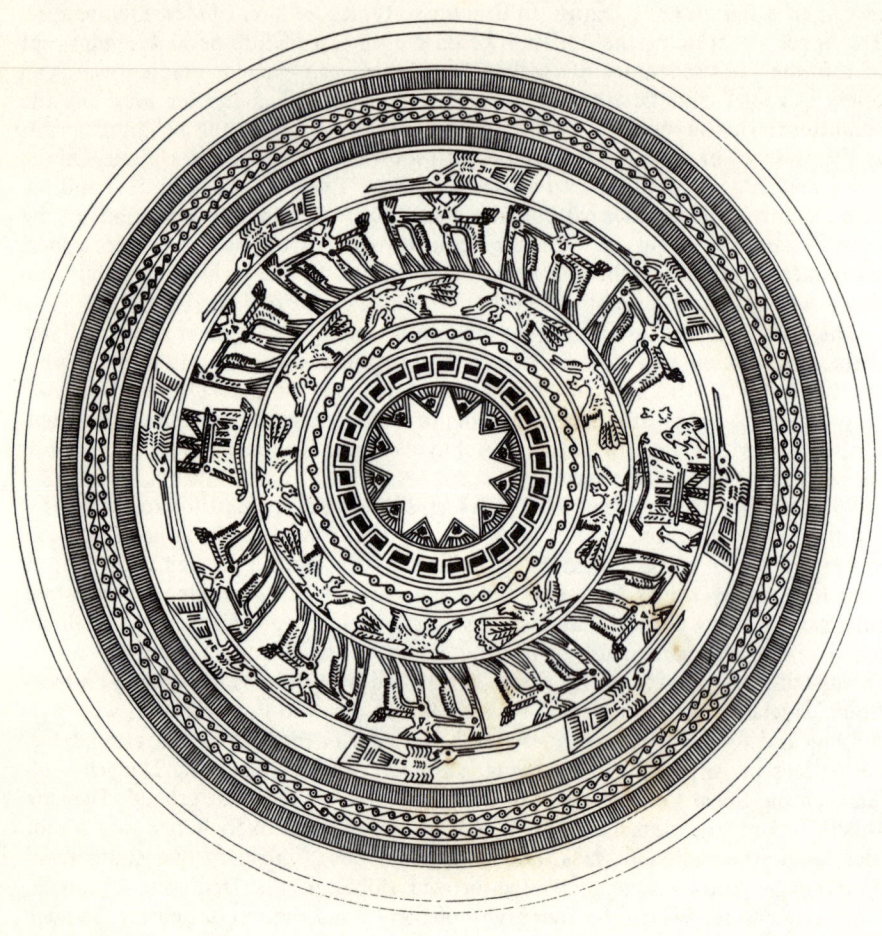

Fig. 1 Tympanon of drum OB 89, from the Ongbah Cave, Kanchanaburi Province, Thailand, now in the National Museum, Bangkok. Note the position of the two 'Indonesian-Style Houses'.

PREHISTORIC HOUSES

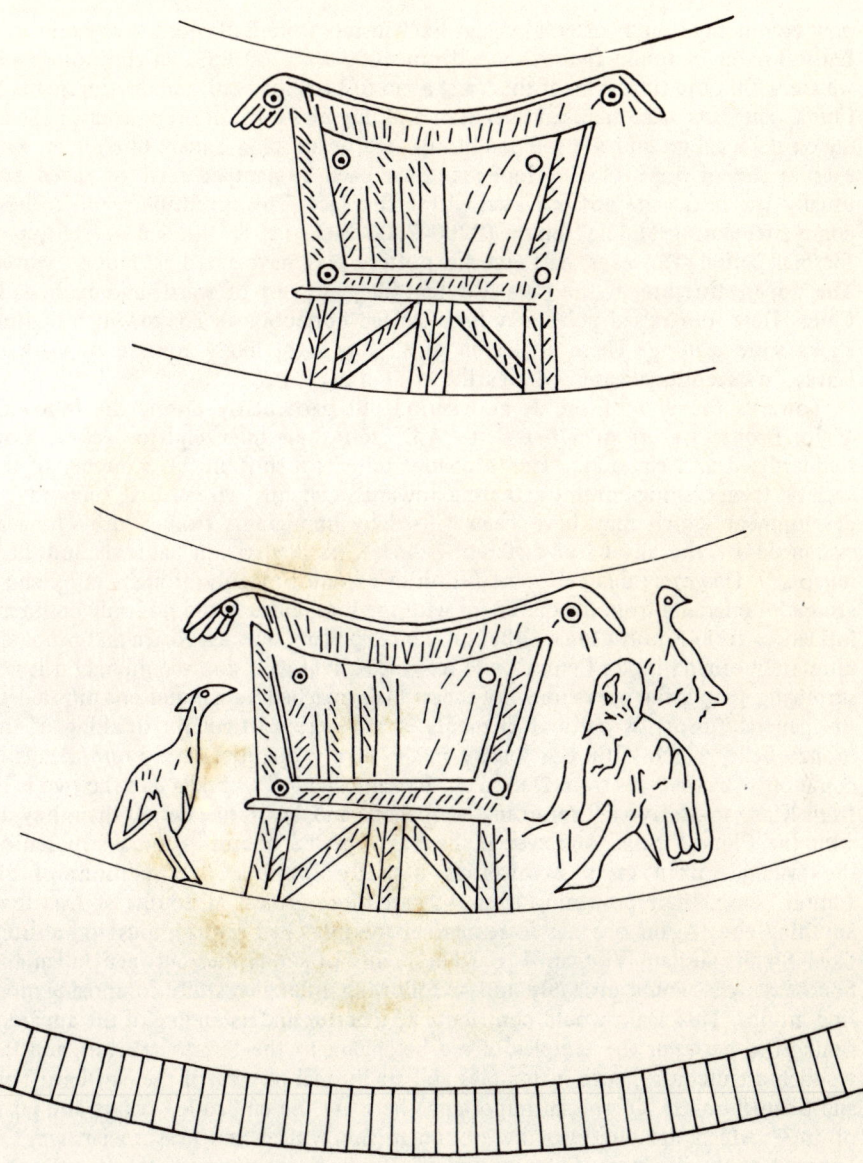

Fig. 2 Drawings based on rubbings of the 'Indonesian-Style Houses' depicted on the Ongbah Cave drum. The slanting lines between the posts of the house probably are the ladders leading up to the living floor.

now commonly found—often in village-like clusters from Early Jomon and onwards. Early Jomon in round figures dates from 5000 to 2200 B.C., so chronologically we are within the time span of the Yang Shao to Lungshan cultural developments in China. The huts—also semi-subterranean and dug down to different levels, depending on the local ground and soil conditions—are, as in China, square or circular, with a usual size of 5 m².[18] The floor may have been of stamped earth or paved, but usually the huts were not provided with a fireplace. This invention seems to have come first during Middle Jomon (2200-2000 B.C.) i.e. at the end of the hypsothermal period. However, earthenware pottery may have acted as 'indoor' stoves. The upper structure of the huts was tent-like, but not of wattle-and-daub, as in China. Here four raised poles may have carried horizontal beams to which slanting sticks were leaning. These sticks, in turn, were most likely covered by bark or leaves—in exceptional cases, with earth.

Towards the end of the Jomon Period but particularly during the following Yayoi Bronze Age from 570 B.C. to A.D. 260, these huts tend to become more standardized and elaborate. This probably reflects a shift in the economy of the society from fishing-hunting-gathering towards a mainly agricultural economy, a development which may have been caused by immigrants from South China as evidenced by the advent of different bronzes, particularly in halberds and TLV mirrors.[19] However, this period of fusion of stimuli probably brought in by small groups of migrants from the continent with the local culture, did not only comprise influences from South China. Other influences passing through Korea and probably ultimately originating in Central Asia may be seen as well, and accordingly it is not surprising that influences from Southeast Asia reached Japan and contributed to the general fusion of cultural elements. I am here particularly thinking of the bronze bells, which—although locally made—in my opinion share more details in common with the bells from Dong-s'on, Battambang in Cambodia and the two bells from Klang in Malaysia[20] regarding both shape and decorative details than they do with the Chinese bells. And even if the Yayoi period houses—as reconstructed on the evidence from many excavations—basically continue the traditions of the Jomon house, their projecting roof ends are more typical of Southeast Asia than anything else. Again one has to remember the modelled bronze house on a drum from Shih-chai-shan, Yünnan.[21] Further points of similarities between Japan and Southeast Asia would probably appear following a detailed study comprising more find groups. This again would contribute to a better understanding of the apparent similarities between the temples of Ise belonging to the Shinto religion, and the wooden architecture, both in temples and traditional houses, of the Northern Thai and Shan/Burmese. Of special importance here are the embedded pillars and posts of Ise[22] which are dug into the ground in the typical Southeast Asian way, as opposed to the distinctly Chinese way of placing the posts on a base stone. Doubtless, we are confronted here with details of a fundamental nature and importance, the still obscure parts of which remain to be discovered.

The only prehistoric houses from mainland Southeast Asia are those reported on in the following paper by Merete Aagaard Henriksen and by O. Janse, who mentions poles from a house in Dong-s'on.[23] Postholes from rotted posts have been also reported from an excavation in Northeast Thailand, but the number was insufficient for a reconstruction.

Fig. 3 Original photo of the house depicted on the Ongbah drum. This kind of drum belongs to the Dong-s'on culture and on Ongbah evidence dates from the period of the fifth to the third century B.C.

From insular Southeast Asia, W. Peterson has recently reported the discovery of two rectangular houses excavated at the Dimolit site, a coastal dune in Palanan Bay, Isabela Province in the Philippines.[24] These houses differ from recent ones in that the floor was not raised above the ground, and may perhaps, on C-14 evidence, be dated to about 1400 B.C. This is all the stranger, as no houses depicted on the bronze kettledrums of the Heger type I—and quite a few are known—are shown on the ground. They are all 'pile-dwellings'. Two different types can be distinguished: the 'mainland type' and the 'Indonesian type'. The 'mainland type' is, for example, represented on the drums from Hoang Ha, Tonkin.[25] They have a sacking saddle-shaped roof with projecting ends supported by poles all down to the floor. In many respects that house type resembles that of the Lao Song Dam, although the latter has a convex roof line. The 'Indonesian type' according to Heine-Geldern, also has a sacking saddle-shaped roof, but has only short unsupported projecting ends. This is the type of house mostly depicted on kettledrums from Indonesia, and a house type still very much in use in the islands. What is peculiar is that none of the drums were ever cast in Indonesia. However, the same type of house was recently discovered on drums from the Ongbah cave in Kanchanaburi in West Central Thailand (figs. 1-3). From this and other evidence the existence of a prehistoric metal-working and trade centre has been hypothesized.[26] Therefore, the possibility cannot be excluded that this type of house is originally derived from the mainland type, even though it is now specific for insular Southeast Asia. And were the 'early centres' of mainland Southeast Asia capable of diffusing ideas of houses and transporting big and heavy kettledrums from the mainland to the Island World penetrating far into New Guinea,[27] then they have most likely also been able to impart impulses to Japan. Certain linguistic evidence is said to support this connection. It should be interesting to see if this evidence is, for example, restricted to the area of the main distribution stream of the bronze bells from Hiroshima on the Inland Sea to Omaezaki Point in Suruga Bay. At least, it is within this area that we also find the Ise temple which, as mentioned above, shows clear Southeast Asian affinities.

However brief this survey of the prehistoric houses may appear it is hoped that it can contribute to the argument that many basic features—both in construction and in adaption to environment—owe their origin to prehistoric man; and further, that house follows man into new and even unfit environments. A recent example of this can be seen in the changed building habits in Southeast Asia in connection with the foreign impact, particularly during the period of the Vietnam War.

Notes and references

1. For details see Merete Aagaard Henriksen's following paper.
2. P. Sørensen, *Archaeological, Excavations in Thailand*. Vol. II. Ban Kao. Copenhagen 1967. P. Sørensen, The Neolithic Cultures of Thailand (and North Malaysia) and Their Lungshanoid Relationship (in *Early Chinese Art and its Possible Influences in the Pacific Basin*. Intercultural Arts Press, Vol. II, 1972, pp.459–507).
3. Yünnan Chinning Shih-chai-shan ku mu ch'ün fa-chüeh pao. Peking Wen Wu Press 1959, Pl.52.
4. *Kaogu*, 1964:12, pp.607–14.
5. *Kaogu hsüeh pao* 1957:1, p.109. See also: W. Watson, *China before the Han Dynasty*. Thames and Hudson, 1961, p.125, fig. 30 which shows a house engraved on a bronze bowl from Chao-ku Hui Hsien, Honan. Both examples date from the Late Chou/Warring States period.
6. P. Sørensen, Preliminary Note on the relative and absolute chronology of two Early Palaeolithic sites from North Thailand (in *Le paleolithique inferieur et moyen en Inde, en Asie Centrale, en Chine et dans le Sud-est Asiatique*. Nice 1976, pp.237–52).
7. Chang, K. C., *The Archaeology of Ancient China*. Yale University Press, New Haven 1968, p.42.
8. Gorman, C. F., Excavations at Spirit Cave, North Thailand. Some Interim Interpretations. *Asian Perspectives*, Vol.13, 1970, pp.79–107.
9. P. Sørensen, *Archaeological Excavations in Thailand*, Vol.II, 1967, pp.8–10. See also H. R. van Heekeren and Count Eigil Knuth, *Archaeological Excavations in Thailand*, Vol.I. Sai-Yok. Copenhagen 1967.
10. The Neolithic Village at Pan P'o, Sian. Institute of Archaeology, Academia Sinica and The Pan P'o Museum. Wen Wu Press, Peking 1963, English abstract pp.306–320 and fig. 10, p.10 to fig. 33, p.33 and IV to XIX.
11. Barnard, N., *The First Radiocarbon Dates from China*. Monographs on Far Eastern History, No. 8, Dept. of Far Eastern History, Research School of Pacific Studies, Australian National University, Canberra 1972. See also Chang,

K. C., Radiocarbon Dates from China: Some Initial Interpretations. *Current Anthropology*, 1973, Vol. 14, No. 5, pp.525-529.

The actual dates given for Pan P'o are:
ZK –   38 = 4115 ± 110 B.C. Bristlecone corrected to 4784 ± 134 B.C.
ZK – 121 = 3955 ± 105 B.C. Bristlecone corrected to 4826 ± 130 B.C.
ZK – 122 = 3890 ± 105 B.C. Bristlecone corrected to 4564 ± 130 B.C.
ZK – 127 = 3635 ± 105 B.C. Bristlecone corrected to 4305 ± 200 B.C.

12. Chang, K. C., *Archaeology of Ancient China*, 1968, pp.97-100.
13. Chang, op. cit., p.34, Note 28 and p.96, Table 4.
14. An Chih-min et al., *Miao-ti-k'ou and San-li-chi'ao*. Wen Wu Press, Peking 1959 Miao-ti-k'ou II (Early Lungshan culture) was C-14 dated:
ZK – 111 = 2.310 ± 95 B.C. Bristlecone corrected to 2.796 ± 141 B.C.
15. Chang, op. cit., p.121. The Ban Kao Culture in Thailand is also regarded as one such Lungshanoid group outside China. This interpretation has been questioned by American archaeologists mainly, but recent C-14 dates from China, as well as the continued research into the material relics of this culture, are still favourably supporting the Lungshanoid relationship of the Ban Kao Culture.
16. Good examples of Hang-t'u techniques may be seen in Chang, op. cit., p.217, fig. 79, and use of it on p.218, fig. 80 with base stones, the further reconstruction of which may be seen on p.220, fig. 81.
17. See note 5.
18. J. Edward Kidder, *Japan before Buddhism*. Thames & Hudson 1959, p.42, fig. 3 and pl.34-35. Vadime Elisseeff, *The Ancient Civilisation of Japan*. Nagel 1974, p.106 and plates 16-17.
19. Elisseeff, op. cit., p.29.
20. Compare Emma C. Bunker, The Tien Culture, *Early Chinese Art and its Possible Influence in the Pacific Basin*. Vol. II, 1972, p.315, fig. 15 A, B and J. Loewenstein, The Origin of the Malayan Metal Age, *Journal of the Malayan Branch of the Royal Asiatic Society*, Vol. 29.2, 1962, p.38, fig. 22, and plates 3 to 5 with Kidder, op. cit., pl.48 to 51. It is here particulary noteworthy that one bell from Kagawa has twelve panels with reliefs, one of which is a typical Southeast Asian house on piles, referred to as a "raised storehouse" (Kidder, op. cit., pl.52, with text p.269) and Y. Watanabe, Shinto Art: Ise and Izumo Shrines. *Heibonsha Survey of Japanese Art*, Vol. 3, 1974, p.105, which also on fig. 86 shows a sherd with a similar house incised on a potsherd from Karako, Nara Prefecture. Although such store houses exist in Japan, (Watanabe, op. cit., fig. 93-96) they do not appear to be common. Besides, it seems even more incredible that architecturally important details should be transferred from such "worldly" purposes to serve in the most sacred of all temples at Ise. I therefore propose that further research into the origin of Ise should be directed more towards traditional mainland Southeast Asian houses than towards "store houses from Sumatra" (Watanabe, op. cit., fig. 93). This gets further support when the ridge support—as found in Mikeden, Geku, Ise (Watanabe, op. cit., fig. 101)—is considered. The ridge pole reaches the ground and is embedded into the ground as it is on pictures of houses incised on bronze kettledrums from the S.E.A. mainland as distinct from those of the Southeast Asian islands (P. Sørensen, The Ongbah Cave and Its Fifth Drum. In *Early South East Asia*, ed. R. B. Smith and W. Watson, Oxford University Press, 1979, pp.78-97).
21. Emma C. Bunker, op. cit., p.300, fig. 6.
22. Watanabe, op. cit., p.53, fig. 36.

23. Janse, O., *Archaeological Research in Indo-China,* Vol. III, 1958, pp.28-32.
24. Peterson, W., Summary Report of Two Archaeological Sites from North-Eastern Luzon. *Archaeology & Physical Anthropology in Oceania,* Vol. IX. 1, 1974, pp.31-32. Hutterer in An Evolutionary Approach to the Southeast Asian Cultural Sequence, *Current Anthropology,* Vol. 17, No. 2, 1967, p.223, notes the unusual feature of the house on the ground, but this was recently disputed by Jules de Raedt in *Current Anthropology,* Vol. 18, No. 2, 1977, p.331, who claims the contrary that living on the ground was not unknown.
25. R. Heine-Geldern, The Drum Named Makalamau. *India Antiqua* 1947, pp.167-176, and pl.XIII, a, d & e.
26. P. Sørensen, The Ongbah Cave and Its Fifth Drum. In *Early South East Asia. Essays in Archaeology, History and Historical Geography*. Edited by R. B. Smith and W. Watson. Oxford University Press. 1979, pp.78-97.
27. J.-E. Elmberg, Further Notes on the Northern Mejbrats (Vogelkop, Western New Guinea). *Ethnos,* 1959: 12, p.73, fig. 1 and p.75, fig. 2.

The First Excavated Prehistoric House Site in Southeast Asia

Merete Aagaard Henriksen

About 30 km west of Radburi in Radburi Province, on the road to Chombung, there is a track to the south leading to the village of Nong Chae Sao. Here in 1962 a farmer wanted to construct a new charcoal kiln. While digging he found two skeletons and some pottery, adzes and beads. The finds were reported to the governor and sent to Bangkok for further investigation. They turned out to be related to the neolithic Ban Kao culture previously known in the Kanchanaburi Province.

During the excavation campaign of the '2nd Thai-Danish Prehistoric Expedition 1965-66' three months were spent in Nong Chae Sao. The reason why the expedition decided to excavate here was to throw further light on the relationship to the Ban Kao culture as the Nong Chae Sao finds appear to be of a younger phase, and the surroundings are different from the site of Ban Kao. Ban Kao is situated on the foreland of river Kwae Noi and a tributary, while the site of Nong Chae Sao originally seems to have been an island in a lake.

The excavation squares were at first put up as close to the charcoal kiln as possible without disturbing it. In this way the excavation went on for a while during the dry season, and finally it was decided to give it up as nothing really appeared. Then suddenly the weather changed, the so-called 'mango-showers' came, and in the wet earth an entirely new picture was seen. There was a very marked difference in the colour of the ground surrounding the kiln, so it became necessary to have it removed in order to find out whether this change of colour was caused by the kiln or not. Now an ellipse appeared, in which the kiln was not centrally placed, so the colour change within the ellipse could not have been caused by the kiln.

The further investigations concentrated on the question as to whether or not the ellipse could be the site of a prehistoric house. If it was a house site, there had to be postholes. However, the technique developed for excavating postholes in Denmark could not be applied to Thai conditions for several reasons. For instance, in Thailand a hole for a post is dug just big enough for the post, whereas in Denmark a pit will be dug into which the post is put, and the hole is then filled up again with soil. Because of the humid tropical climate the putrefactive process is much faster and more powerful than is usual in Europe. Another problem again is termites. Once they have started eating away the timber, dry rot gets easy access too. In excavating the 'supposed postholes' care must be taken not to confuse them with animal passages and tree roots by excavating them in sections. Six holes were found, four of them arranged in a rectangle and the remaining two placed at each end of the long axis. When 10 cm of the soil covering the whole of the site was removed, the six postholes were still there contrary to the animal passages and tree roots (fig. 1).

During the continued excavation a group consisting of four pots and two adzes (fig. 2) were found within the house site, having most likely been placed on the original surface under the house, while the two skeletons had been buried half a metre under the house.

To the north around the posthole in the long axis a collection of charcoal was

Fig. 1 (a) One of the six postholes found during the excavation. The diameter is c.40 cm. (b) Modern post in the process of rotting (see text p.17). It was found near the site.

found. Whether this is the remains of an open fireplace cannot be determined (fig. 3).

On a slope a little to the south of the house site some almost disintegrated potsherds were found together with fragments of adzes and grindstones. The potsherds were water-worn, and the adze and grindstone fragments were also marked by water. A few fragments of shell implements appeared to originate from freshwater mussels. This supports the idea about a house on an island. The complete assemblage of pots, sherds and fragments of stone implements are, without doubt, recognized as Ban Kao culture.[1]

Finding such a house site and postholes always leads to the question of what the house actually looked like. The present reconstruction (fig. 4) has emerged through studies of present day Thai village houses, the majority of which are built on poles. The space under the house is often used as a stable for the cattle, as the place for the woman's loom, or as a fireplace. No matter what this space has been used for, there is one thing that all houses have in common: the ground is usually muddy. This may be due to water dripping from the dwelling platform, to the presence of pigs, dogs and chickens, or more directly to the rainy season.

Considering all these things it is most likely that what we have found is the remains of a house built on poles with a living platform and an oval thatched roof. The difference in the colour of the ground would not have been so marked if the dwelling had been directly on the ground.

As already mentioned this is the first excavated neolithic house site in Southeast Asia, but other neolithic house sites are known in East Asia. In China on the Pan P'o site in Shensi Province rounded as well as square houses on the ground or slightly dug down are known. They belong to the Yang Shao culture. In a later phase of the same culture there are houses with rounded gables. This feature is again found in the following Lungshan period, out of which the Ban Kao culture in Thailand develops. The Ban Kao culture is dated by means of C-14 to have lasted from 1800 B.C. to 1300 B.C.[2]

The way of living for present day Thai farmers does not differ very much from that of neolithic farmers. Accordingly, the question can be asked whether any similar house types are known today. The answer is in the affirmative.

Some 150 years ago a group of Black Thais (Lao Song Dam) were transferred by the military from the area around Vientiane in Laos to the region between the towns of Radburi and Petchaburi at the base of the Malay peninsula. The descendants of these people still live in houses on poles with roofs thatched with a special type of grass. The roofs have rounded gables at each end. In 1966 the oldest remaining house was 130 years old, and the only renewal made had been the changing of the roof every third year (fig. 5). Also in this type of house the space under the house was used as a stable, and storage place for the woman's loom and for the big rice container made of wicker work plastered with mud. This population group still sticks to the old traditions as already described in the Chinese annals from the second century B.C.[3] These people have not totally avoided influence from the surrounding Siamese population as some houses have a rounded gable at one end—and only one end—of the house.

According to the ethnological literature on Southeast Asia houses on poles and

Fig. 2 Remnants of the group of four pots found in the south-eastern corner of the house, here shown *in situ*. They are placed on top of pillars of earth, the surrounding soil having been removed. The front pot is type 15 and the one behind it is type 6, according to Per Sørensen's typology published in *Archaeological Excavations in Thailand*, Vol. II: Ban Kao, Copenhagen 1967. In the lower right-hand corner one of the adzes may be seen sticking out from under the pot. The tent peg indicates the location of the south-eastern posthole (see also fig. 3).

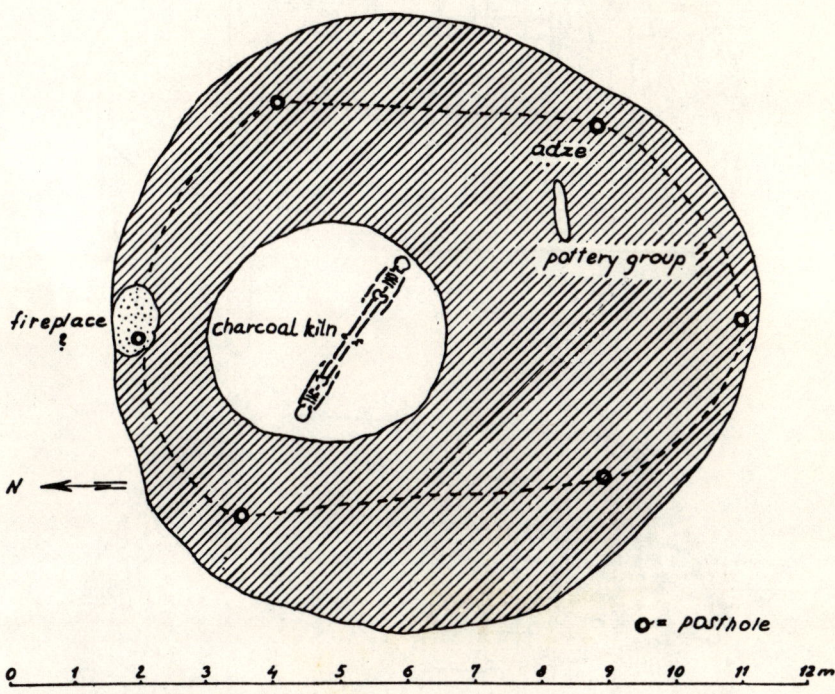

Fig. 3 Map showing the size of the 'colour-changed' ground and the location of the postholes. The roof of the house probably was slightly smaller than the 'colour-changed' ground, i.e., about 9.5 m long. The dwelling platform was only about 4.5 by 5.5 m.

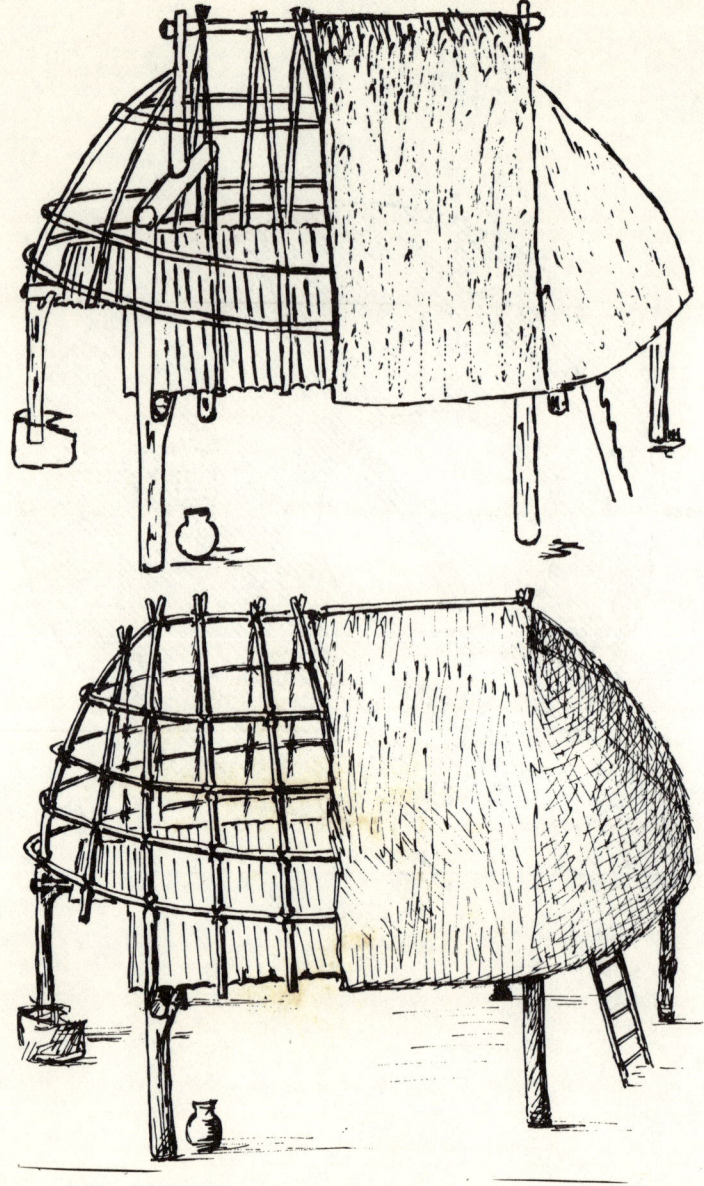

Fig. 4 The proposed reconstructions of the house at Nong Chae Sao. The total length including the rounded gables was probably about 9.5 m.

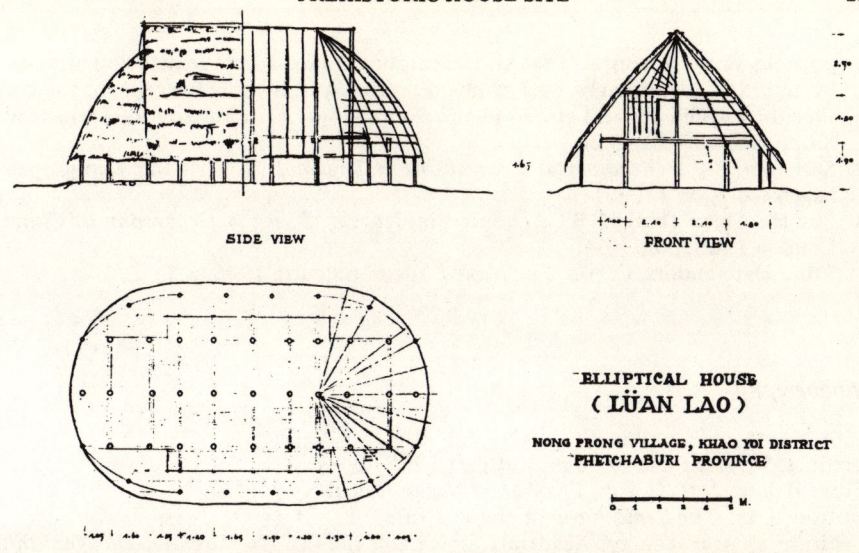

Fig. 5 Plan and section of the 130-year-old house near Petchaburi. (Courtesy of Arphon Na-Songkhla, The National Museum, Bangkok.)

with rounded gables are known in the Shan States. Here this particular type of house is simply called the 'Shan-house', and in the descriptions it is compared to a tortoise shell or described as 'the house with the egg-shaped roof on poles'. It is also said that the house forms a rectangle with ray-like rafts at each end to be compared to half an umbrella frame. The building materials and the size of the house all depend on the builder's economic position. A less well-off person will build a house totally of bamboo with six supporting poles in the rectangular dwelling part of the house. Usually the house is 4.25 m wide and 8.75 m long, the two rounded gables included. The entrance is always at the gable and is reached by means of a ladder.

The Nagas in the western part of the Shan States have also adopted this type of house. Fürer-Haimendorf writes about these: "Entering the Naga hills one leaves behind the twentieth century and is surrounded by people who follow the mode of life not essentially different from the style in which some five thousand years ago neolithic man lived in Southwest China, Indo-China and probably also in a good many parts of India."[4]

The Nong Chae Sao finds seem to confirm this statement and may perhaps support the opinion that there is a cultural relationship between the neolithic Ban Kao culture and certain groups of the present Thai population.

Notes and references

1. Unfortunately, all this evidence in the form of all the excavated finds has been destroyed. Everything was transported to the National Museum in Bangkok to be stored, but in 1970 it appeared that rain had penetrated the roof during the

previous rainy season, so that all the cardboard boxes were soaked and attacked by termites. Accordingly, everything excavated was discarded except for the two skeletons which are still stored in the Sood Sangvichien Museum of Prehistory, Siriraj Hospital, Bangkok.
2. Sørensen, P., *Archaeological Excavations in Thailand.* Vol. II: Ban Kao. Copenhagen 1967, pp.110-111.
3. Ssu Ma Chien (b. 145 B.C.), quoted in Tregear, T. R., *A Geography of China,* London 1966, pp.63-64.
4. Fürer-Haimendorf, C. von, *The Naked Nagas.* Calcutta 1946, p.3.

Bibliography

Credner, W., *Das Land der Tai.* Stuttgart 1935.
Fürer-Haimendorf, C. von, *The Naked Nagas.* Calcutta 1946.
Hutton, J. H., *The Sema Nagas.* London 1921.
Institute of Archaeology, Academia Sinica and the Pan P'o Museum, *The Neolithic Village at Pan P'o, Sian.* Peking 1963.
Janse, O., *Archaeological Research in Indo-China,* Vol. III, 1958.
Mills, J. P., *The Lhota Nagas.* London 1922.
Milne, L., *Shans at Home.* London 1910.
Scherman, L., Wohnhaustypen in Birma und Assam. *Archiv für Anthropologie.* Band 42, Neue Folge XIV, 1915.
Sørensen, P., *Archaeological Excavations in Thailand.* Vol. II: Ban Kao. Copenhagen, 1967.
Tregear, T. R., *A Geography of China.* London 1966.

The Tradition of Chinese Building

Else Glahn

The traditional Chinese house is raised on a platform of stone and covered by a curved roof with long, projected eaves. The roof is carried by wooden pillars, and the weight of the roof is transferred to the pillars by sets of wooden brackets, which form a collar around the building between the pillars and the roof (fig. 1).

The building is rectangular with the long sides to the north and the south. To the north, east, and west the spaces between the pillars are filled out by light walls, while to the south some of them are fitted with doors and windows. The walls are made of sun-dried bricks and covered by plaster. They are vulnerable to the climate, to sun and rain, and in order to protect them the eaves of the roof are stretched far out. The outer part of the bracket set carries the eaves while the inner part carries the roof. The roof is curved by letting the rafters span only from one purlin to the next in an increasingly wide angle between rafter and crossbeam from eave to ridge. The purlins are supported by struts which stand on the crossbeam below.

Timber being the most important material carpentry achieved the level of true craftsmanship at an early age. The craftsmen's skills were handed down from master to apprentice. The characteristics of Chinese buildings were not created as a conscious, artistic style. They developed gradually in accordance with the natural qualities of timber and in step with the increasing skill of the carpenters. The designing of a building was not an art but a craft. There were no architects, only supervising officials and craftsmen. For public buildings craftsmen were employed by the government. Court and government buildings were erected by such drafted labour, and the work was supervised by officials in the Board of Construction under the Ministry of Works. In the highly bureaucratic state building operations were strictly organized and rationalized, as can be seen from the two building manuals edited by the Board of Construction.

The first manual, the *yingzao fashi*, was printed in 1103. Its author, Li Jie, was at that time Vice-Director in the Board of Construction and supervisor of the work of government buildings in the capital, Kaifeng. Later he was responsible for the building of palaces for the Emperor Huizong. He was a gifted and learned man, and when he compiled the work, he 'researched into the classics, histories and many other books, and at the same time he questioned craftsmen who explained everything', as stated in his introduction. The manual is well organized; it describes preliminary calculations, foundations, carpentry, joinery, manufacture of bricks, tiles, and paints, etc. It continues with calculation of labour service and materials and ends with drawings of constructions, of various types of buildings, and of decorations. In the section about carpentry first the use of standard dimensions is described, and then the basic rules are given for the construction of each detail of a building.

The other manual, the *gongbu gongcheng zuofa zeli*, was published in 1734. It is far more bulky and not as well organized as the *yingzao fashi*. In the first twenty-seven chapters carpentry rules for twenty-seven different sizes of buildings are given,

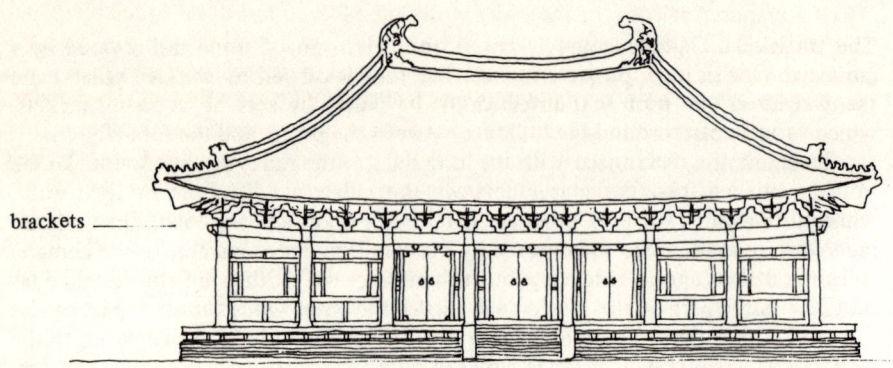

Front of building from the 10th century

Front of building from the 18th century

Fig. 1

measures for each structural member of each building, though the traditional use of standard dimensions is uninterrupted. Definition, placing, and carving of each member are not clearly described, and no drawings are included.

The study of the history and development of Chinese architecture began when in 1919 a manuscript copy of the older work, the *yingzao fashi*, was found. The printed edition of 1103 had disappeared before 1500, but a few manuscript copies had survived. One of these manuscripts was reproduced in photolithography, but it was soon realized that both text and drawings had suffered badly through transmission. Readers were puzzled to see that constructions in the drawings were different from those known in the Imperial Palace in Peking. Chinese tradition was at that time still regarded as unchangeable and unchanged. A new edition of the manual was carefully prepared, different manuscripts being compared in an attempt to reconstitute the original text. The drawings were rather unintelligible, and therefore a master-carpenter from the Imperial Palace reconstructed them and added colours to the decorations. The result was published as a very beautiful book in 1925.

Inspired by this publication a group of scholars founded the Society for Research in Chinese Architecture in Peking in 1930 and began to publish a bulletin. The enthusiastic and learned member of the society Liang Sicheng described and measured old Chinese buildings and published his results in the bulletin. Members of the society studied the two manuals, but they were very difficult to read, partly because most of the characters for technical denominations are only found in these books. Further, each of them uses different denominations for the same structural members. The study group then consulted the old craftsmen from the Imperial Palace, and with the later manual as a textbook and the craftsmen as teachers they gradually obtained an insight into building methods from the eighteenth century. Through Liang Sicheng's and his colleagues' work on buildings of the period from the ninth to the twelfth century knowledge of the early architecture spread, and gradually it became possible to understand important parts of the *yingzao fashi*.

No government buildings or palaces from that time exist today, but in remote places temples are still left. Research members of the society travelled around and made reports. Through temple chronicles it was possible to know when a temple building was erected and when and to what extent it was repaired. The research was interrupted by the wars, but has been taken up again in the years after 1950, which have seen so many archaeological activities. Recent results are published in archaeological periodicals, but the extensive notes of Liang Sicheng, who died a few years ago, are still unknown. Although much work remains to be done, it is now possible to see the outline of the Chinese architectural tradition. We also have some idea of the changes which this tradition has undergone through the ages.

Two facts are common to the two manuals, the use of standard dimensions of timber and the attention paid to the bracket sets. The bracket arm was taken as the standard dimension; the measure of its cross-section is the starting point for the measure of every single structural member of the whole building.

In the early manual it is written: 'All rules for constructing houses have the standard dimension as their base . . . The height and depth of the eaves of each house, the size of each nameable structural member, the force of the bent and the straight of each curve of the roof, accordance with the measuring instruments of the carpenter: the pair of compasses, the square, the plumb-line and the ink string, in every case the units of standard dimension constitute the rule.'[1]

According to the *yingzao fashi* there are eight grades of standard dimensions, used for different sizes of buildings. In all standard dimensions the depth is subdivided into 15 units and the width into 10 units. Thus the size of the unit varies with the size of the standard. The biggest dimension is 9 by 6 inches, and consequently the unit is 0.6 inches. This size is used for the biggest buildings with ten to twelve pillars in the front, the long side. The next grades are gradually smaller until the last, the eighth, which is 4.5 by 3 inches with a unit of 0.3 inches. This dimension is used for small pavillions with complicated brackets.

On top of the standard dimension can be placed a rectangular piece of wood, the so-called wedge, the height of which is 6 units, or the same size as the free space between two tiers of bracket arms (fig. 2). When a wedge is added the dimension is called 'full standard', 21:10 units. Without the wedge it is called 'single standard'.

In the early manual the measures of each structural member is given in units, the subdivision of standard or one tenth the width of the bracket arm. In this way the description of a structural member is relevant to any size of a building, big or small, as the size of the unit varies with the grade of the standard. In the later manual the cross-section of the bracket arm is again used as standard dimension. The ratio of the height to the width is 2:1, almost the same as the earlier full standard, 21:10. The single standard of the later manual is 1.4:1. In early buildings most members were based on single standard, while later full standard was used more widely.

Both manuals pay the same attention to the bracket sets. The description of them takes up as much space as the combined description of all the other carpentry members, pillars, beams, purlins, rafters, etc. A bracket set consists of different sorts of structural members (fig. 3). A square piece of wood called a *dou* constitutes the base for the curved horizontal arm called a *gong*. An arm is supported under the centre and stretches out to both sides. It carries, like a yoke, weight at each end, where other bases can be placed, each carrying other arms or boards (fig. 3).

A long straight piece of single standard is the so-called *ang*, an important member which rests on a base in the centre of the bracket set above the head of the pillar. One end goes down in an oblique line beyond the bracket arms and carries the eave; the other end goes up in the roof where it supports a purlin. It acts as a lever arm (fig. 3).

The upper tiers of bases carry long horizontal boards, *fang*, which connect the bracket sets. In the uppermost tier a small horizontal member protrudes at right angles to the front. It is called *shua tou*, or head.

In the *yingzao fashi* are described four kinds of bracket bases. All of them supports other members: arms, levers, boards, etc. But as their positions are different, so are their sizes, forms, and names. The biggest base, called *lü dou*, is placed on top of a pillar or on the lintel at the bottom of the bracket set. It carries the heaviest weight and is cut in a cross to receive two mortised arms (fig. 2). It is 20 units deep and 32 units wide and long. The height is divided into three parts, the ratio of which is 8:4:8. The upper part has a mortise 8 units deep and 10 units wide, the width of the arm. The middle part, the body, is 4 units high and the lower part, curved to fill the pillar head, is 8 units high. The other bases are only 10 units

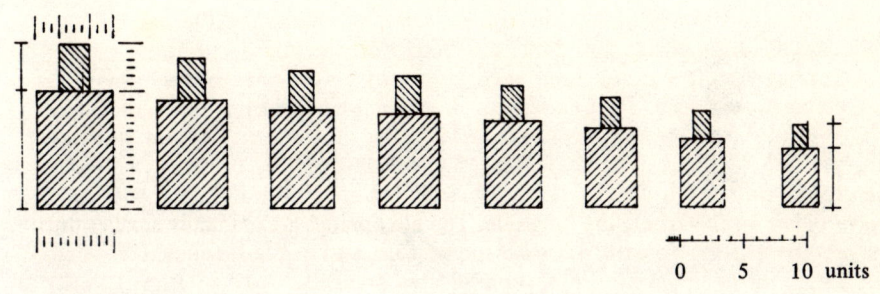

standard dimensions 1103

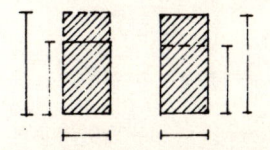

standard dimensions 1734

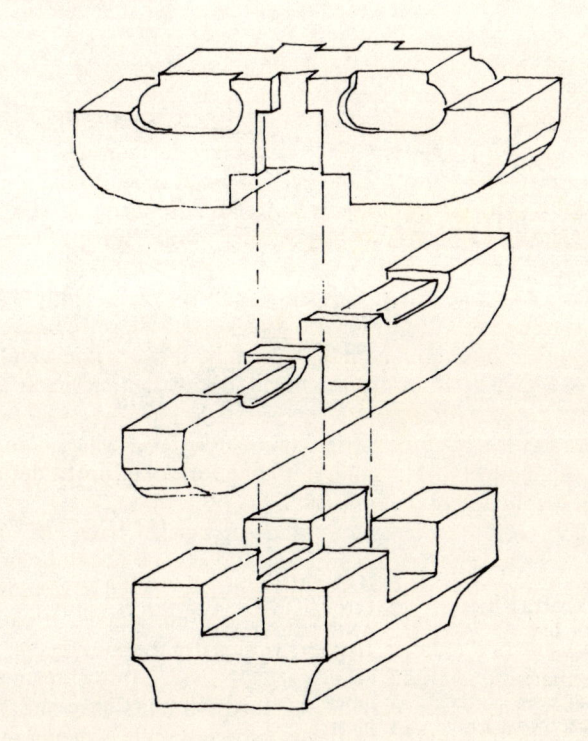

flower arm

wall arm

big base

0 5 10 units

Fig. 2

single standard
full standard

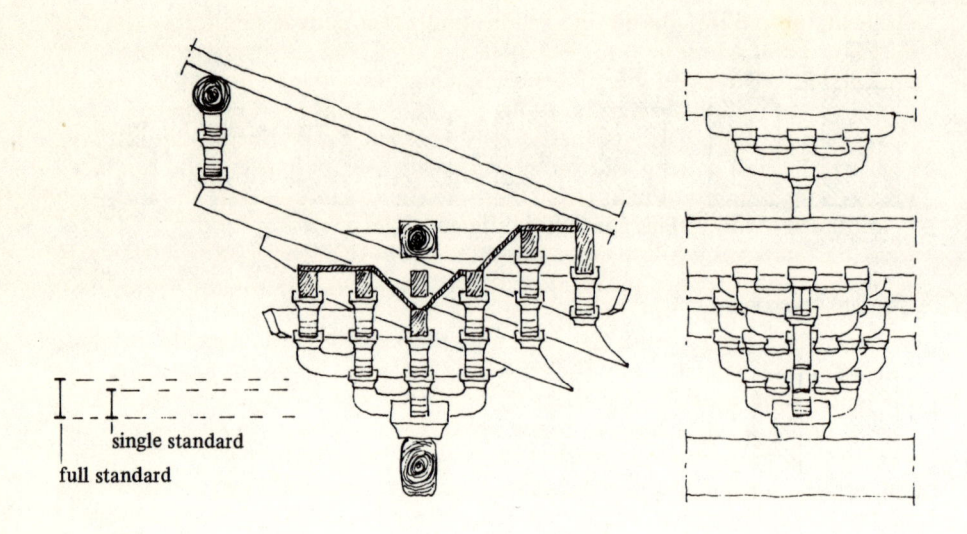

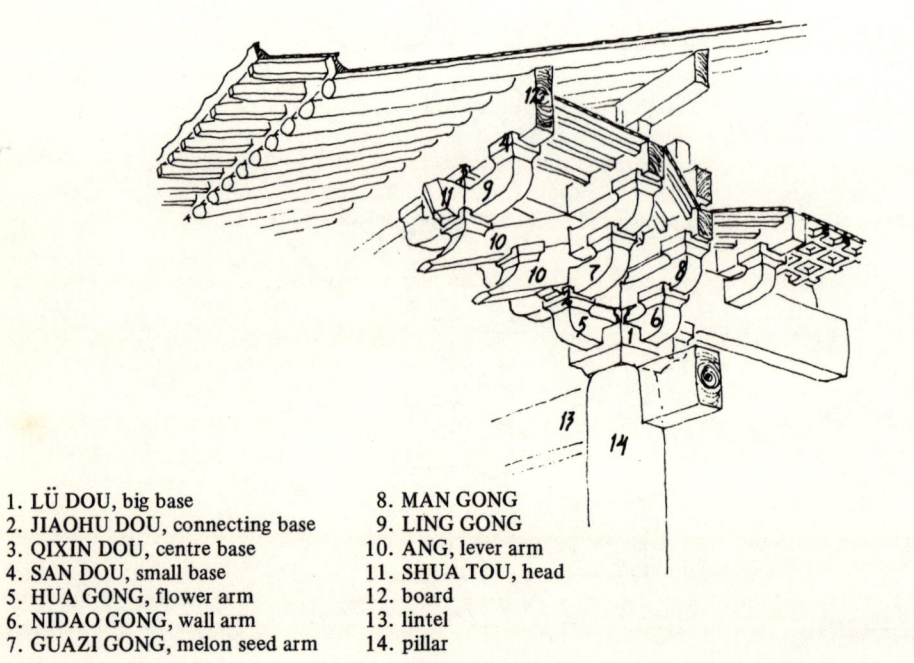

1. LÜ DOU, big base
2. JIAOHU DOU, connecting base
3. QIXIN DOU, centre base
4. SAN DOU, small base
5. HUA GONG, flower arm
6. NIDAO GONG, wall arm
7. GUAZI GONG, melon seed arm
8. MAN GONG
9. LING GONG
10. ANG, lever arm
11. SHUA TOU, head
12. board
13. lintel
14. pillar

Fig. 3

high, but the ratio of the upper, middle, and lower parts is still 4:2:4. The base placed on top of a lever or at the end of an arm stretching out at a right angle to the buildings, is called *jiaohu dou*, or connection base. Its top is 18 by 18 units (fig. 3). On top of the centre of an arm carrying the centre of an arm above is a base called *qixin dou*, or centre base; its top is 16 by 16 units. Finally there is the *san dou*, small base, placed at each end of an arm parallel to the building and carrying a board. Its top is 16 by 14 units (fig. 3).

In the same work details about five different types of arms are also given. One of these, the *hua gong*, or flower arm, stretches out at right angles to the building. In the bottom tier it rests in the big base. It is 72 units long. In the upper part of each side two 'eyes' are cut out 4 units down the sides (fig. 2). A flower arm is usually based on full standard, while the other arms are based on single standard. In case it is based on full standard, only the centre and the 'eyes' are 6 units higher and their top touches the under-side of the arm in the tier above. The under-side and the sides of the centre are cut out to be mortised with the *nidao gong*, or wall arm. This is also placed in the big base, flush with the wall and at right angles to the flower arm. It is 62 units long and always based on single standard. In its centre is cut a mortise, 10 units deep, in order to join this arm with the flower arm. A third sort of arm, parallel to the wall and stretching to each side on top of the end of the flower arm or the lever, is the *guazi gong*, or melon seed arm, which is 62 units long and rests in a connection base (fig. 3). Further, there is the *man gong* in the tier above the melon seed arm and the wall arm. It is the longest of the arms, 92 units long. It rests in a centre base (fig. 3). Finally, there is the uppermost arm, the *ling gong*, 72 units long, which at the centre carries a centre base and at each end a small base. The three bases carry a horizontal board.

The number of members in a bracket set varies. A set can consist of a single arm or a single lever with the corresponding transverse arms, or it can be very complex with two flower arms and three levers with all the corresponding transverse arms and bases. Their sizes are counted in tiers from one up to five. The complexity depends on the placing of the set. The biggest ones are those on top of the pillars in the front of a building. The sets on the lintel between the pillars are smaller, and the smallest are placed inside a building where they carry a beam in the roof construction.

There are four sorts of bracket sets: the pillar sets on top of each pillar, the corner sets on top of the pillars at each corner of a building, the bay sets on the lintel between each pillar, and finally, the balcony sets which carry a balcony. On murals and paintings from the time before about 1300 some buildings are placed on a series of balcony bracket sets instead of a platform. No such constructions exist today.

Several details in the traditional Chinese building constructions have changed in the course of time, but the main principles of the frame construction are the same. Roofs of big buildings are curved, a western-type principal is never seen. The purlins carry the rafters, which only go from one purlin to the next. Before about 1400 each purlin was supported by oblique struts resting on the crossbeam below, while after this time the supporting struts became vertical.

The brackets have changed even more through the centuries. The earliest have

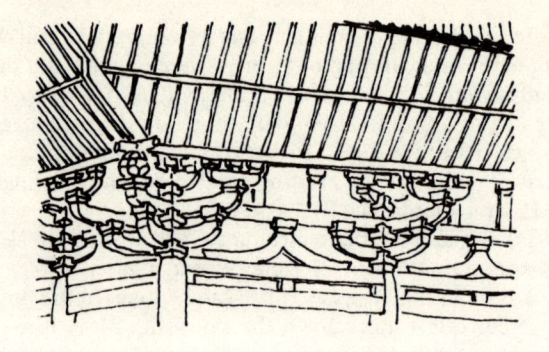

RENZI GONG, bay bracket 701

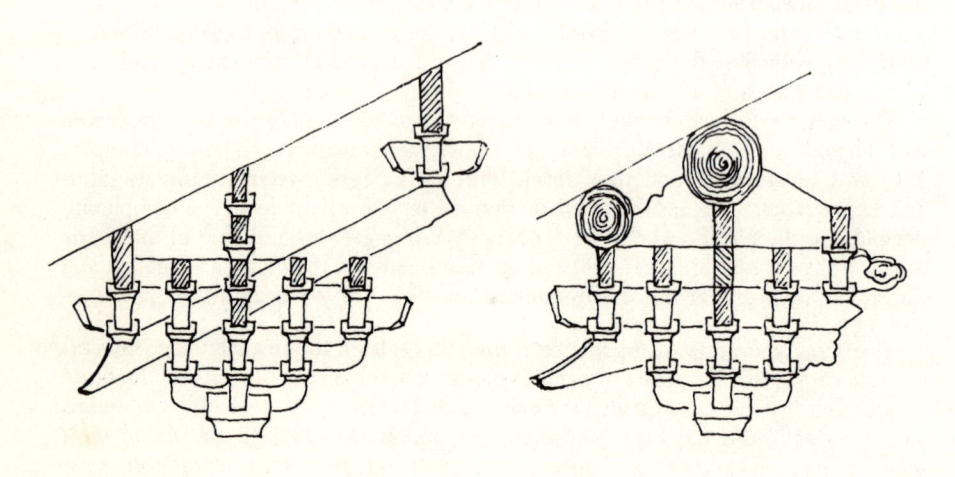

bracket set, 1103

bracket set, 1734

Fig. 4

CHINESE BUILDING

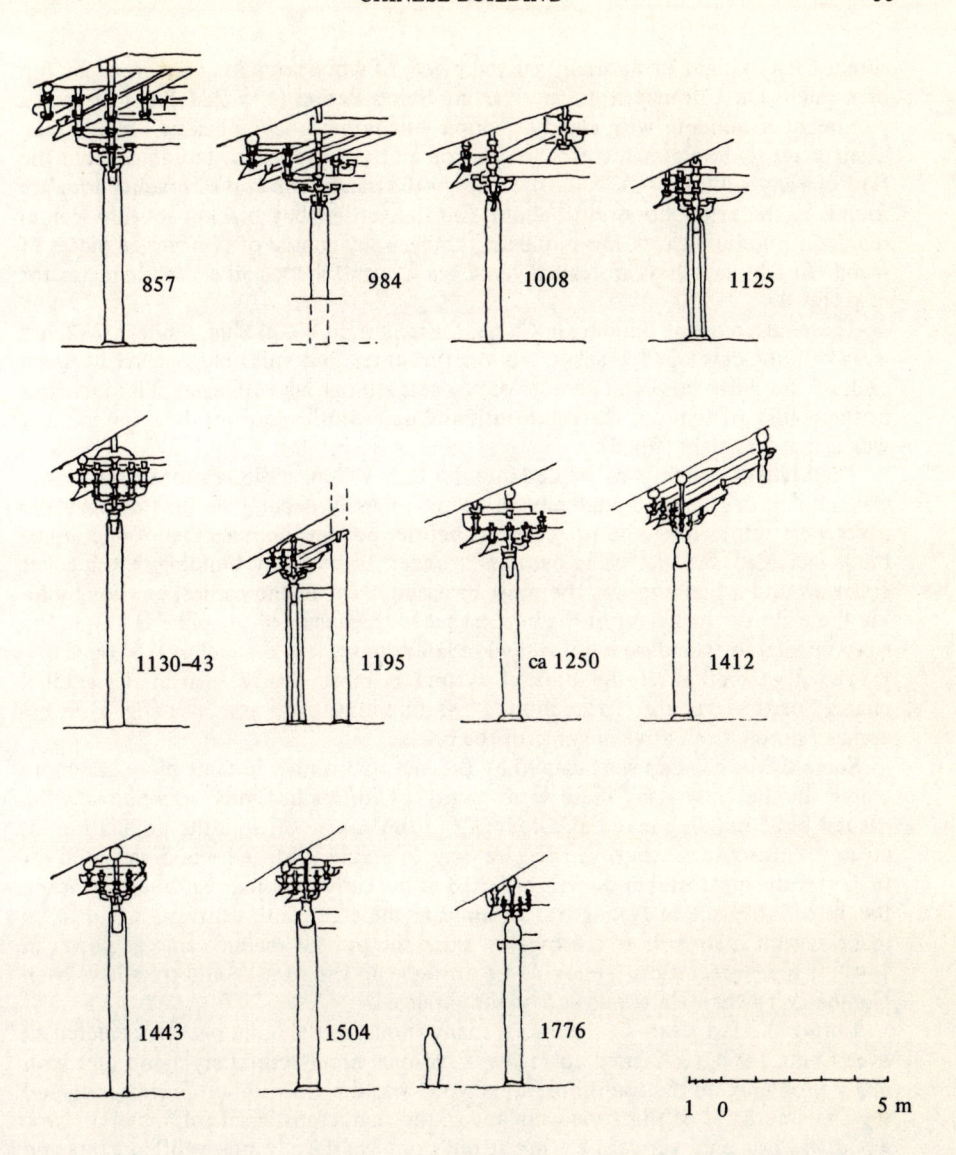

857   984   1008   1125

1130-43   1195   ca 1250   1412

1443   1504   1776   1 0   5 m

Fig. 5

surely been straight or naturally curved pieces of wood stretching out from the top of a pillar. On a bronze from the Warring States Period (475-221 B.C.) there is a picture of a building with clearly defined, but rather uncomplicated bracket sets. Their gradual development can be seen on pottery models of buildings from the Han dynasty (206 B.C.-A.D. 220), where both straight and curved bracket arms are found. In the next period until about 800 the earliest bay bracket sets are seen in reliefs in Buddhist caves and murals in tombs. They consist of two curved pieces of wood. In Chinese they are called *renzi gong*, arms shaped like the character for man (fig. 4).

The oldest existing building in China, *foguang si*, in Wutai Shan, built in 782, has already fully developed bracket sets on the lintel, but still only one set between each of the pillar sets. The number of bay sets alternating with each pillar increases in the course of time; in the eighteenth and nineteenth centuries the usual number was as many as eight (fig. 5).

The bracket system was created in order to have long eaves as protection for the walls, but it degenerated gradually to become merely decorative. In later times the eaves were not as long and projected as before, perhaps because the production of brick increased and the walls became stronger. In the early buildings the bracket collar around a building was the most imposing part. In the earliest existing building the ratio of the height of the bracket set to the height of the pillar is 1:2; in the early manual the standard is 1:2.5, and in later houses it is as small as 1:5 (fig. 5).

The degeneration of the bracket system is most clearly seen in the gradual changes of the lever arm. After about 1400 it no longer acts as a lever (fig. 5). It becomes a purely decorative member of the bracket set.

Some of the changes were caused by the fact that timber became more and more scarce. In the early days there were plenty of forests in China, so wood was the natural basic building material. Gradually in the course of time the population increased, forests were destroyed to give way to arable land, the wood was used for fuel, and the great timber dimensions used in the early buildings became rare. When the Imperial Palace in Peking was repaired in the eighteenth century, it had to be made several metres shorter. However, since the present regime came to power in 1949, it has been official policy to try to recreate the forests, and trees have been planted everywhere, in towns and on mountains.

During the last years of the 1950s many monumental buildings were erected all over China. Architects tried to create a national architectural style and met with many problems. In the traditional style wood was the most important material, and the characteristics of this style were due to the characteristics of this material. Now wood was not only very scarce, but it did not have the advantages of concrete and steel. Some of the architects tried to apply brackets and curved roofs to these modern materials, not always with success. They were, not without reason, accused of wasting the people's means on unnecessary decorations. But whatever the aesthetic values of these attempts may be, the craftsmanship is as excellent as ever.

Note

1. Ch. 4, pp.1A and 2A, 1925 ed.

The House of Swidden Farmers as a Special Object for Ethnological Study.[1]

Lucien Bernot

The house, in the broadest sense of the word—a closed-in space more or less isolated from the rest of the world by its shell of wood, stone, bricks, earth, canvas, ice (the igloo) or branches, made up of more or less specialized areas, a place for everything and everything in its place—is doubtless, thanks to its universality, one of the most useful, if not the most precious object of all ethnographical study.

The house also frequently represents one of the most dominant tangible and tenacious features of an ethnic group, remaining typical in several generations. This seems fairly obvious in the case of our Western style houses which are built to last. But this is equally true of the perishable 'grass house' of Southeast Asia with which we are dealing in this paper. Such a house cannot last several decades and a man must build several houses in his lifetime. And yet a permanence exists, for the old house is copied, and both the new and the old, generally identical, are themselves copies of another, still older house. In other words, even though the bamboo house is less durable than the house of brick or stone, it possesses lasting characteristics.

Of course, bamboo houses, built of perishable materials, are incapable of leaving traces that will defy the centuries, whereas it is still possible to read in the ground the signs of Roman dwellings two thousand years after their destruction and neglect. Among the Marma (Arakanese living in Bangladesh), we had the opportunity of visiting sites of villages abandoned about ten years before. Sometimes, a line of mango trees recalled the path to a bamboo monastery, also destroyed, or, the even edges of an artificial lake (tank) reminded us that the place was formerly inhabited by men. But of the village itself absolutely nothing remains. The obviously dried-out building materials (wood and bamboo) have been transported little by little to the new village where they are used as firewood. Generally it is the presence of some plant or other which also testifies to the existence of the abandoned village. Therefore, to prove the existence in former times of a rural village in Southeast Asia, archaeology is of little use. The first and foremost reason why we can study today cities such as Angkor, Halingyi and Pagan, is that ruins of stone and brick are still visible there. Admirable objects for comparative study. But where the peasant house in Southeast Asia is concerned, the secular dimension will always be lacking. We have in fact a historical dimension, but spanning a few generations only. Because, except for certain details that will be considered presently, when drawings or old photographs of travellers allow a comparison, the house of today is in reality the house of, say, a hundred years ago, for any given ethnic group.

Certain details do differ but they concern mainly construction materials and less the shape and lay-out of the house. Corrugated iron may have replaced straw roofs, beams are shaped with a saw instead of barked with an axe, wooden boards instead of pans of woven bamboo are used as walls; a wooden door, or even a glass window with handles for opening and closing them within casings installed by a carpenter, have perhaps taken over from the former sliding partitions or open parts of the bamboo wall. But such transformations—and we could mention others such as the Westernization of furniture—do not seem to have greatly affected the whole: the type and style of the house.

We find ourselves confronted by a seemingly paradoxical situation. As we said before, the peasant abode, in particular because of its thatched roof, is incapable of withstanding time. What is more, building such a house, although apparently simple, cannot be an individual undertaking. It is well known that in Southeast Asia, houses are built or repaired during the dry season, the builders being the inhabitants of a village. Thus, a Southeast Asian peasant (farmer), 30 or 40 years of age, has already been called upon to participate in the building of several houses. Not only does he know how to build, but he also knows to perfection the models that must be copied. This technical routine also contributes, perhaps, to fixing the style of the house. In other words, when one studies a peasant house in a given ethnic group, one studies, in fact, the traditional abode of this group.

The same goes for the house as for the arts of cooking and dressing: they are all tenacious cultural traits. When there is a desire for change, it often results in imitation, either of the conqueror, or of the most powerful neighbouring group, or the foreigner who has a certain prestige. Field-work reveals how the ethnographer can benefit from what A. Leroi-Gourhan called 'consumer techniques', from whom, we might add, these remarks have been borrowed. To build such houses, without a nail, without metal, only one tool is necessary: the *dao* or brushsword.

The house not only allows a comparative study with neighbouring houses and is the proof of the weight of tradition, but it is also the basis for every ethnographical study—and one should really list the study of the building materials, tools, techniques of manufacture, etc., as well.

But the house is much more. This object which can be looked at, described, photographed, sketched, blue-printed, visited, measured, (all excellent approaches for the ethnographer), is also the meeting point for two dimensions, one spatial, 'the refuge', the other temporal, 'the rhythm of daily life', as A. Leroi-Gourhan has said. In reality, to make the demonstration clearer, the ethnographer dissociates the different parts of the house from the different moments of daily life within this house. For the inhabitant, this arbitrary distinction is much less marked, as far as the interior of the house is concerned.

The peasant house is always built in a village. The land registry, not always in existence, allows building where one pleases, within the clearing or the village space, but this freedom is limited by certain choices: there are social imperatives regarding the orientation of the house, more concerned with whether it should be up-stream or down-stream, with the degree of incline, with sunrise and sunset, than with north, south, east or west, and which also depends on the nearby houses already built.

True, the typical house of the ethnic group will be copied, but according to the social position of the head of the household, certain details in the lay-out or decoration may become subject to other rules. For example, only the village dignitaries may surround their garden with a wall. The height of the piles, that is, the height of the floor above the ground, also depends upon hierarchy. A Naga or a Chin can boast such a feature only if he has given a special feast and he alone will have the right to put up on the wall the skulls of his sacrificed buffaloes.

One enters these houses by means of a rough wooden ladder having an uneven number of steps. The ladder leads through a door to the platform from which one or several doors open into the house itself. The notched ladder, like the door, is the way that a visitor must necessarily pass to enter or to leave the house, and here certain miniature *rites de passage* take place. Ritualistic objects, (such as the pod of *Entada pursoetha*), are present in this passage and allow arrival and departure formalities, somewhat too hastily named 'etiquette'. The stranger will no doubt be invited to sit down, and a mat will be rolled out for him in the part of the house considered to be the most noble, sometimes across from the hearth, often near the space where the master of the house sleeps. There, too, he will be offered tea, betel-nut, tobacco, beer, or alcohol.

This house of wood and bamboo, covered with leaves or grass, built without nails, stone or cement, is nevertheless affected by all the social norms of the ethnic group, as we have seen.

Excepting the low table, approximately 30 cm high, around which everyone sits crosslegged, there is no furniture, neither chairs nor tables nor beds. The cooking, basket-making, weaving, and changing of the baby, all take place sitting on the floor, and people sleep on mats on the ground. Close to the ground, holes made in the bamboo wall let you see what is happening outside, but from the outside, unless you glue your eye to these openings—a deed which is severely punished—you cannot see what is going on inside the house.

For cooking purposes, a permanent hearth is made up of a thick layer of earth placed upon the floor. A metal tripod, or three clumps of beaten earth, are used to support one pot. Five stones will support two pots at a time. There may be two quite separate hearths, one on which the mother cooks for the older generation and one on which the daughter-in-law cooks for the younger generation. It would not be possible for them to cook together, even on a five-stone hearth. Over the hearth there are three shelves which, being constantly exposed to the smoke, are dry and safe from insects. There the salt, some dry peppers, a few balls of yeast, and possibly a little meat, are kept.

The woman and her husband, when they are young, can sleep side by side, their heads towards the outside wall and their legs stretched into the middle of the room. As they grow older, they may grow apart; the woman then sleeps with the young children and the girls, the man with his sons. In some ethnic groups, the boys, after the age of ten, may sleep in the common house, a kind of 'club' often looked after by the Buddhist monastery. The young girls may also sleep together, in a house that does not have many inhabitants.

Couples can have a certain privacy under the mosquito-net, usually made for two, which is almost a room within the room, once the household is asleep.

The hearth for cooking is equipped with its kitchen utensils and even some provisions (mentioned above). The paddy is kept elsewhere in the house, or in a granary separate from the house. The beer is kept in the least sunny room, or part of a room, of the house. The same goes for the water, although a bowl of clear water is placed near the entrance, for washing bare feet or for drinking purposes. The water reserve is renewed daily by the women and young girls after they have bathed in the river. Near the kitchen hearth, always built against the wall, are the utensils and the still. A hole in the ground evacuates the dirty water (water for washing vegetables, dishwater or excess broth).

Men's and women's garments are very rarely mixed; they are put away in separate baskets and hampers. This separation is also scrupulously observed when the clothing is hung up to dry.

Firewood—dead wood stripped of its bark, thus limiting the risk of smoke—is stored below the house. It is the women who gather firewood.

The mats are kept rolled up and the baskets upside-down, on bamboo poles placed across the room on a level that we would call the ceiling.

The latrines may be in the house, near the kitchen. Since the bamboo floor is at this point very loosely woven, the excrements drop onto the ground beneath and the pigs, dogs and chickens take care of the cleaning up. In the room used as kitchen, a bamboo partition and a sliding board hide you from view. Sometimes, too, there are latrines in the village; if not, one can go behind the bushes on the edge of the clearing, where the pigs are.

Of course, the different parts of the house will vary in lay-out according to the ethnic group. As we have said, each group has developed its particular arrangement. However, in every group there exists the same division into areas for honouring guests on the one hand, and secondary areas (kitchen, latrines), on the other, and these areas considerably affect daily life within the house.

Buddhists, Hindus, Animists and even Christians, give great importance to the 'noble' section of the house—which is where the head of the house sleeps, and where the guest is received—and it is there that they place, on altars, the objects considered sacred: small statues of the Buddha, flowers in their vase, colour prints, calendar, skulls of cattle, pods of liana, a portable altar brought back from the fields and theoretically connecting the house to the field several hundred metres away, by a thread obviously broken innumerable times since its unwinding.

And the beam, the doorsill, a post considered primary, might also inspire signs of respect, fear and hope, being witnesses to the invisible world.

But in fact, and we have already alluded to this, it is during specific moments of the day, or appointed times of the year, that these sections of the house become, for a period of minutes or hours (or days), particularly affected by life's rhythm.

Strictly prescribed for the preparation of ordinary meals, the kitchen hearth may at rare times, in winter (when the temperature can go down to just a few degrees above freezing), become a central meeting point. Another hearth, moveable if need be, (simply a chunk of beaten earth on which to build a fire), is at such times set up in the middle of the noblest room. And if the house is to offer a meal to several dozen people, a rather common occurrence, especially in winter during holidays, the cooking will then be done out of doors and the men will do the women's job. Likewise, the manufacture of lime (from shells) necessary to making quids of tobacco, is done out of doors.

To gin the cotton or to card it, to dry the freshly-dyed threads or to dry laundry, usually washed every day, one chooses preferably a sunny spot. But to spin, or to lay out tobacco leaves to dry, one must have shade, and preferably humid shade close to the ground for warping hemp and for weaving (female occupations).

It seems that men also prefer slightly humid shade for making their baskets. But for these swidden farmers there is no need to have a special place for agricultural tools, since they have none, and their place of work remains the swidden. To these people who are farmers and only farmers, the house is more a 'dwelling' than an 'agricultural workshop', to quote A. Demangeon speaking of Europe. So, except for weaving and basketry, the life of the household consists essentially of sleeping, cooking, eating and caring for the children.

The family rises before sunup; the fire is lit (sometimes it only needs stoking at dawn), the household has its first meal of the day, often the left-over boiled rice, cold, from the previous night. A second meal is taken in the middle of the day, a little before noon, and a third at sundown. True, three meals a day has become the rule today, but it seems that two or three generations ago, two meals a day only was the rule, one at daybreak, the other at nightfall. Travellers have explained this by saying that at those times of the day mosquitoes (night insects) and flies (day creatures) will leave one in peace. In so far as the swidden farmers are concerned, their hard labour (bigger fields further and further away from the villages) forced them to add the third meal. The longer working day also has imposed a break in the middle of the day. Of course, we must neither accept nor reject summarily such attempts at explanation.

However, given these three meals to prepare, the paddy to be husked and whitened each day, the peasant woman also spends long hours at the hearth or at husking the paddy.

Reunited at mealtimes, the members of the household take their place around the huge plate of rice—up to three pounds of dry rice—for four or five people. The midday meal does not always take place at the same time, it is eaten when 'ready', and the latecomer's portion is kept for him. We recorded in the case of one family the hours of their midday meal: anywhere between 9.45 and 2.30 p.m. . . It is rather the organization of the work itself than the absence of watches which is responsible for this fluctuation. Swidden farmers, though they attribute great importance to the exact moment (exact in their eyes) when calculating horoscopes, live without clocks, or with clocks which are only ornamental, and depend on the position of the sun or on the observation of natural phenomena (flora or fauna). Appointments may well be made, and kept, by these farmers without clocks. But daily life for the household is therefore punctuated mainly by the female occupations.

Every evening, the house becomes the 'refuge' once again. At calling distance from the nearby houses, each household feels safe within the village, everyone has long since returned to his house, or else is known to be in safety somewhere else, and nobody, during night time, will risk going on the trails that connect the clearings.

But at a certain time in the year, when the work in the fields requires the greatest effort, from June to September, and which also corresponds to the monsoon, the village dwelling may be abandoned for a short time. It is obviously a waste of time to go each day to a field one or two hours away by foot, so the household goes to live temporarily in a house built in the field, naturally much more primitive than the one in the village. In this house—often given a special name—one is of course more isolated than in the village. The inhabited clearing is replaced by the cultivated field. So, whereas in their village house a woman and her young children can well sleep alone, in this temporary house there are always one or more men (brothers, brothers-in-law or sons) who will spend the night.

It should be noted that the agrarian rituals are most abundant during this time of the year.

As Max Sorre has said: 'The final expression of a life-style, the dwelling place is the instrument of its permanence. Its stability denotes the moment when a human group has taken root.'

Note

1. Translated from French into English by Mme Gabrielle Benguigui-Varro.

The Two-door House: the Intha Example from Burma[1]

Lucien Bernot

In our previous presentation, we tried to illustrate the importance of the house for ethnographical study in Southeast Asia. Such a study puts the ethnographer face to face with technology, economy, religion, jurisprudence, social and family life. To a Westerner accustomed to houses 'made to last', the Southeast Asian house is fragile and built with great speed. It nevertheless bears great resemblance, on the whole, to the lay-outs of our own modern flats.

Hearth of the house, altar, female areas and male areas, all these zones and the objects belonging to them, have been arranged in an order characteristic of each ethnic group. We think we discovered such an organization in the Marma house, as we wrote in 1967. (Bernot, 1967 a, pp.419-422.)

Southeast Asia, especially in its insular and southeastern parts, is also the land of the longhouse, by which is meant a house where several couples or nuclear families live at the same time (fig. 1a).[2] American Indians also had longhouses and L. H. Morgan, in a work recently republished and prefaced by P. Bohannan (Morgan, 1881), situated these longhouses in his diagram of evolution and explained them by talking about native promiscuity (fig. 1b). Towards the end of the chapter dedicated to the North American Indians, he said: 'It is made reasonably plain, I think, from the facts stated, that in the Upper Status of savagery, and also in the Lower Status of barbarism, the Indian household was formed of a number of families of gentile kin; that they practiced communism in living in the household, and that this principle found expression in their house architecture and pre-determined its character' (id., p.139).

It detracts nothing from the importance of Morgan, to whom the ethnologist is and remains indebted, to say that this explanation is probably false. These longhouses of America and Asia, so admirably organized as they are into cells, are but so many individual houses placed end to end. One might, at least for Southeast Asia, propose a totally different hypothesis.

If it is true, as we think today, that wet paddy fields came before swidden, these 'longhouses' inhabited by swidden farmers would seem to be, in reality, a more recent type of habitat: the dwellings of people who, after having cultivated the lowlands (on the plains) were forced to flee before the invaders and take refuge in the hills where they cultivated dry rice, by swidden, grouping their individual homes in 'longhouses'.

We need not emphasize that this is pure hypothesis and that a rigorous comparative study might disprove it.

A good number of excellent monographs about Southeast Asia exist, which generally present very detailed descriptions of the houses. Certain authors, such as Nguyen van Huyen (1934), have even attempted a synthesis of these sources. L. Scherman's covers a somewhat more limited area (1915). However, when we consider the number of ethnic groups (distinguished according to linguistic criteria,

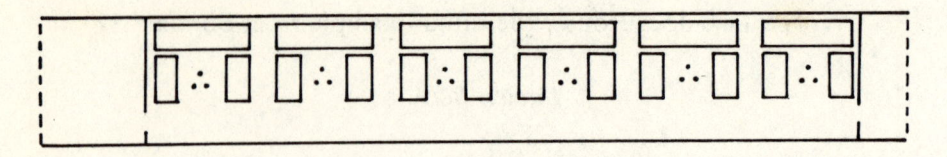

Fig. 1a Plan of Dafla House (approximately 50 m x 6.50 m). (After Shukla, 1959 p.13.)

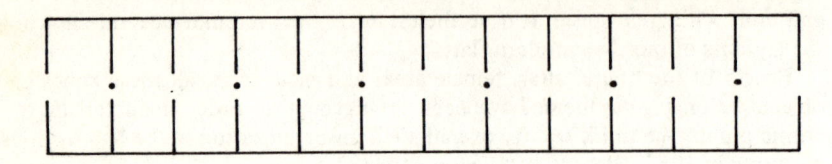

Fig. 1b Ground plan of Seneca-Iroquois Longhouse (approximately 30 m x 6 m). (After Morgan, 1881, p.126.)

insufficient perhaps, but practical), we are forced to recognize that for 100 'languages' spoken there are no more than fifteen or sixteen which have been described. Therefore, any systematic synthesis is for the time being premature, and we can only suggest a method, based on information gathered in the existing literature or on our own field work.

In our first paper (see above, p.35), we stated that every ethnic group had its own type of house. Yet, when we lived with the Intha of Inle Lake (Southern Shan States), we counted five types of house. This diversity does not appear to contradict our first statement.

First a few words to try and clarify our description. The Intha (Bruneau, 1972) such as the Arakanese, the Tavoyan, etc., speak 'old Burmese' but they can read, write, understand and speak Rangoon Burmese as well. They live in houses, built on the ground or on piles, around the flood-prone banks or in the Inle Lake. Each house owns at least one boat. They are therefore a lacustrian (lake-dwelling) population. Apart from this characteristic, this ethnic group of approximately 60,000 inhabitants differs from the other ethnic groups in Burma from other points of view as well.

In the poorest houses, one makes do with gardening (on 'floating islands') and a bit of agriculture on land; in other houses, however, besides these activities, certain crafts make these people richer than the first: they sew garments (uniforms ordered by the government, for example), weave traditional costumes, prepare food products liable to be preserved. A third group has totally abandoned agriculture, gardening and fishing, and devotes itself to artisan work; these are obviously the ones who are best off. They are weavers, tailors, makers of preserves (three activities done by both women and men), but also, among the men only, there are boat builders, carpenters and woodworkers, blacksmiths, goldsmiths, potters, etc.

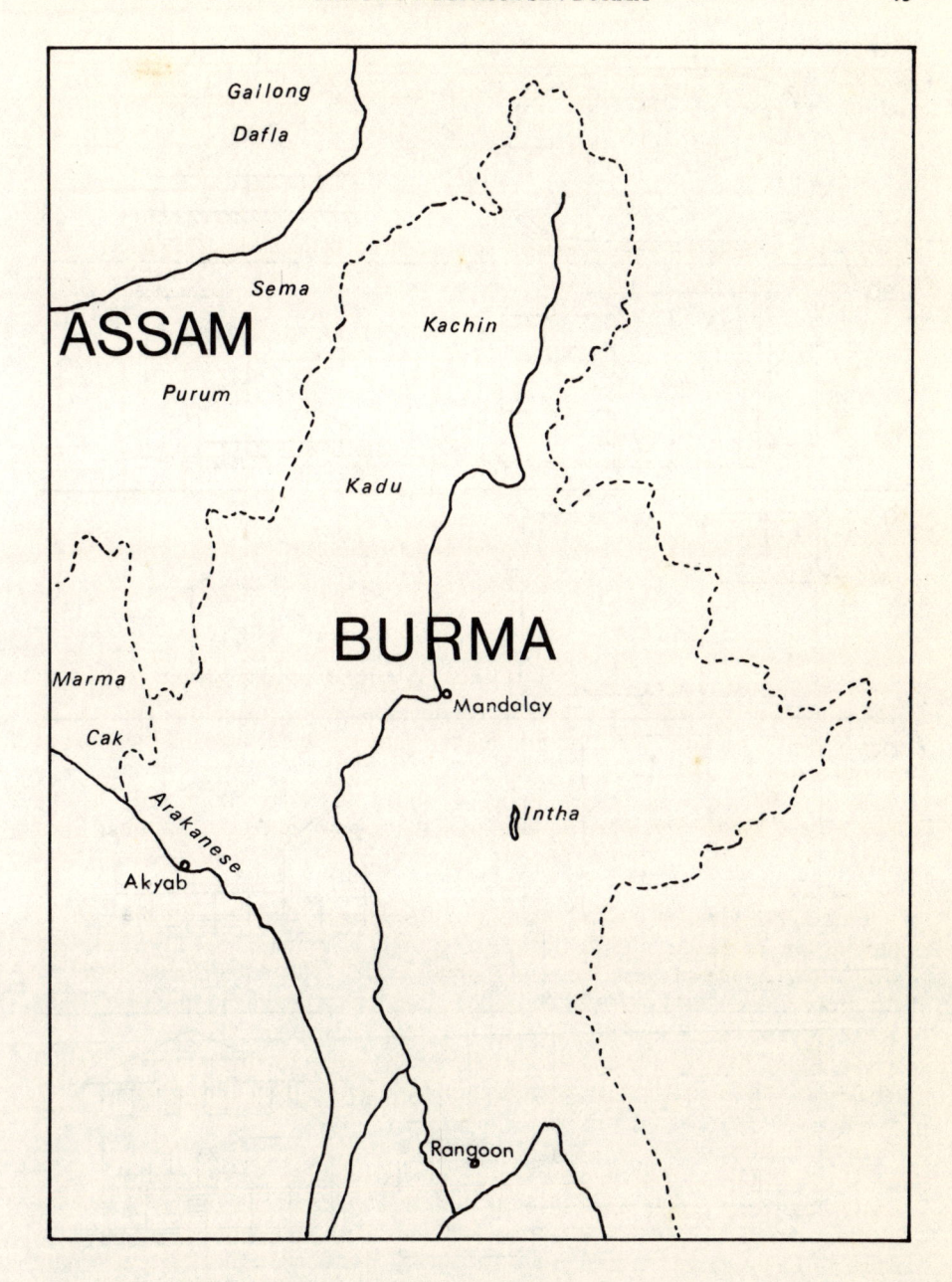

Fig. 2 Sketch map of Burma and Assam.

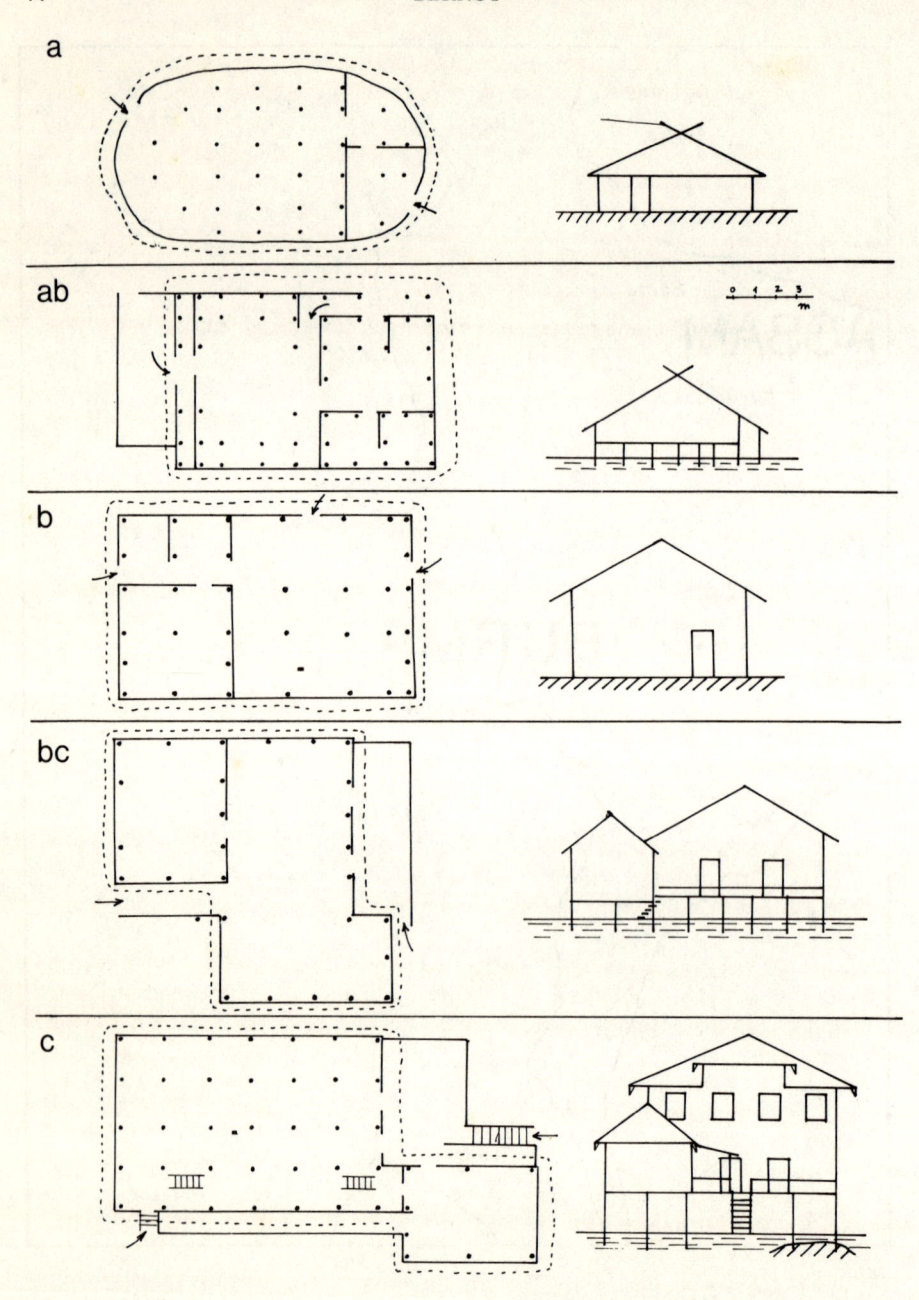

Fig. 3a, ab, b, bc, c   Plans of the Intha Houses. Arrows indicate doors.

This somewhat long introduction seemingly diverted us from our subject; but in fact it ties in with it, since for each of these groups we noted three different types of house (A, B and C). Even though it was our Intha informants themselves who suggested it, this classification is somewhat over-simplified and we shall refer also to intermediary types (AB and BC).

House A (fig. 3a)
The house is built on the ground, the walls are of sun-grass panels (*Imperata cylindrica C*) and the roof is covered with the same grass.

Two persons (brother and sister) live in this house and do agriculture in the rice-fields surrounding the lake. The brother also practises some alchemy in a small shed near his house.

Living space: approximately 80 m^2; height of the topmost beam: 3.50 m; two doors.

House AB (fig. 3ab)
The house is built over the water, thus on piles, the walls are made of panels of grass or bamboo, the roof is thatched.

Four people—the father, the mother and two young children—live in this house. The father is a gardener and a weaver, the mother also weaves. This house, though of broken-down appearance, is considered one of the most lasting, and its owner proudly tells how on stormy days many a neighbour comes to seek shelter in his home. This house is supposed to be quite old, at least its supporting posts; some of them, or parts of them, are carved. (We believe that these posts are perhaps one hundred years old.)

Living space: approximately 80 m^2; height of the topmost beam above water level: 3.80 m; two doors.

House B (fig. 3b)
The house is built on the ground. The walls are made of boards and of bamboo and the roof is covered by corrugated iron.

Ten people live in this house: the father (a widower), a son and a daughter (both about thirty years old and unmarried), one married daughter, her husband and their five young children. They make their living by agriculture (paddy, betel leaves), and by selling grain.

Living space: approximately 115 m^2; height of the topmost beam: 6.50 m; three doors, two of which are side by side.

House BC (fig. 3bc)
The house is built over the water, and on piles. Walls are made of bamboo and boards, the roof is thatched, or of corrugated iron. Windows have shutters, but windows, because of scarcity, have zinc, instead of pane-glass.

Four people live in this house: a man, his wife, their young daughter and the wife's sister (unmarried). They are tailors, and have one sewing machine.

Living space: approximately 100 m^2; height of the topmost beam above water level: 6 m; two doors.

House C (fig. 3c)
The house is built over the water and was entirely constructed by woodworkers and carpenters. It is made of boards assembled tongue-and-groove, its roof of corrugated iron. This house has two storeys, the first floor can be reached by two inside staircases made of teak. Both storeys have teak floors and the posts of the octagonal section are also of teak. There are 26 pairs of windows (with pane-glass) and 26 pairs of shutters. It is obviously a wealthy house, but by no means the only one. The inhabitants sleep and eat on the floor, but things are put away in English-type furniture.

Four people live in this house: father, mother, daughter (20), son (23). The first three are tailors, there are three sewing machines and they cut and put together the uniforms ordered by the government (for the work forces) and sub-contract work to other tailors in the village as well.

Living space: approximately 220 m^2; height of the topmost beam above water level: 9.50 m; three doors, two side by side.

After this quick sketch, which we have kept to a minimum of details, we must note that, when going from the poorest to the richest house, modifications are obviously apparent. On the other hand, people eat and sleep in the same manner, wear the same type of clothing, cook more or less the same kind of meals, whether rich or poor. Finally, and in spite of the modifications in the houses, one fact remains: there are almost always two doors, one at each end of the house.

It is difficult for the Inthas to explain the existence of these two doors, and they get around it by speaking of tradition (which does not help), by commenting on the disappearance of tradition (which is obvious) and pointing out those houses which have only one door (which do exist). As to remarks we can formulate from the notes we kept daily during our stay, they come down to this: one uses the most convenient door according to the job one has to do. Discussions teach us that one door was in the past necessarily used by the daughter-in-law who came to her new family's house for the first time, and that the other door was reserved for the exit of the dead before their immersion in the mud of the lake.

When stopping with the Arakanese peasants in the region of Akyab (Jan. 1974), we saw two-door houses, whereas we noted that the Marma—who are Arakanese refugees since the beginning of the nineteenth century in what is now called Bangladesh—live in houses which have only one door. (Bernot, 1967 a, p.429). We noted two doors in the Cak house of today's Bangladesh (Bernot, 1967 b, pp.70 ff) but in December 1973 we saw only one door in the Kadu house, near the source of the River Mu. The Kadu are linguistically very close to the Cak and, besides, they call themselves Cak.

Ethnographical literature tells us that the Purum have two doors (Das, 1945, p.245, cf. fig. 4a). So do the Kachin (Gilhodes, 1922, p.159; cf. fig. 4b) and the Sema Naga (Hutton, 1921, pp.40–41, cf. fig. 4c). Further north in the N.E.F.A. (now Arunachal Pradesh; in northeastern India) L. Srivastava has noted that the Gallong house not only possesses two doors but also two encased beams leading to these entrances. On the author's diagram are clearly marked 'entrance for men' and 'entrance for women' (Srivastava, 1962, p.16; cf. fig. 4d).

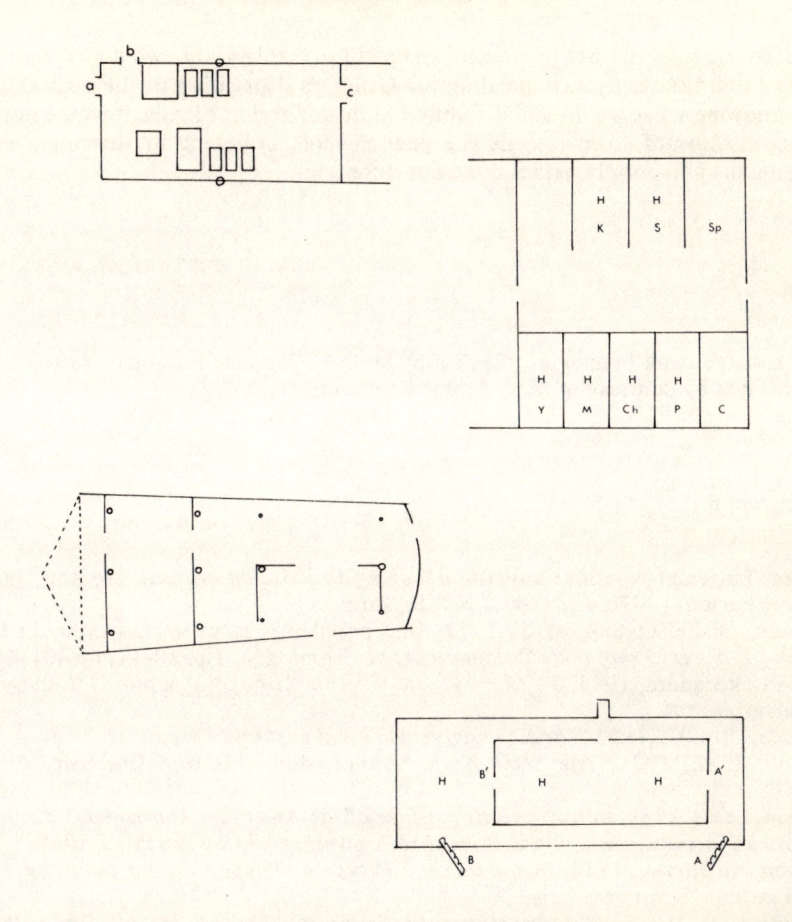

Fig 4a   Ground plan of Purum House (after Das, 1945, pl.XIX, Figure 74 and pp.45 sq.)
a and b, back doors; c, front door.

Fig. 4b   Plan of Kachin House (after Gilhodes, 1922, p.159). H: Hearths; K: Kitchen; S: Sitting-room; Sp: Spirits; Y: Youngsters; M: Married son; Ch: Children; P: Parents; C: Cellar.

Fig. 4c   Sketch of Sema Naga House (after Hutton, 1921, p.41).

Fig. 4d   Plan of Gallong House (after Srivastava, 1962, p.16). A: Women's ladder; A': Entrance for women; B: Men's ladder; B': Entrance for men; H: Hearths.

Of course it would not be a sound argument to 'explain' the two doors observed in the Intha houses by extrapolating the Gallong's segregation of the sexes. However, knowing what we do about family life in this region of Asia, it would not be completely absurd to investigate the phenomenon, beginning by drawing a map situating the two-door houses and the one-door ones.

Notes

1. Translated from French into English by Mme T. Gabrielle Benguigui-Varro.
2. Drawings by courtesy of Mme Sophie Charpentier (EHESS).

Bibliography

Bernot, Lucien, 1967a, *Les paysans arakanais du Pakistan oriental.* Mouton, Paris.
Bernot, Lucien, 1967b, *Les Cak.* C.N.R.S., Paris.
Bruneau, Michel et Bernot, L., 1972, Une population lacustre: Les Intha du Lac Inle. *J. d'Agr. Trop. et de Botanique Appl.*, Tome XIX, No. 10–11, pp.401–441.
Das, Tarakchandra, 1945, *The Puruns, an old Kuki Tribe of Manipur.* University of Calcutta.
Gilhodes, Rev. C., 1922, *The Kachins, religion and customs.* Calcutta.
Hutton, J. H., 1921, *The Sema Naga.* Second edition. Oxford University Press, 1968.
Morgan, Lewis, 1881, *Houses and House-Life of the American Aborigines.* Ed. 1965, with an Introduction by Paul Bohannan. University of Chicago Press, 1965.
Nguyen van Huyen, 1934, *Introduction à l'étude de l'habitation sur pilotis en Asie du sud-est.* Geuthner, Paris.
Scherman, L., 1915, Wohnhaustypen in Birma und Assam. *Archiv für Anthropologie*, n.s. No. XIV. Transl. into French by Barbara Wall, ASEMI, 1975, Vol. VI, No. 2-3, pp.159–199.
Shukla, Brahma, K., 1959, *The Daflas of the Subansiri region.* Shillong.
Srivastava, L. R. N., 1962, *The Gallongs.* Shillong.

The Lao House: Vientiane and Luang Prabang[1]

Sophie Charpentier

As Pierre Clément and I have given elsewhere a more complete view on the Lao house in the regions of Vientiane and Luang Prabang,[2] I shall limit myself here to a few points illustrating the subject. I shall first make a short survey of the general environment, the village, its location, introducing here the only edifices which do not belong to the village—that is the temporary houses in the fields. Then I shall say a few words about the rules governing residence, and present the Lao house by analysing two plans characteristic of the two regions of Vientiane and Luang Prabang. This will lead us to a brief typology. The second part will deal with building.

The village

The Lao live on the plains, in the valleys and along the rivers. They are rice farmers, cultivating irrigated fields. The houses are clustered in villages; in the country no isolated house is to be seen. This seems to be a frequent phenomenon in Southeast Asia. The villages, *baan2*, are frequently settled along the streams, the Mekong or its tributaries, the best location being the mouths, *paak*, of these tributaries;[3] thus we have Ban Pak Suang and Ban Pak Ou where the tributaries Nam Suang and Nam Ou join the Mekong. On plains, in the middle of irrigated fields, one often sees villages on earth banks, *dOOn*, which also means island, so that the villages are called Ban Don Mo or Ban Don Noun. Nowadays more and more villages stretch along the roads.

The Lao village varies in size from about ten dwellings to one hundred and fifty. An examination of eight villages on the plain of Vientiane gave an average of 60 houses per village. At first one is struck by the plantations of bamboos and coconut trees among which the houses are set up in the village. At second sight, the houses look homogeneous, no house being much bigger or more richly decorated than the others. The only other buildings are the *wat* (the Buddhist temple) and the school.

We have distinguished two main types of villages, the first one being loosely grouped, the second one compactly grouped. In the former, typical of the rice plains, around Vientiane for instance, the houses are surrounded by yards, between which run paths. The yard is used as a farmyard, with outbuildings bound to agricultural activities, such as granaries, barns or pigsties. In the second type, representative of some villages near Luang Prabang, the houses are close to one another, without yards. They are set parallel to each other, along streets running down to the stream.

The only isolated houses are those we can see in the paddy fields, used temporarily as shelters when the people work in the fields. They are built on piles like the other houses, but are of smaller dimensions. They are called *thyeng naa* (fig. 1). When the paddy fields are far from the village, all the family moves to come and live in this small edifice, at sowing time for instance, or during the transplantation

Fig. 1 A temporary house in the fields.

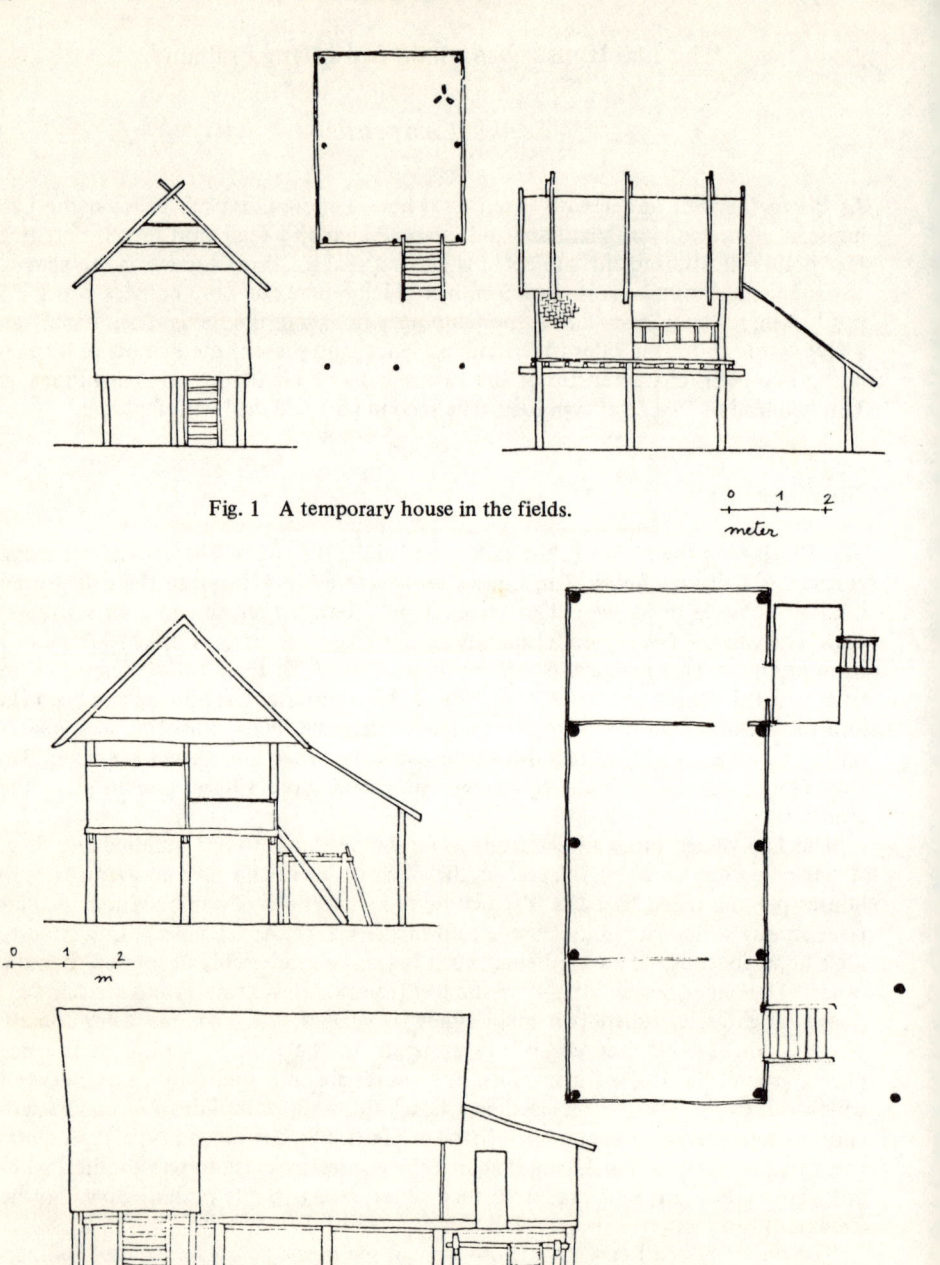

Fig. 2 A Lao house at Ban Pak Tuan.

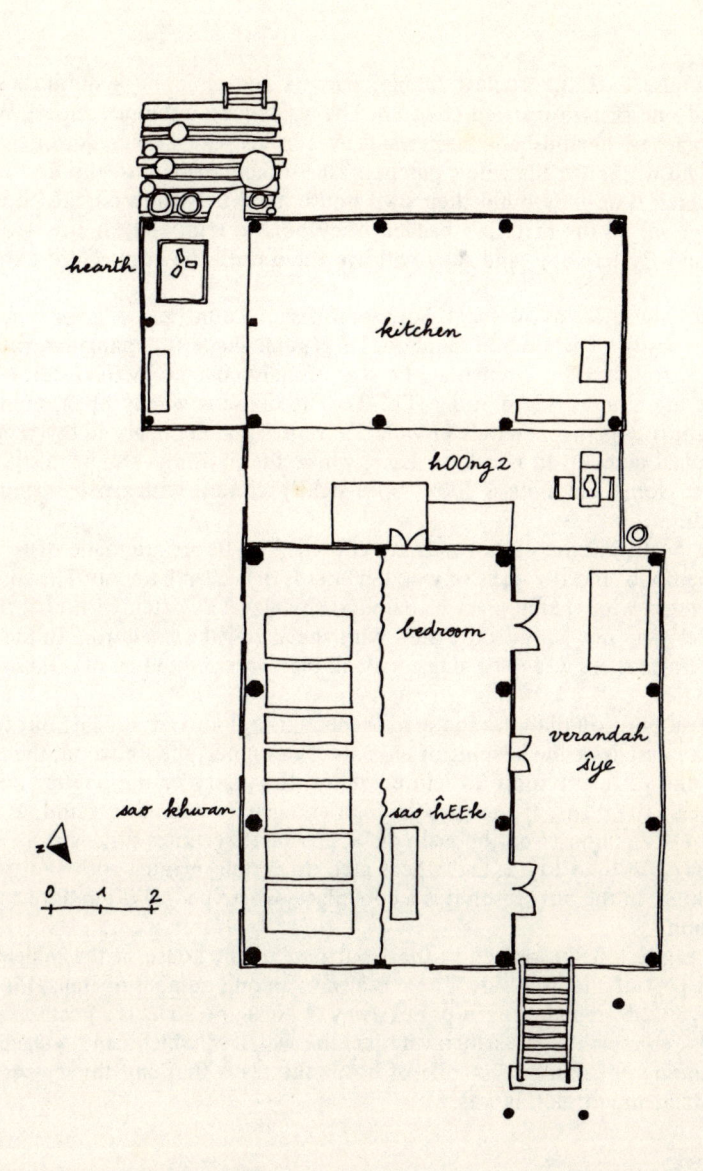

Fig. 3 Plan of a house at Ban Don Noun (near Vientiane).

and the harvest. Sometimes, several of these *thyeng naa* clustered together form the nucleus of a new village closer to the fields.

The house

In a Lao house lives the nuclear family, parents and children, sometimes grandparents and one or two married children. The residence is often uxorilocal. When a daughter marries, her husband comes and lives in his wife's house for one or two years, and he works for his wife's parents. This usually lasts until the first child is born, at which time they build their own house, near the wife's parents' house. If they cannot get all the materials needed, they build a temporary house with light materials, chiefly bamboo, and they will live there until they can afford a stronger house.

The Lao house is, as in most Southeast Asian countries, a 'grass house' on piles made mostly of wood and bamboo. Its general shape is rectangular, with one or two main roofs, and a kitchen at the rear, usually covered by its own roof. The main roofs are simple ridged roofs (fig. 2). The house is widely open, with large verandas, and the plant materials provide the ventilation necessary in this region of humid tropical climate. In Northern Laos, where the mornings can be misty in the cool season, some old houses look more tightly closed, with small openings in wooden walls.

For the posts, the hardest woods are chosen. The floors are made of wood or flattened bamboo, and the walls of wooden boards or woven bamboo. The roofs are usually covered with thatch grass or bamboo shingles, less often with clay tiles or wooden tiles, and nowadays sometimes with sheets of galvanized iron. In the traditional buildings, there was not a single nail; all pieces were fixed by pegs, and rattan or bamboo ties.

The house built on piles has the space beneath the floor free and laid out for the storage of materials or the keeping of animals. The timber, the firewood, the thatch grass, and the different tools are stored there; the pigsty or the poultry house is built between the posts. If the space is high enough for people to stand, as is the case in most of the houses on the plain of Vientiane, it becomes a living place where women weave on their looms and where men do certain manual activities, such as basket making. In the hot season it is a cool place, where people often have a nap in the afternoon.

The stairs are usually located in the front part of the house, at the gable end or in the first part of the long side. There is always an odd number of steps, for a Lao proverb says: 'odd remains, even passes away.'[4] Near the stairs is a post *sao nam2*, 'water post', supporting an earthenware jar, the water of which can be reached by people standing in the house. A rule of hospitality says that any thirsty passer-by can go upstairs and drink this water.

The floor level

Now let us go up into the house. At this level, the inside organization differs in the two regions of Vientiane and Luang Prabang, so we shall present two plans charactiristical of the two regions.

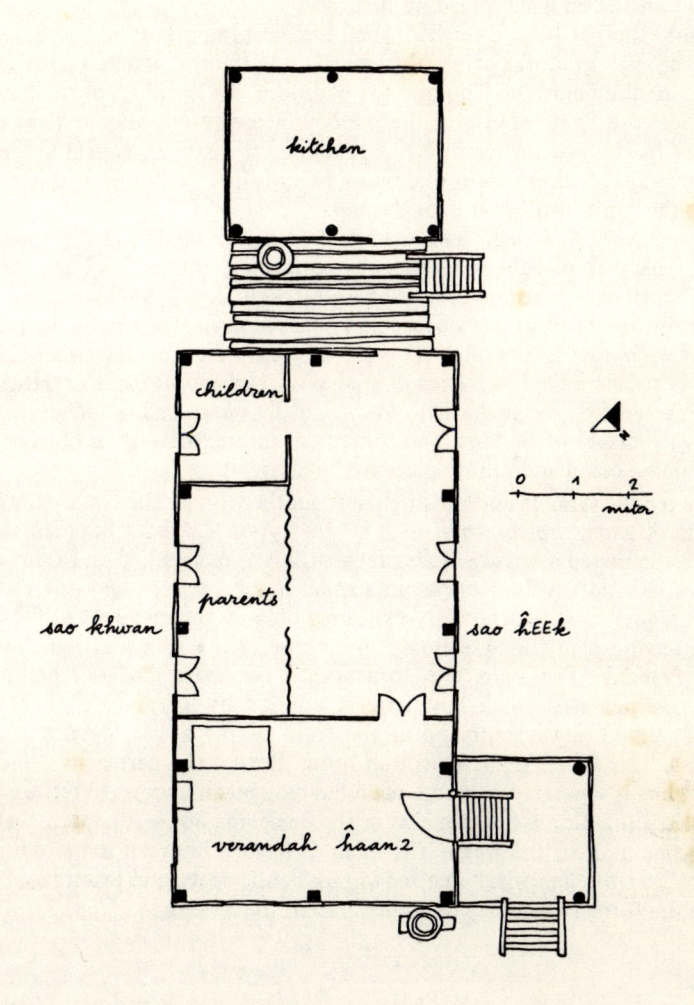

Fig. 4 Plan of a house at Ban Don Mo (near Luang Prabang).

The first house is in the village of Ban Don Noun, near Vientiane (fig. 3). We enter a lengthwise veranda, *ŝye*, covered by a lean-to roof. This roof is sloping very low on the outer side and prevents the sunshine from coming in. This veranda, completely open, is only delimited by a low railing. This is the place where visitors are received, sitting on mats spread on the floor.

Behind the partition is the bedroom, the most important part of the house. Two doors and one window open to the veranda, the floor of which is a little lower than the one of the bedroom. To enter the bedroom, the members of the family use the rear door, the front door and the window being always closed. They are opened only for feasts, when a ceremony, a wedding for instance, is held inside the room. Traditionally, strangers are not allowed to enter the bedroom, because they could disturb the spirit of the house, *phii hùùan*.

There is very little light inside the bedroom, the windows being small and often closed. This lack of light is a good way to protect privacy, for one cannot look inside. The room is partitioned lengthwise by a curtain, behind which are spread the mattresses, the head of the sleeper being placed against the outer wall. The second post of each row is a 'principal' post, to which the Lao attach a spiritual value. These posts are called *sao khwan* 'soul post' and *sao ĥEEk* 'first post', the latter being erected first. Near the *sao khwan*, on the outer wall, is the domestic altar, a shelf with images of Buddha, and sometimes magic formulae or objects. This is the most noble, sacred and private place in the house.

Between the veranda and the kitchen is another room called *hOOng2* (i.e., room), then the kitchen, *hùùan khw*, with its own roof. Clothing, kitchen utensils and goods are gathered along the walls, the hearth is at one end, in an extension covered by a lean-to roof. A door opens on a small terrace, *saan*, where the water jars are kept. A ladder allows a secondary exit, used only by the members of the family.

The second plan (fig. 4) belongs to a house of the village of Ban Don Mo, near Luang Prabang. The stairs are divided into two parts laid out perpendicularly, between which is a small low terrace, covered by a lean-to roof. One enters a veranda, *haan2*, always situated at the front of the house, opened by two large windows. This *haan2* is the reception room. Behind the partitions is the bedroom. The kitchen is separated from the main building by an uncovered terrace with water jars, whose function is the same as in the preceding house, that is, a 'wet' place for the kitchen and for the toilet. The main difference between the two houses lies in the fact that the imaginary line separating public space and private space is lengthwise in the former example, and transversal in the latter one.

Typology

We will now classify the houses we encountered into a few general types. For this purpose we will adopt criteria used by the Laos themselves, listing the types identified by the Lao language. This typology is based on the general aspect of the houses, determined by the shapes of the roofs. We shall distinguish here between the two regions, and shall treat separately the problem of the kitchen. The following types refer to the main part of the house.

In the region of the Vientiane we can distinguish three main types: type 1, with a simple gable roof covering the bedroom and an open veranda; type 2, *hùùan ŝye*, with a gable roof covering the bedroom, and a lean-to roof added on one side, covering an open veranda, *ŝye*; type 3, *hùùan fEEd*, 'twin house', with a double roof, one covering the bedroom the other covering the veranda. To these three types can be added a front veranda called *labyeng*, thus giving three new variations (fig. 5).

In the region of Luang Prabang the houses are more homogeneous, and here we can distinguish only two types: type 1, with a simple gable roof, covering the front veranda, *ȟaan2*, and the bedroom; type 2, similar to type 1, to which has been added a lengthwise veranda, *ŝye* (fig. 6).

In both regions the kitchen is situated at the rear end of the house and may be placed under the main roof; under a lean-to roof; under a gable roof, the ridge of which is at right angles to the ridge of the main roof; or under a gable-roofed building separated from the main building by a terrace (fig. 7).

The building of the house

The construction work cannot be considered separately, isolated from other aspects of the Lao's life. So before recounting the technical facts, we should like to mention briefly the social, economic and ritual aspects bound to the building of houses, answering the questions: Who builds, how, and when?

Social and economic aspects

In Laos houses are built during the dry season. The building period stretches from the end of the harvest to the beginning of the rainy season, when there is no hard work in the fields, so that the people have time off.

The building process can be divided into several phases. The first one is devoted to the gathering of materials. Wood and bamboo are cut in the forest, or now, near urban areas, bought from a trader. Then the materials are prepared by the householder, occasionally assisted by some male members of his family. The timber is squared, cut off to the right length, the mortises are bored, the bamboo are woven, everything is highly prefabricated. This is the most extensive stage, it usually lasts a few months, sometimes a year or two.

Then the framework is erected in one single day, "between a sunrise and a sunset"[5], with the help of the villagers; for many workers are needed to erect the heavy pieces of wooden frame. Formerly, the girls of the builder's family were sent to invite all the men of the village to participate in the building. Everyone was invited to a feast the night before the work was to start, with a large meal washed down with rice alcohol, and with music and dance that could last all night. The number of workers coming was the reflection of the social importance of the family; the size of the house was determined by the number of people helping. Thus traditionally house building was a collective work, such as the other community jobs of the village, harvesting, for instance, or digging the wells and repairing the roads.

But nowadays, who builds? From our field observations, we made out three

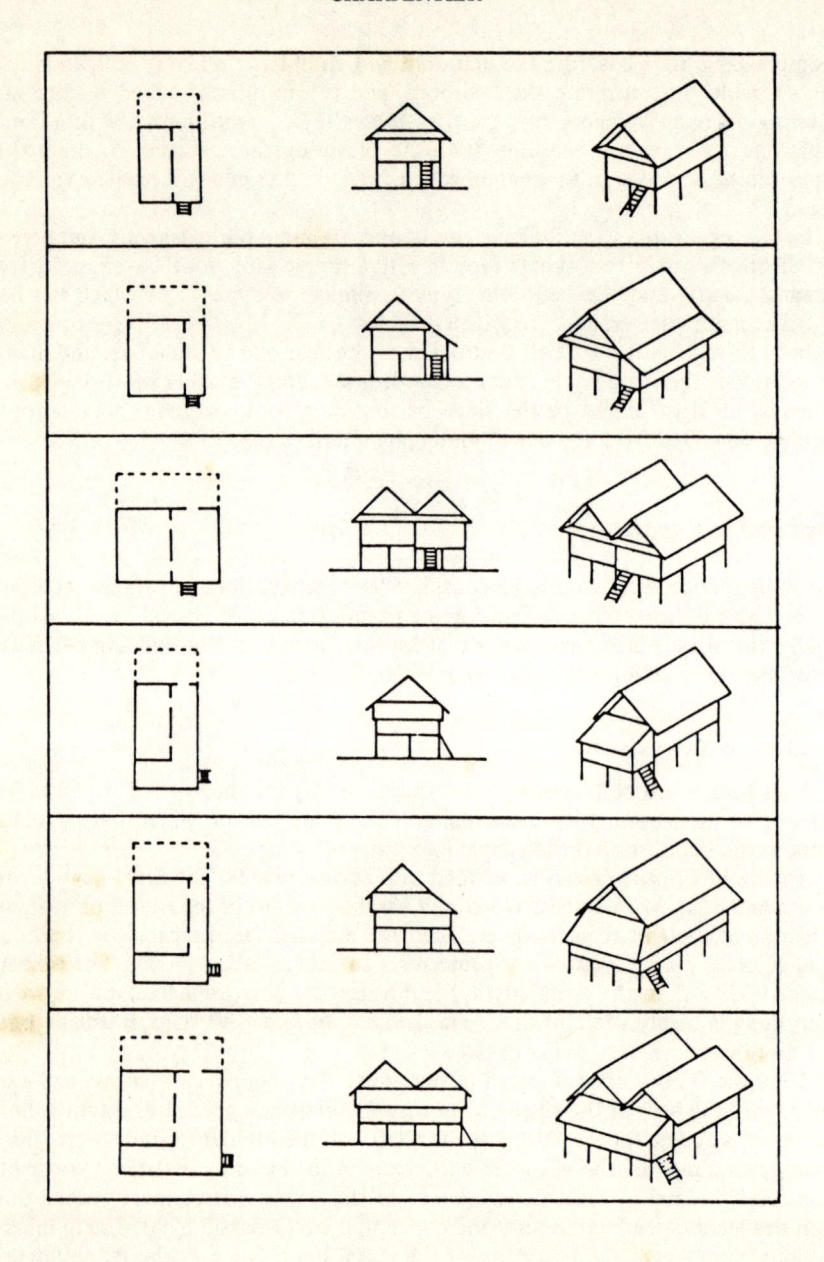

Fig. 5 Types of houses in the region of Vientiane.

THE LAO HOUSE 57

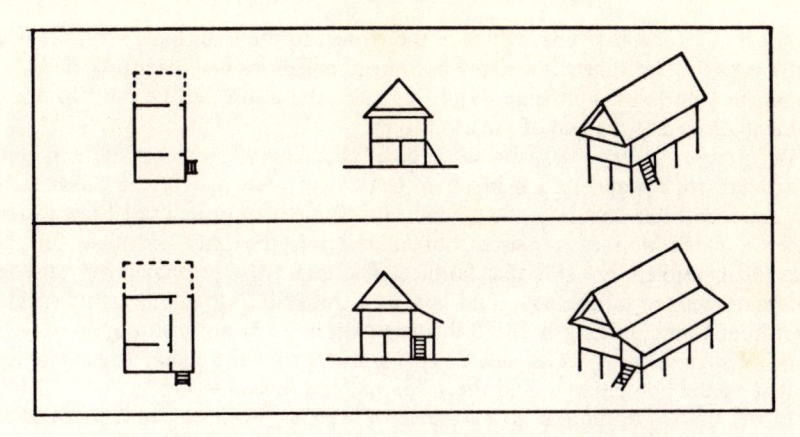

Fig. 6 Types of houses in the region of Luang Prabang.

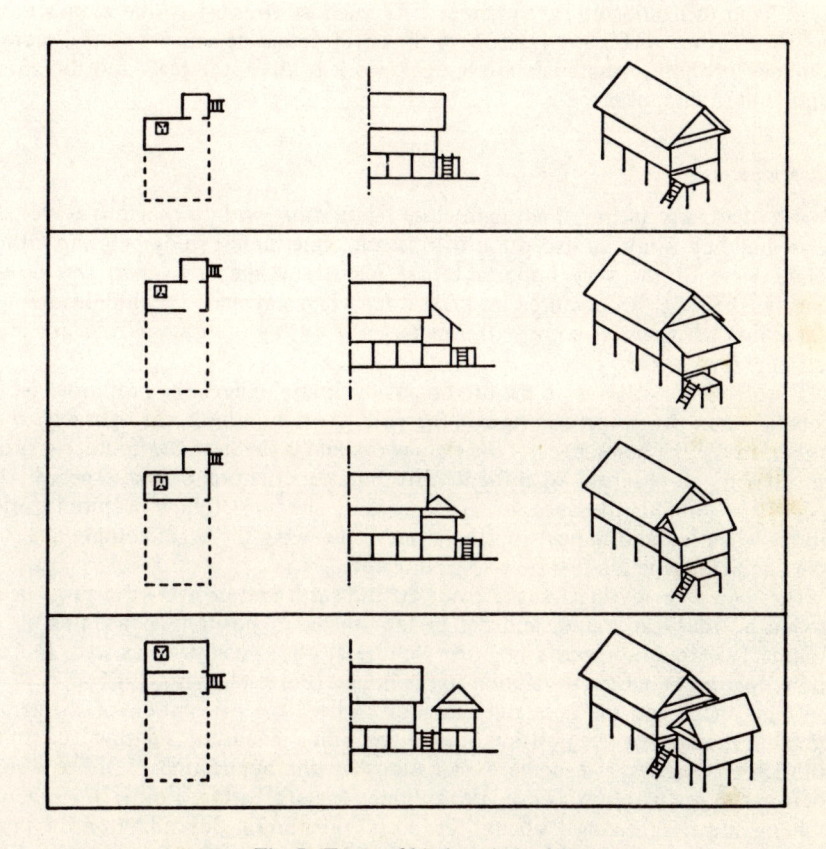

Fig. 7 Types of kitchens in both regions.

main cases. In the first one, which is the closest to the traditional way, the builder is the householder himself, assisted by unpaid collaborators, parents or neighbours, whom he will assist next time. With this help, the house can be built in one day, and inaugurated at the end of the afternoon.

But now, near the cities, the situation is changing. If the householder living in a village has, for instance, a job in town, he can ask a few men of the village to build his house, and this illustrates the second case. These men form a small team working under the direction of a master builder, who is the only one paid, but these occasional builders are still rice farmers. The materials are prepared by the team, the frame erected in one day. And last, as a third case, we can now find specialists for whom housebuilding is the only occupation. They are paid day by day, they work by themselves, or with one or two workers to assist them. The materials are bought by the householder, and the work may last several weeks.

In the first case, there is an exchange of services, in the second and third cases, a remuneration of hired work. The abandonment of tradition is connected with economic changes. Formerly, with the mutual aid, there was no money passing from hand to hand, but only indirect gifts, such as offerings to the monks during the rites, or largess for the feast. Now the construction depends more and more on a money economy: materials are bought, work is hired, the feast and the gifts in kind tend to disappear.

Ritual aspects

For the Lao, any technical act is in close relationship with its religious aspect, and house-building is not an exception to this rule. One cannot study building without being aware of the very important part played by the astrologer, *hmOO hon*. Usually, the latter has acquired his knowledge when staying at the Buddhist temple. Sometimes he possesses a copy of a manuscript stating the general rules for many acts of everyday life.

The astrologer chooses, in the lifetime of the householders, the propitious period to build, then the propitious time in the year, the right month, the right day to cut timber, to dig the holes, to raise the framework and inaugurate the house. He knows the rules to be observed to prevent disturbing supernatural beings, especially the god of the ground, the *naga*, or *nak*. For that, one must follow propitious orientations when laying the posts on the ground, throwing the earth coming out from holes, and choosing the first hole to be dug out.

The *naga* is a mythical snake living in the earth and in rivers. He turns in the ground all the year round, and lies in four different positions depending on the month. This tradition exists in other Southeast Asian countries as well. In Cambodia, the *nak* is quoted in relation to the house. (Porée-Maspéro, 1961, p.217). We can find the origin of these rules in India, where the orientation of the tantric temple is dictated by the position of the *naga*. Some manuscripts dating back to the 10th-13th centuries give some explanations on the application of these esoteric doctrines to architecture. (Bose, 1932; Boner & Rath Sarma, 1966). In 1969, on a building site near Luang Prabang, the posts' orientation depending on the *naga's* position was still observed by the master builder, who told us that the top of the

THE LAO HOUSE 59

Fig. 8   Framework in the region of Luang Prabang.

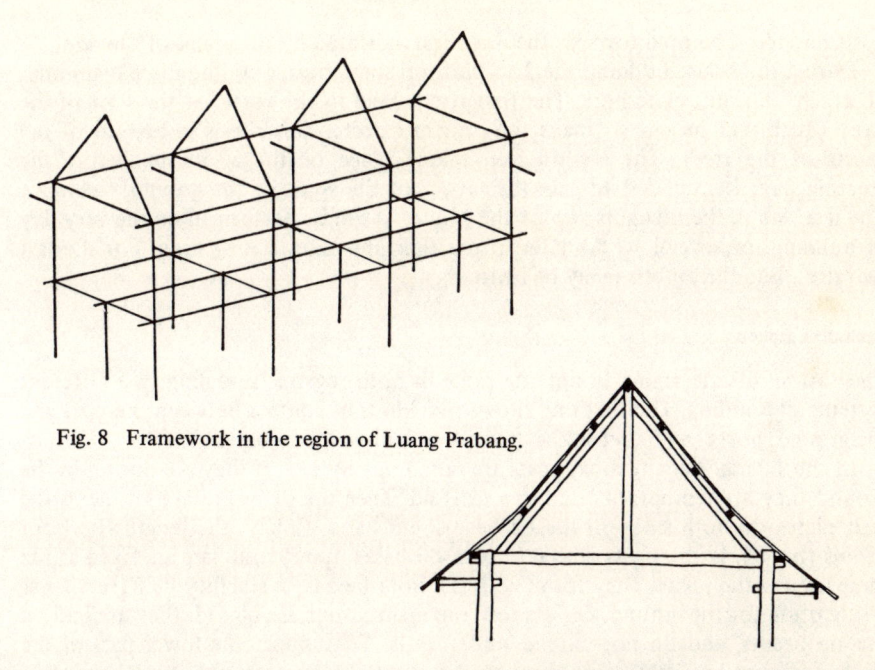

Fig. 9   Brackets and shape of the roof in the region of Luang Prabang.

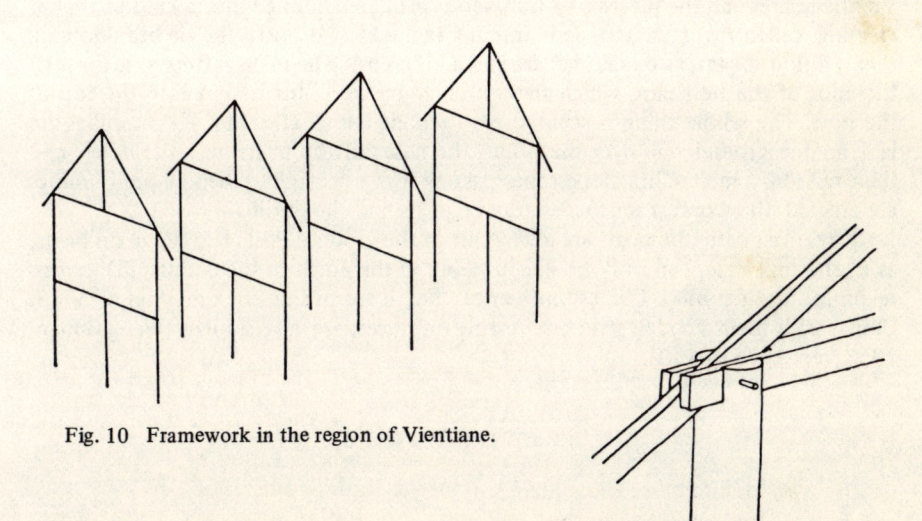

Fig. 10   Framework in the region of Vientiane.

Fig. 11   Joint of post, tie-beam and rafter.

posts had to be pointed towards the direction indicated by the scales of the *naga*.

During the house-building the Lao perform some rites, only the three main ones of which we shall relate here. The first rite is held in the forest at the foot of the trees which will be cut to make the principal posts. This rite is in honour of the spirits of the trees. The second rite, taking place on the afternoon before the erecting day, is intended to gain the favour of the spirit of the ground, the *naga*. The last one is the inauguration of the house. It can be performed on the very day of building, or several weeks later, if the finishing takes a long time. For the last two rites, Buddhist monks may be invited.

Technical aspects

The setting of the frame is not the same in both regions, revealing two different systems of building. The first one allows two kinds of contact between the post and the ground; posts can be set in the ground, or laid down on bases.

In the Luang Prabang area, posts are raised one by one; if they are not set in the ground they are temporarily tied to a scaffold. Then the tie beams are set, next, the wall plates on both sides on the tie beams' ends and, finally, the lengthwise floor beams (fig. 8). If the posts are laid down on bases, transversal bars are fixed at the same level as the joists. They form, with the floor beams, a 'stability belt', serving as a substitute for the ground. On the top, the main rafters are placed, they are laid on the tie beams, and do not extend underneath. To support the lower part of the roof, one uses brackets going through the posts. This creates the special shape of the roofs in this region (fig. 9).

In the Vientiane area, the traditional way of building is different. We were first puzzled by the fact that here, by way of contrast, the main floor beams were transversal. This can be explained by the peculiar constructional system used in the Vientiane area: all the pieces of a transversal plan are trimmed into a kind of timber framing, called *hvii* (fig. 10). This framing includes two posts, the tie beam joining them, a floor beam, two main rafters and a king post. The main rafters pass through the ends of the tie beam, which themselves lodge in a mortise cut into the top of the post. The whole thing is secured by a wooden stick (fig. 11). The framings are laid on the ground one over the other, the bases of the posts near the holes, and then raised by men pulling long ropes passing over a scaffold. When all the framings are erected, the workers set the lengthwise joists and the purlins.

In this last case, the posts are always set in the ground. Posts laid down on bases, as in the first case, can only be encountered in the north of the country. Does this technical fact denote a Chinese influence? For it seems that the buildings of South China, with their wooden structure resting on socles, are very similar. (Wang Cuilan, 1963, rep. 1975, p.150).

Notes and References:

1. The paper presented here is the result of a joint undertaking by Pierre Clément and myself. Our work is here set forth in three separate articles because it was necessary to present it in this form at the colloquium. The English translation has been checked by Mme G. Benguigui-Varro.
2. Charpentier & Clément, 1975.
3. For the transliteration of Lao words (in italics), please see note 2, p.00.
4. Only temples and spirit houses have stairs with an even number of steps; for the Lao believe that supernatural beings do everything the reverse way from humans.
5. Traditional expression.

Bibliography

Archaimbault, Charles, 1973, *Structures Religieuses Lao (Rites et Mythes)*. Vighagna, Vientiane.
Bernot, Lucien, 1967, *Les paysans arakanais du Pakistan Oriental. L'histoire le monde végétal et l'organisation des refugies Marma*. Mouton, Paris.
Boner, Alice and Rath Sarma, S., 1966, *Silpa Prakasa*. (Transl. from Ramacandra Kaulacara.) Brill, Leiden.
Bose, Nirmal Kumar, 1932, *Canons of Orissan Architecture*. R. Chatterjee, Calcutta.
Charpentier, Sophie, and Clément, Pierre, 1975, *L'habitation Lao dans les région de Vientiane et de Louang Prabang*. Thèse de 3ème cycle. Paris.
Charpentier, Sophie, and Clément, Pierre, 1975, "Deux systèmes de construction Lao. Contribution à l'étude des charpentes en Asie du Sud-Est." *ASEMI*, Vol. 6, Nos. 2-3, pp.101-132.
Condominas, Georges, and Gaudillot, Claude, 1959, *La Plaine de Vientiane. Etude Socio-Economique. Rapport d'étude*. BDPA, Paris.
Condominas, Georges, n.d., *Essai sur la société rurale Lao de la région de Vientiane*. Ed. Ministre des Affaires Rurales, Vientiane, roneo.
Doré, Pierre Sylvain, 1971, *La divination dans l'état de Lane Xang Khao*. Thèse de doctorat de 3ème cycle, Paris, roneo.
Halpern, Joel M., 1964, *Economy and Society of Laos. A brief Survey*. University of Southeast Asian Studies, Yale.
Haudricourt, André-Georges, 1968, La technologie culturelle. Essai de méthodologie. *Ethnologie Générale*, Encyclopédie de la Pléiade, Nrf, pp.731-822, Paris.
Porée-Maspéro, Evelyne, 1961, Kron Pali et rites de la maison. *Anthropos*, Vol. 56, No. 28, pp.179-251, pp.548-628, pp.883-929.
Wang Cuilan, 1963, Habitations populaires Thai à la frontière du Yunnan. (Transl. from Chinese by M. H. & G. Métailié). *ASEMI*, Vol. 6, Nos. 2-3, pp.147-158.

The Spatial Organization of the Lao House[1]

Pierre Clément

The orientation of houses has been dealt with by Professor Bernot, while Sophie Charpentier introduces the Lao house with a brief typology. The intention here is to analyse the plan of the house, trying to understand it in different ways and from its various aspects: physical, social, ritual, functional ... in relation to spatial organization. For this purpose we are to consider:

1. The system of orientation used by Lao people,
2. The rules governing the orientation of the houses,
3. The internal orientation,
4. The rules of access and moving through the houses,
5. The rules governing the space structuring, at first in the village, then from a theoretical point of view relating to architectural composition.

The orientation system

Lao people, cultivating wet rice in the flat country, will place their villages near a stream, which is the foremost physical element in the orientation system. Such a stream is at first an axial line of orientation with two directions: *hnùùa*,[2] i.e. upstream and *tae2*, i.e. downstream (fig. 1). Then it divides space into two parts: one bank (*f̂aak*) and the other bank (*f̂aak nai*), corresponding to two stretches of land and enabling one to identify two other directions: the bank where we are and the other one. In most cases, villages are placed on one bank only. These two directions are referred to differently, depending on the site and the location of the village or the town.

In Vientiane, for example, the Lao make a distinction between *t̂haa1*, i.e. the bank and *t̂hong1*, i.e. the plain (fig. 2). In Luang Prabang, where the flat country is not very wide and the town surrounded by mountains, they say *t̂haa1*, i.e. the bank and *baan2*, i.e. the village (fig. 3).[3]

But, fortunately, major streams are flowing mostly from the north to the south, which is at least the direction of the Mekong serving as an axial line of orientation in the whole country. So *hnùùa* and *tae2*, i.e. upstream and downstream, were used to indicate north and south, as opposed to the sunrise, *taavan 9OOk*, and sunset, *taavan tok*, direction (fig. 4).

In addition to this system, the terms of which are specific to Thai languages, Lao astrologers will use Indian terms.

Thus *hnùùa* and *tae2* are given various practical meanings, applying to various cases:
       — one in a local situation with reference to the stream,
       — another one, on a national scale with reference to the Mekong,
       — another one, on a universal scale with reference to the cardinal points.

Thus we have a multi-scale orientation, like a nest of elements.

THE LAO HOUSE: SPATIAL ORGANIZATION   63

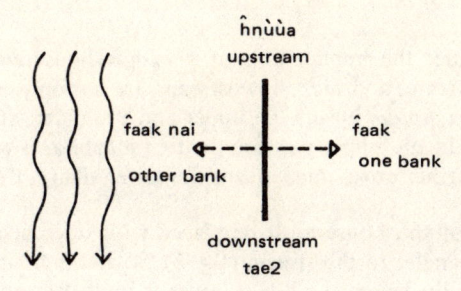

Fig. 1 The basic system of orientation.

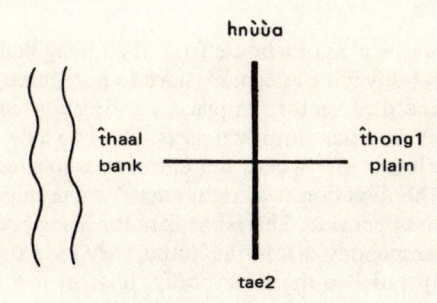

Fig. 2 The orientation in Vientiane.

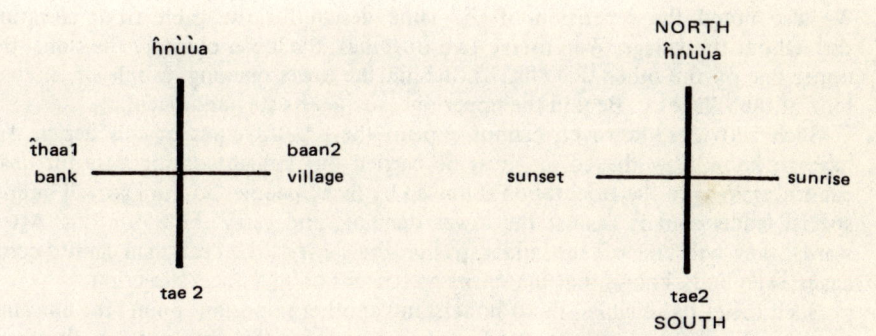

Fig. 3 The orientation in
Luang Prabang.

Fig. 4 The orientation with
reference to cardinal points.

The orientation rules of the houses

We shall now consider the implications of placing a house with reference to this system. *hnùùa*, upstream, and *tae2*, downstream, are not only spatial, but temporal and social references. *hnùùa* means the upper and the older village, the top or the head of the village. In the upper part are the first inhabitants while the newcomers will settle a little further down. *tae2* means the lower village, the tail or the bottom of the village.

First, the ridge of the house must be placed with reference to the stream, the ridge purlin being parallel to the stream (fig. 5). So all the houses will have parallel ridges. But what really happens when a house is built near another one? To find out, we have to look inside the house.

The internal orientation

Let us take for example a plan of a house from the Luang Prabang area. We see the position of someone's body lying asleep. We have to note three points if we consider this body like a geometrical vector: its place, its direction and the position of its head. The ridge divides the house into two parts. The Lao have to sleep in the upper part opposite to the lower one where the entrance is located and through which they have to move. The direction is at right angles to the ridge purlin and the head is directed towards the upper side. This is the case for living people (fig. 6).

In contrast, when somebody dies in the house, they have to put him in the other part, the lower part, parallel to the ridge purlin, his feet facing the front elevation of the gable (fig. 7).

The rules of access and moving through the house

We also noted the repetition of the same design for the gable front elevation throughout the village. We observe two openings: the lower one near the stairs, the upper one on the other side (fig. 8). Behind the lower opening, people sit, discuss, look at the village ... Behind the upper one, the guests stay and sleep.

Such activities, however, cannot explain the repetitiveness of this design. We have to know how the coffin must be carried out straight on, because the dead cannot again take the orientation followed by living people. So the Lao will build a special ladder, put it against the lower opening, and carry the coffin out. Afterwards, they will take off the ladder, so that the spirit of the dead man cannot come again; everybody knows that the spirits go straight on in a linear direction.

Such belief has enabled us to understand another important point: the entrance location. We have already noticed various places for the entrance: on the front gable in Vientiane and on the side in Luang Prabang. At first we thought that there was a difference between the two areas, but then we noted some other locations on the side in the Vientiane area if the house had a *labyeng*, i.e. a front veranda; on the front gable in Luang Prabang if the house had a *ŝye*, i.e. a lengthwise veranda. As we

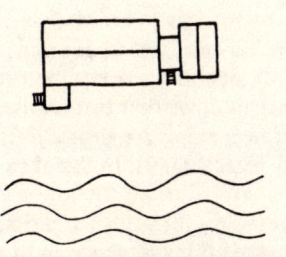

Fig. 5   The ridge purlin is parallel to the stream.

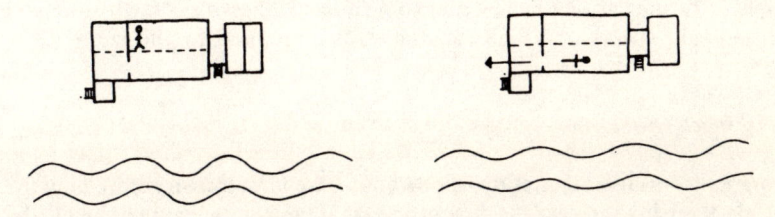

Fig. 6   The orientation of living people.   Fig. 7   The orientation of dead people.

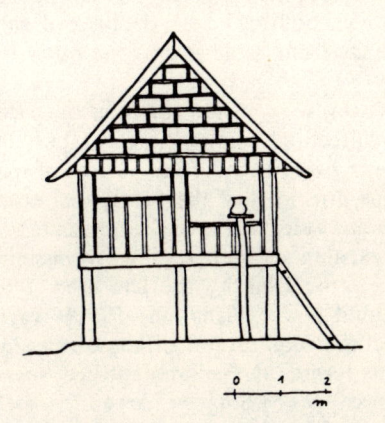

Fig. 8   The design of the gable front elevation.

shall see, the principle will be the same in both areas. In order to protect the inside of the house from intrusion, especially the bedroom, the Lao when entering follow a direction parallel to the door opening into the next room, so we cannot go straight on through the room; the guest knows that this is where he must stop.

This rule, which consists in making a right-angle turn after entering or leaving a room, is illustrated in many cases (fig. 9). In the examples stated we are going from the inside to the outside.

If we go out of the bedroom, we must turn at a right angle and, if there is a front veranda then turn left. The same thing is shown in the houses of the Luang Prabang area. We have to notice that, when changing direction, we must also go down a little further. The spatial hierarchy is marked by various levels in the location of rooms. The highest place being the bedroom, we go down slowly, step by step. The same principle of turning at right angles and going down is shown again when we go backwards and take the second flight of stairs which are used by the family as service stairs.

Rules of space structuring

We now return to the orientation of one house. We have shown before how the Lao will settle their houses near the stream and what happens when they build a second house next to the first one.

First of all, as nobody is allowed to place his feet towards somebody else's head, the dweller in the next house must place his head opposite to his neighbour's head or his feet opposite to his neighbour's feet (fig. 10). In the same way, the back cannot face the front of the neighbouring house; the back of one house will be against the back of another, and the front gable against the other front gable opening on the street (fig. 11).

Behind regional differences, we can find the rules of space structuring and their implications as regards architectural composition. A table (fig. 12), is used to show a way of schematic synthesis giving a theoretical pattern of spatial organization.

The headings state some principles of the Lao spatial organization: orientation, hierarchy, social partition and rules of moving. Immediately below these are given some general principles existing in both regions; we assume that such rules are general rules of the space structuring by the Lao even if some of them are unconscious and hidden behind new explanations or new ways of use. In the lower half we have the architectural implications of these rules in both areas of Luang Prabang and Vientiane. As regards the column entitled 'social partition', we must refer to the analysis of house types by Sophie Charpentier (see pp.00-00). As regards the column 'functional partition' which we have not yet dealt with in this paper, we must say that all the houses are divided into three parts: one public space for receiving guests, one private space for the family and one space for service. These three elements are not distributed in the same way in both areas: linear in Luang Prabang, radial in Vientiane. They can be divided in two elements: a served space and a serving space.

We intend to use this pattern of spatial organization to compare the houses of the various Thai ethnic groups.

THE LAO HOUSE: SPATIAL ORGANIZATION

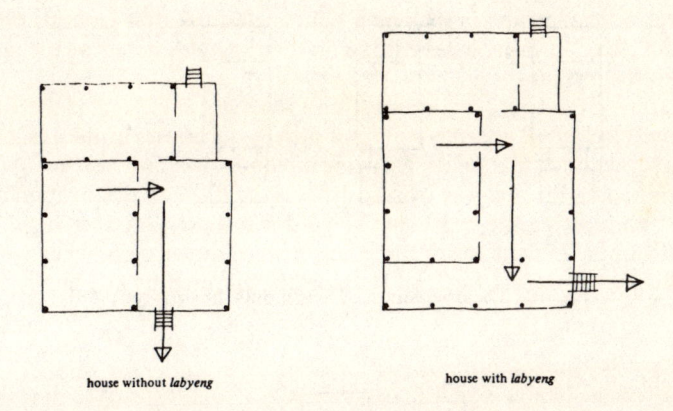

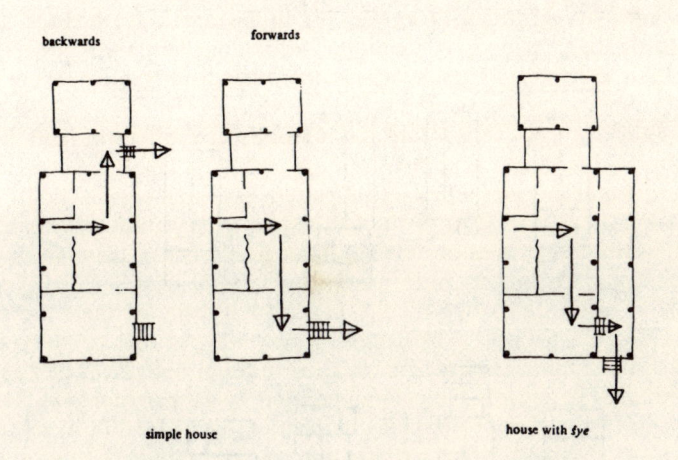

house without *labyeng*

house with *labyeng*

backwards forwards

simple house

house with *fye*

Fig. 9 The principle of moving through the house.

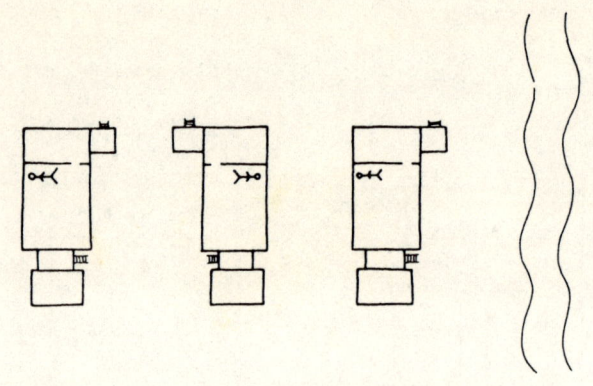

Fig. 10 The orientation of neighbours' houses (see p.66).

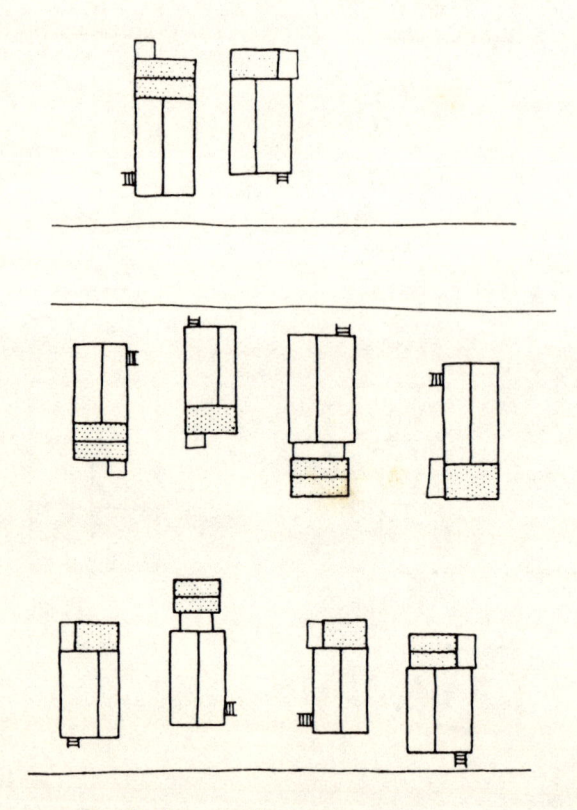

Fig 11 A group of houses (see p.66).

Architectural implications	Orientation	Hierarchy	Social partition	Functional partition	Moving
General laws	– Ridge purlin **∥** to the stream or **∥** the sun's orbit E — W – Living people and dead people Living ⊥ ridge dead **∥** ridge	– Opposition head/foot – Internal organization up + down – – Group of houses	Opposition: inhabitants/guests closed/open	– In 3 areas: reception/living/services – Binary dissociation of each area: served space/serving space	Opposition spirits/living people – linear for spirits and dead people – right angles for living people
General rules *Luang Prabang*			Transversal:	ĥaan2/room/services 1 2 3 linear distribution	– Dead's window – Access
Vientiane			Longitudinal:	ŝye/room/services 1 2 3 radial distribution	– Access

Fig. 12 The rules of space structuring.

Notes and References

1. The paper presented here is a result of a joint work between Sophie Charpentier and myself, translated into English with the aid of Chantal Thérond, translator at the Institut de l'Environment.
2. For the transliteration of Lao words Sophie Charpentier and I have used the system of Marc Reinhorn, Professor of Lao at the Institut National des Langues et Civilisations Orientales, Paris.
   The aspirated consonants are written: (1) with an 'h' after k, t, p; (2) with an 'h' before n, m, l (also written in Lao).
   The consonants k, t, p have three forms: one normal k, one high aspirated kh, one low aspirated k̂h.
   The consonants s and f have two forms: one normal s, one low ŝ.
   The consonant h has two forms, both aspirated: one high h, one low ĥ.
   The ñ indicates the 'gn'.
   The 9 indicates the glottal stop.
   The long vowels are repeated, e.g., aa. The O and E indicate an 'open' o and e.
   The figures 1 and 2 written after the words indicate the accent, '1' a rising accent, '2' a low and modulated accent.
3. As regards the orientation in Luang Prabang, see: Luc Mogenet, La conception de l'espace à Louang Prabang, *Bulletin des Amis Royaume Lao*, Nos. 7-8, pp.166-196.

Bibliography

Archaimbault, C., 1963, Contribution à l'étude du rituel funéraire lao. *Journal of the Siam Society*. Vol. 51(1): 1-63. Repr. in: *Structures Religieuses Lao (Rites et Mythes)*. Vientiane, Vithagna, 1973.

Bernot, L., 1955, Contribution à l'étude internationale des structures sociales: l'espace et le temps. *Bulletin international des Sciences Sociales*. U.N.E.S.C.O. Vol. 7(4): 643-52. Paris.

Bernot, L., 1967a, *Les paysans arakanais du Pakistan Oriental–L'histoire, le monde végétal et l'organisation sociale des réfugiés Marma (Mog)*. Mouton, Paris/La Haye.

Bernot, L., 1967b, *Les Cak, contribution à l'étude ethnographique d'une population de langue loi*. C.N.R.S. Paris.

Maspéro, H., 1923, Les coutumes funéraires chez les Tai Noirs du Haut Tonkin. *Bulletin de l'Association Francaise des Amis de l'Orient*. No. 6, pp.13-26. –Repr. in: *Les Religions Chinoises*. Paris, 1950.

Mogenet, L., 1972, Notes sur la conception de l'espace à Louang Prabang. *Bulletin des Amis du Royaume Lao*. Nos. 7-8, pp.166-96.

Pétonnet, C., 1972, L'Espace, distance et dimension dans une société musulmane. A propos du bidonville marocain de Douar Doum à Rabat. *L'homme*. Apr.-June, pp.47-84.

The Lao House among the Thai Houses: A comparative survey and a preliminary classification[1]

Pierre Clément

Before starting this presentation, we must say that, if the first part of our contribution referred to a work already finished, the second part will deal with a research that we have just begun[2] (Charpentier, 1975). We formulate some questions, some hypotheses not yet confirmed. But, as we thought that it would be very interesting to discuss our approach with the participants of the meeting, we have agreed to state it at our own risk.

In our first paper above we considered the spatial organization of the Lao house. That study originated from field-work, from direct observation of dwellings, of everyday life, of ritual ceremonies. Such work was a comparative study between the houses of the Vientiane and the Luang Prabang areas, only as regards Lao people. In addition to the house distribution and in order to go further than the mere static analysis of typology and morphology, we tried to make a dynamic approach by observing the various uses of houses, the continuous movements inside, and inside and out. We tried, then, to define some rules of space structuring, common to both areas.

We now want to know if these rules refer to Lao people only or have a wider distribution and are valid for other Thai ethnic groups as well. We shall ask the following question: is there one set of rules governing the spatial organization of houses? And since in ethnology linguistic classification is used to make comparative studies we shall approach the problem in the same way. But if such a comparative study results in a positive answer to the above question, we shall then have to compare the Thai spatial organization of houses with that used by the other linguistic groups in Southeast Asia. For example, the pile dwellings have a very different meaning in Laos where the Thai-Lao are the majority, from what they have in Vietnam where the Vietnamese majority have their houses on the ground.

But, at a first stage, we will limit the comparison to Thai people, and if we find a significant pattern, we shall try to compare it with the patterns of the other linguistic groups.

We are aware that when comparing within the Thai linguistic group we risk committing the sin of evolutionism. We are tempted to classify the houses from the simplest to the most sophisticated ones, and thus to formulate historical conclusions (An Nimmanahaeminda, 1966). In order to avoid such historicism we shall compare the systems of relationship between elements (e.g., rules of movement), instead of the elements themselves (e.g., number of doors). Further examination of these problems through the study of Chinese historical documents will be carried out later on.

In this second part of our presentation, our study is hindered by various obstacles. Thus the lack of bibliographic sources limits our study to the plan of the houses as we have insufficient information about the use and significance of the house. Limiting our study to the plans alone, we may be subjected to the same criticism already

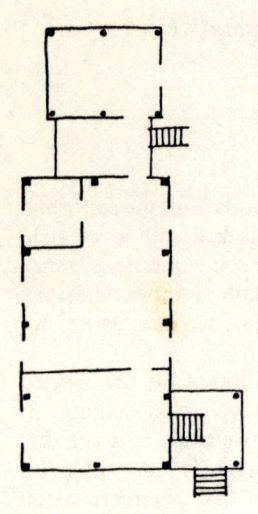

Fig. 1 Lao house, Luang Prabang area.

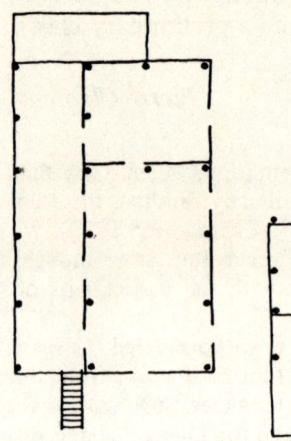

Fig. 2 Lao house, Vientiane area: 'simple'.

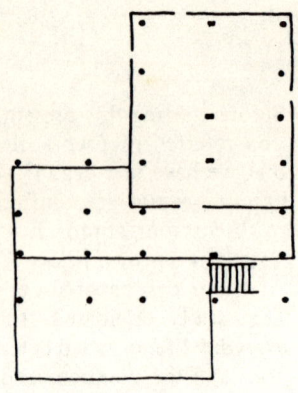

Fig. 3 Lü house, Chieng Kham area.

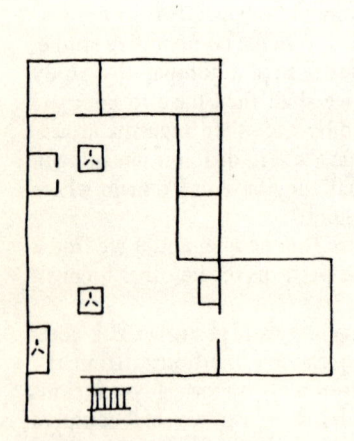

Fig. 4 Tho house, Red River (Lunet de Lajonquière).

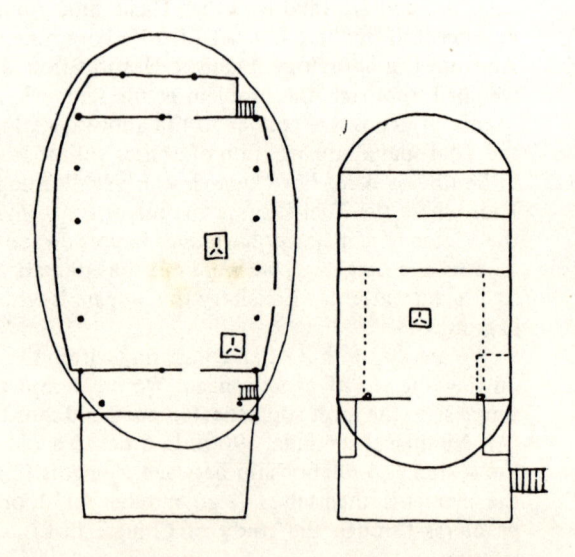

Fig. 5 Black Thai house (Dang Nghiem Van).

Fig. 6 Shan house (Scherman).

Fig. 11 Zhuang house in Jingxi (Sun Yitai).

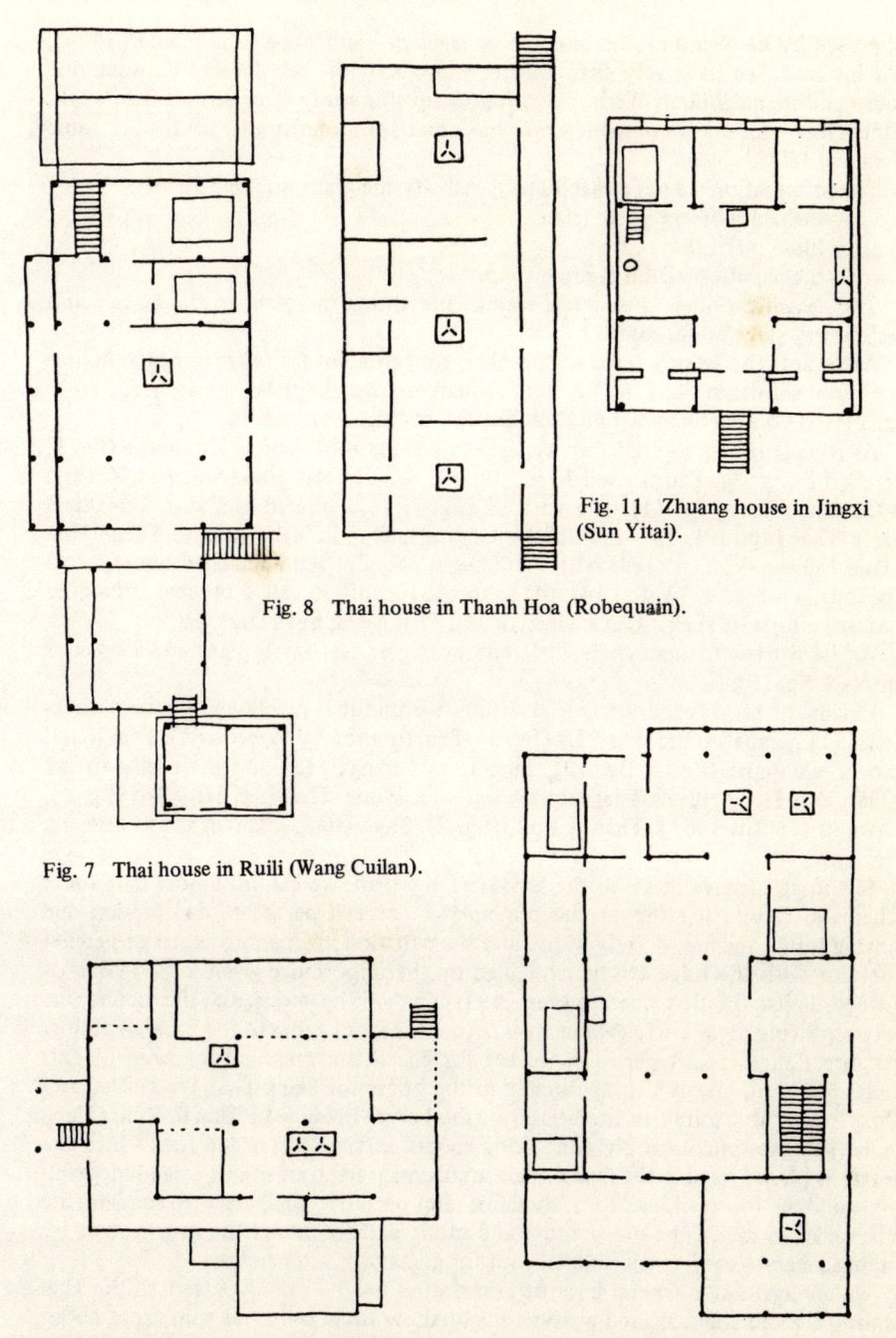

Fig. 8 Thai house in Thanh Hoa (Robequain).

Fig. 7 Thai house in Ruili (Wang Cuilan).

Fig. 10 White Thai house (Dang Nghiem Van).

Fig. 9 Zhuang house in Longji (Sun Yitai).

expressed by us regarding the research of Nguyen Van Huyen (Charpentier, 1974). For instance, we have very little information about the relationship between one house and its neighbour. We hope to follow up this study after further field work. (Since this paper was completed, we have had the opportunity of visiting some Shan and Lü villages.)

The information we have enables us to classify the plans on the basis of:
— the overall form of the plan
— the type of the roof
— the partition of the internal space

This classification is a practical way of presenting the plans of the houses at a preliminary stage in our research.

As regards the overall form of the plan, we can identify: (1) rectangular houses like those shown in fig. 1 to fig. 9; (2) square houses like those shown in fig. 10 to fig. 14; (3) isolated Siamese buildings like the one shown in fig. 15.

As regards roofs, we find four types: (1) a gable roof: simple Lao house (fig. 1, fig. 2), Lü (fig. 3), Tho of Red River (fig. 4), Shan of Mae Hong Son area, Zhuang in Guangxi (fig. 9, fig. 11), Thai in Ruili (fig. 7); (2) a hipped roof with four sides: White Thai (fig. 10), Tho (quoted by Gourou), Thai in Nghe An and Thanh Hoa (Dang Nghiem Van, p. 184); (3) a double A roof for semi-detached houses: Lao (fig. 12), Yuan (fig. 13, fig. 14); (4) a 'tortoise' roof (so called because it has the shape of a tortoise shell): Black Thai (fig. 5), Thai Neua, Shan (fig. 6).

We have tried to map these different examples of overall plans and shapes of roof (see fig. 18).

Finally, as regards the internal partition, we find that it follows two main directions: (1) parallel to the ridge: Lü (fig. 3), Thai (quoted by Robequain), Thai Neua, Lao in Vientiane (fig. 2, fig. 12), Zhuang in Guangxi; (2) at right angles to the ridge: Thai Deng, Black Thai (fig. 5, fig. 17), White Thai (fig. 10), Tho (fig. 4), Khampti (Census 1961), Thai in Ruili (fig. 7), Shan (fig. 6), Lao in Luang Prabang (fig. 1).

But if we observe in detail the layout of the plan, we can read more than these schematic results relating to the principles of access, partition, distribution and moving inside the house. In fact, the internal partition in a perpendicular or parallel direction with the ridge can be explained by the importance given to two types of privacy limits: the first one between the family and the guests, and the second one between living areas and sleeping areas. From the front gable to the back we follow the direction of social partition: places for guests, for men and for women. This social partition, clearly distinguishable in the houses of Black Thai, White Thai and Shan is now also found in the houses of the Lao or Siamese or Thai in Ruili (Wang Cuilan) as the functional division: living rooms, service (water and fire)—since the hearth is placed outside the living space, under a special roof or in a small independant building for cooking. In a dynamic approach we shall have to explain the tendencies to divide the house more and more, and to extend the original core by adding a lean-to roof, or an isolated roof for granary or kitchen use.

We are again at a general level of observation on the overall pattern of the Thai houses; a more sophisticated analysis might show some other relevant facts, about the location and the direction of the stairs and about the rules of moving inside the

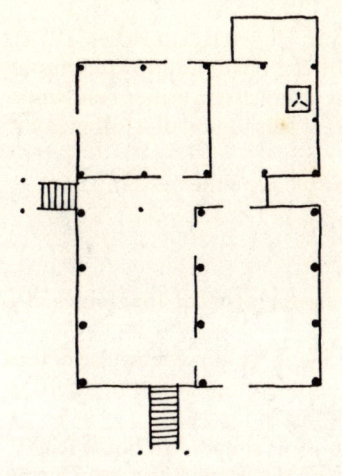

Fig. 12 Lao house, Vientiane area: 'semi-detached'.

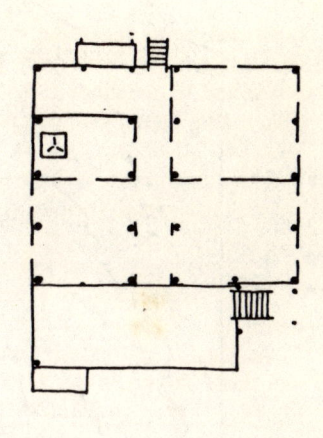

Fig. 13 Yuan house near Sayaboury.

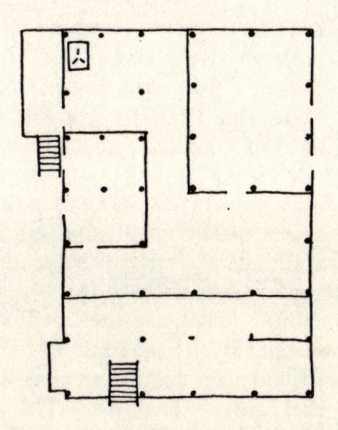

Fig. 14 Yuan house, Chieng Mai area.

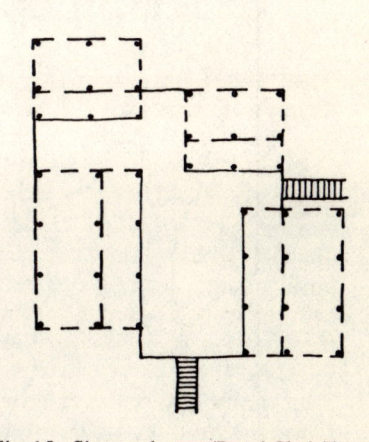

Fig. 15 Siamese house (Rutai Chai Chongrak).

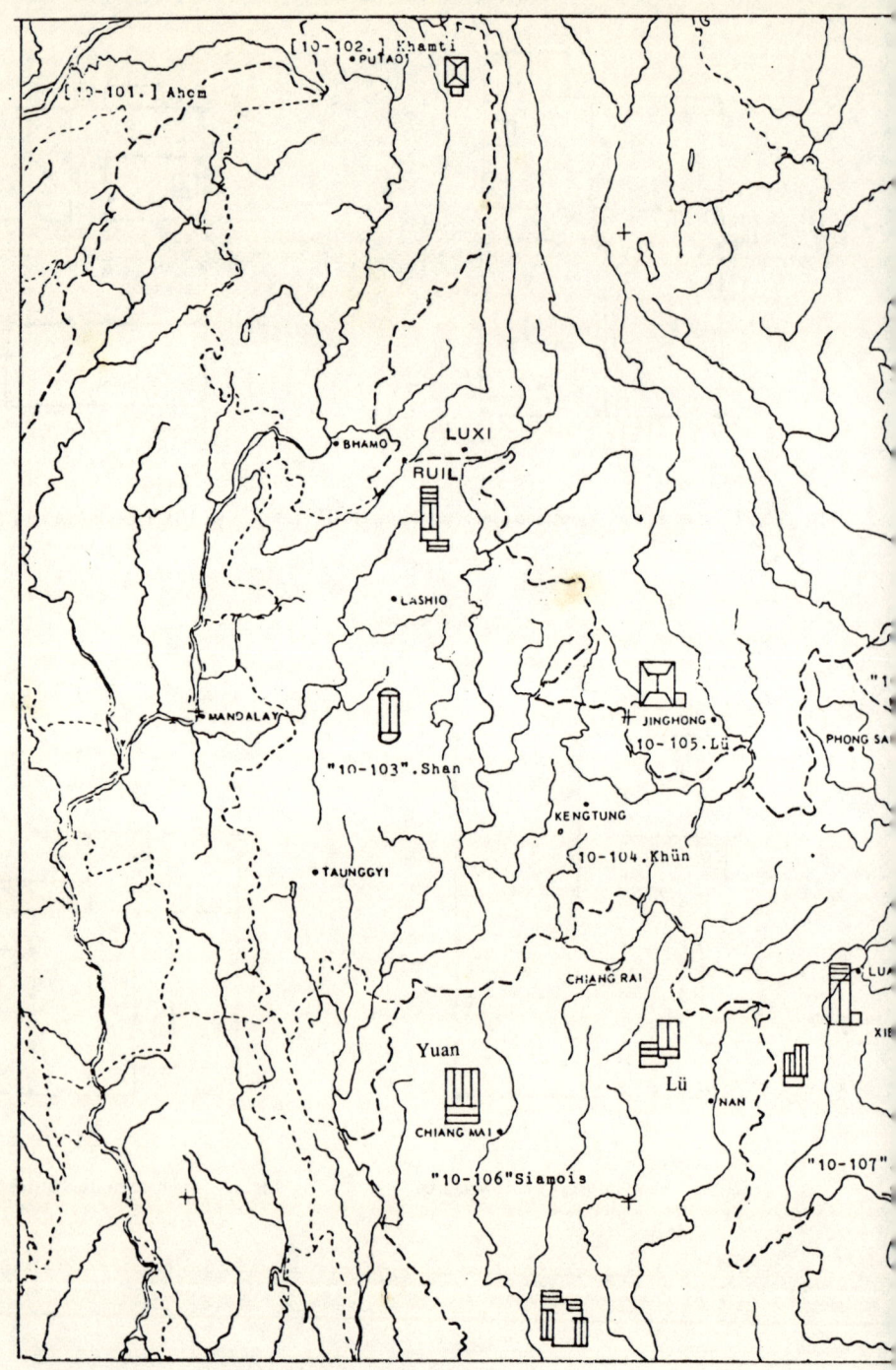

Fig. 18 Thai groups and types of house: form and roof.

77

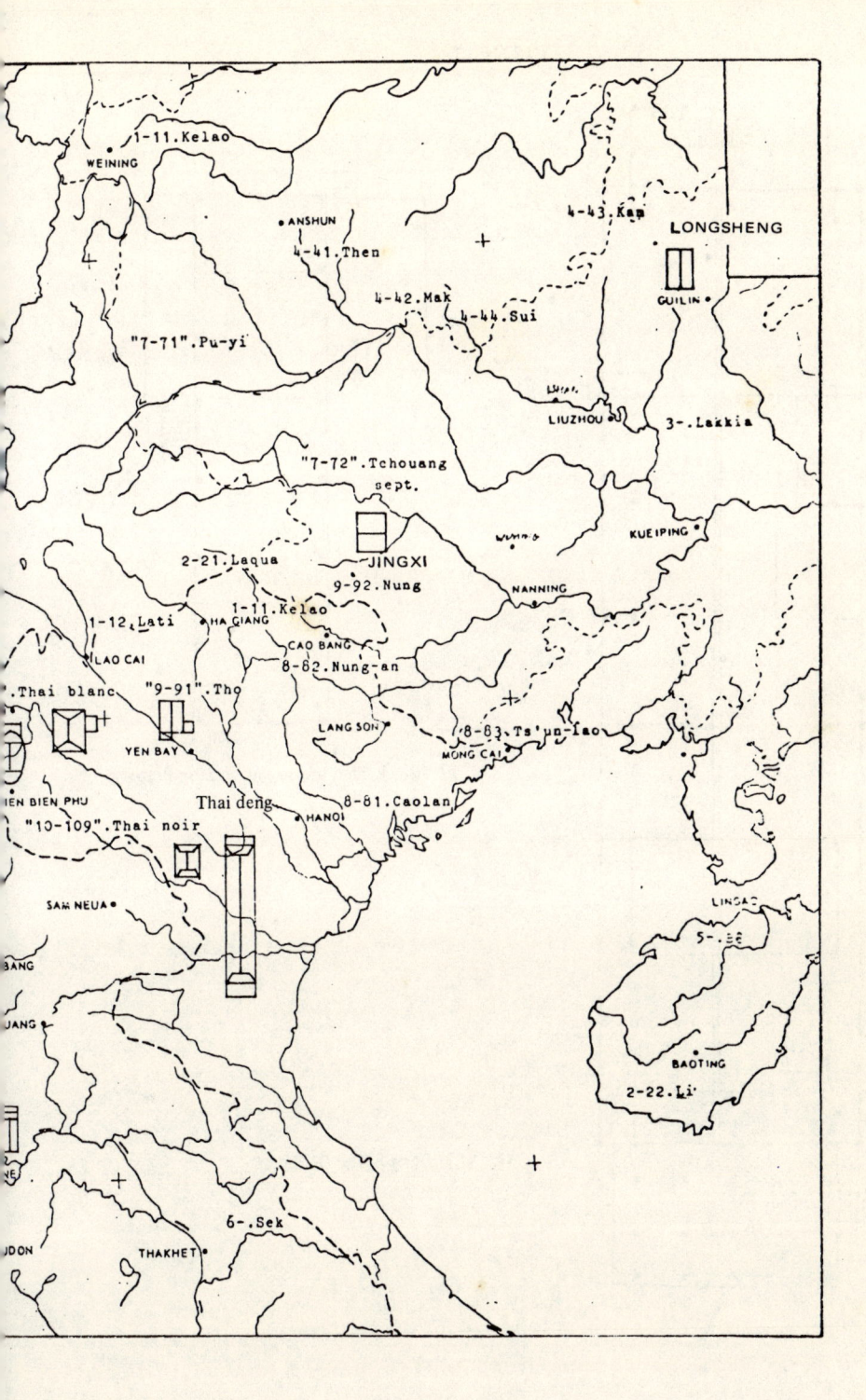

1-11.Kelao
WEINING
• ANSHUN
4-41.Then
4-43.Kam
LONGSHENG
4-42.Mak
GUILIN
4-44.Sui
"7-71".Pu-yi
LIUZHOU
3-.Lakkia
"7-72".Tchouang
sept.
KUEIPING
2-21.Laqua
JINGXI
NANNING
9-92.Nung
1-12.Lati
1-11.Kelao
HA GIANG
LAO CAI
CAO BANG
8-82.Nung-an
.Thai blanc
"9-91".Tho
YEN BAY
LANG SON
8-83.Ts'un-lao
MONG CAI
Thai deng
8-81.Caolan
DIEN BIEN PHU
HANOI
"10-109".Thai noir
SAM NEUA
LINGAO
5-.Be
BANG
JANG
BAOTING
2-22.Li
UDON
6-.Sek
THAKHET

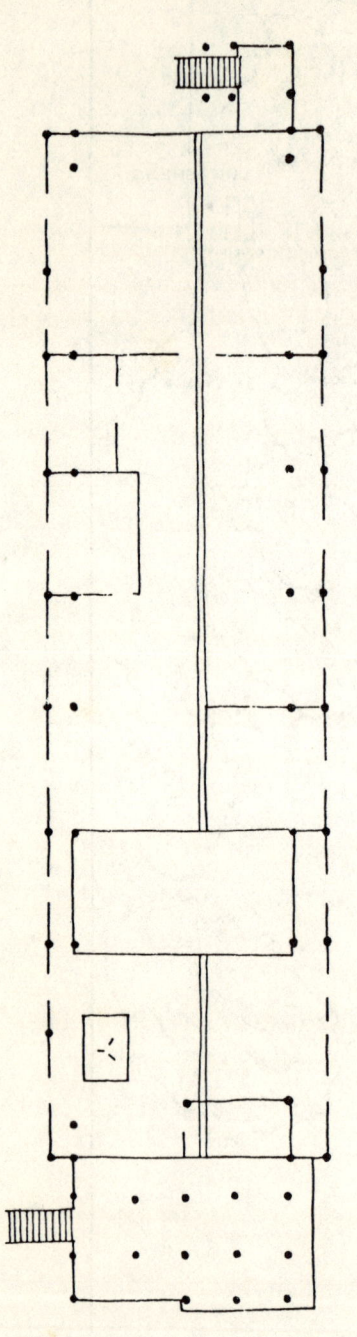

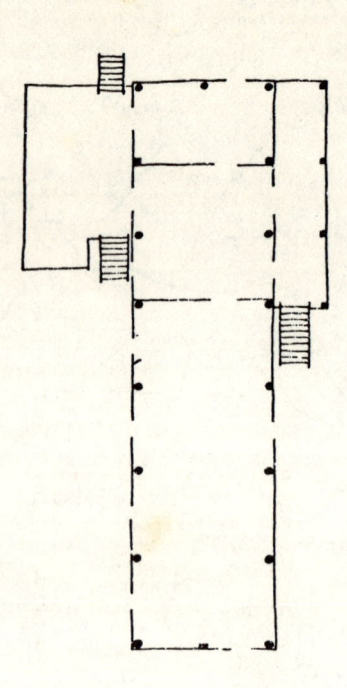

Fig. 17 Black Thai house near Luang Prabang.

Fig. 16 Thai Deng house (Robert).

house. The house has one flight of stairs (Lü, Shan) or two flights of stairs; the main stairs being in the front and the secondary stairs, if any, (service stairs for women or family use) in the back in Lao, Yuan, Black Thai, White Thai, Thai Deng and Tho houses. The main stairs are in the front part of the house, in the front gable or just near it on the long side: generally they are on the opposite side of the sleeping area. In addition, their direction depends on the orientation of the long side of the area to which they lead, this direction always being parallel to the entrance of the next room, protecting the inside privacy, and compelling one to make a right-angle turn in order to enter the next room. As for the Lao house it appears clearly that the inhabitants protect themselves against the visitors' eyes, but also against the spirits who always move straight on. One example is at variance with this principle. Reference is made to the Zhuang house at Jingxi (Guangxi) where the stairs are on one central axis. Undoubtedly we have here the mark of Chinese influence, for the composition of the Thai houses is never based on a principle of symmetry. We intend to go further in our analysis, but our purpose in this contribution is to indicate some methodological directions and some elements of the corpus of our current research, and is not meant to provide all the answers. In addition, the methodological approach will have to be most strictly applied to real life, and other more accurate examples will be collected.

But from now on, we can note that the pattern structuring the Lao space throws light on the other types of houses of Thai groups from a novel point of view, anticipating a relevant comparative study of this linguistic family within the context of architectural research.

Notes and References

1. The paper presented here is the result of a joint work between Sophie Charpentier and myself, translated into English with the aid of Chantal Thérond, translator at the Institut de l'Environment.
2. Since this paper we have published the following book on the same subject: *Eléments comparatifs sur les habitations des ethnies de langues thai*. Paris: Centre d'Etude et de Recherches Architecturales, 1978. 259 pp.

Bibliography

Abadie, Maurice, 1924, *Les races du Haut-Tonkin de Phong Tho à Lang Son*. Sociéte d'Editions Géographiques, Maritimes et Coloniales. Paris.
An Nimmanahaeminda, 1966, Thai traditional domestic architecture. In: *The Kamthieng House* by J. J. Boeles, pp.39–47.
Boeles, J. J. & Sternstein, L., 1966, *The Khamtieng House. An introduction*. Siam Society, Bangkok.

Census of India, 1961, *Report on House Type and Village Settlement Patterns in India*. Vol 1, part IV.A (iii). Govt. of India Press, Delhi.

Charpentier, S. & Clément, P., 1974, Notes sur l'habitation sur pilotis en Asie du Sud-Est. *ASEMI* V (2): 13-24.

Charpentier, S. & Clément, P., 1975, Pour une approche ethno-architecturale de l'habitation. In: *Histoire et Théorie de l'Architecture*. Institut de l'Environment, pp.127-130, Paris.

Dang Nghiem Van, 1971, Aperçu sur les Thai du Viet Nam. *Etudes Vietnamiennes*. Données ethnographiques, I (32): 163-222.

Diguet, Col. E., 1908, *Les montagnards du Tonkin*. Challamel, Paris.

Gourou, P., 1936, *Les paysans du delta tonkinois: étude de géographie humaine*. Rep. 1965. Mouton, Paris/La Haye.

Haudricourt, A. G., 1970, Les arguments géographiques, écologiques et sémantiques pour l'origine des Thai. In: *Readings on Asian Topics*, pp.27-34, Copenhagen.

Izikowitz, K. G., 1962, Notes about the Tai. In: *The Museum of Far Eastern Antiquities Bullet*. XXXIV: 73-91. Stockholm.

Lévy, A., 1972 a, Les Langues Thai. *ASEMI*, III (1): 89-113.

Lévy, A., 1972 b, Présentation des feuilles de cartes de la famille thai. *ASEMI*, III (4): 21-25+ cartes.

Lunet de Lajonquière, Ct. E., 1916, *Ethnographie du Tonkin Septentrional*. Paris.

Raquez, A., 1902, *Pages Laotiennes*. Hanoi.

Robequain, C., 1929, *Le Thanh Hoa, étude géographique d'une province annamite*. Van Oest, Paris/Bruxelles.

Robert, R., 1941, *Notes sur les Tay Deng de Lang Chanh*. Hanoi.

Rutai Chai Chongrak, 1975, *The Old Thai House* (in Siamese). Silpakorn University. Bangkok.

Scherman, L., 1915, Wohnhaustypen in Birma und Assam. *Archiv für Anthr*. n.s. 14. Transl. by Barbara Wall, *ASEMI*, V (2-3): 159-199.

Sun Yitai, 1963, Présentation sommaire des constructions surélevées *malan* des Zhuang du Guangxi. Transl. by M. H. et G. Métailié, *ASEMI*, V (2-3): 133-146.

Wang Cuilan, 1963, Habitations populaires thai à la frontière du Yunnan. Transl. by M. H. et G. Métailié, *ASEMI*, V (2-3): 147-158.

Two Houses in Thailand

Jørgen Rahbek Thomsen

The farmer's house

About 20 kilometres north of the town of Lampang in North Thailand on the highway to Ngao and Chieng Rai a laterite track branches off from the main road into the dense forest. The road looks fairly newly constructed, and a sign gives the reason for the existence of the road to be the construction of the Kew Lom Dam on the Wang River about 20 kilometres further into the forest. But not all the traffic on the road is from the dam site. Small local buses crowded with villagers and their bundles and baskets tell us that the road also serves a number of remote farmer settlements located in the jungles. It is a new mode of transportation for the villagers who for years have had to use the river, one of the reasons why the villages have been located so close to the river.

One such village is Ban Mae Mai situated close to the new road. The village is on a fairly high river bank on a place where the River Wang is met by a small tributary, Nam Mae Mai, forming a kind of "traffic junction" for the traditional transportation system, a typical location of settlements in Thailand.

The village consists of about 60 households living in compounds of different sizes. The average plot of land within the village area is about 1,000 square metres. Most compounds have access to the small lanes forming the internal communication system in the village, but despite the neat fences of bamboo and wood enclosing the compounds, everybody seems to cross everybody's land. In accordance with the joint family system several generations normally inhabit each compound which can have one or several houses, almost all built according to the traditional architectural and structural concept.

A typical compound is No. 23, according to the numbering system used in the local census, which tells furthermore that the household consists of 10 persons. The compound covers an area of 900 square metres. The buildings consist of a dwelling with two separate bedrooms, a terrace, and a kitchen. In front of the living quarters in a rather auspicious setting is the rice granary. It is built on heavy stilts leaning inwards. The importance of this building to the family is indicated by its setting alone. In a corner of the compound is a shed covering the rice pounder, from which you can hear the characteristic sound, such as can be heard as the background rhythm in

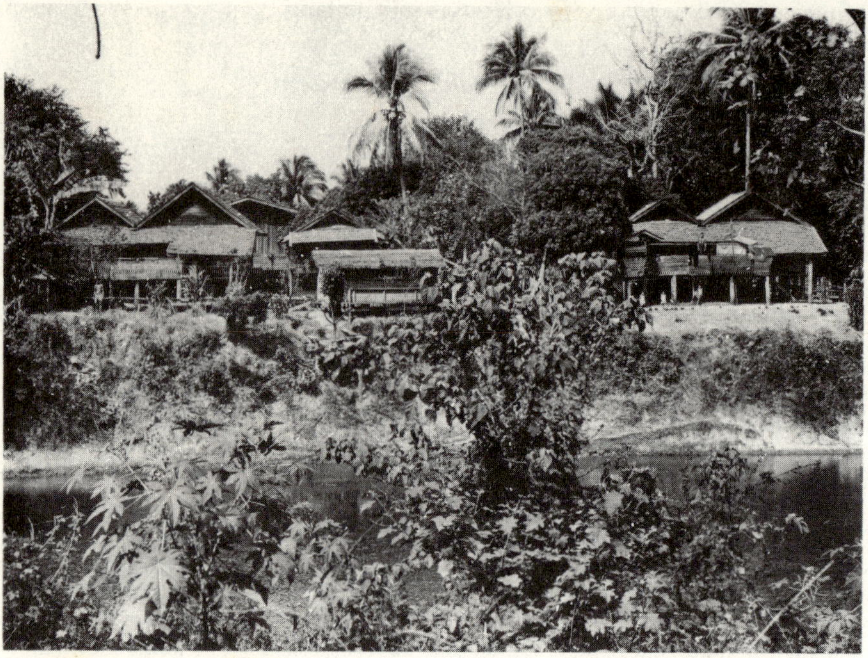

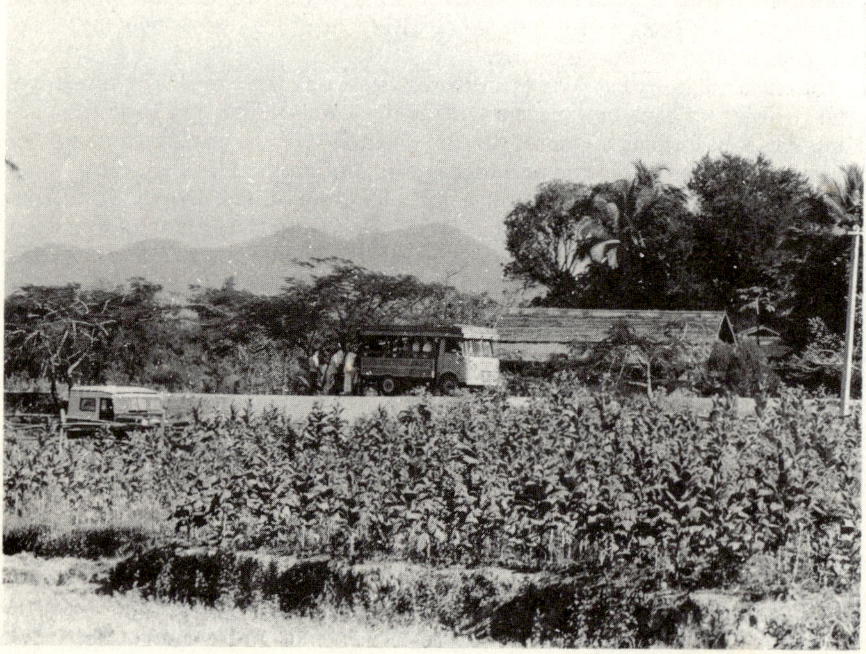

TWO HOUSES IN THAILAND

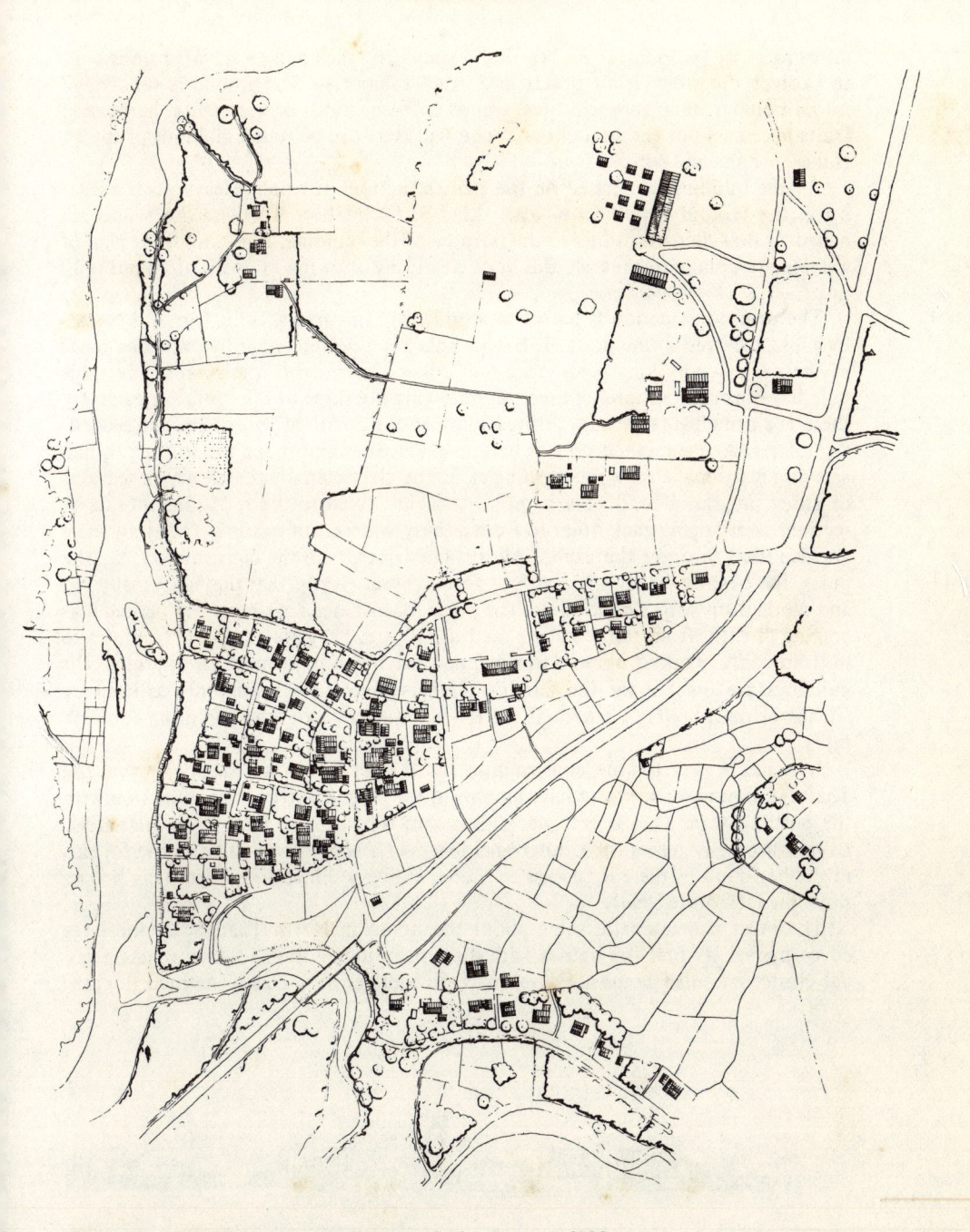

Plan of Ban Mae Mai and surrounding area. Scale approx. 1:6000.

all villages. In addition to this we find a small cart shed and an elevated floor built to protect the straw from floods and other calamities. The ground is subdivided into a number of small enclosures, where different kinds of vegetables, herbs, and fruits necessary for the household are grown. Here can be found all kinds of spices, chilies, banana and papaya trees.

All the buildings are based on the same structural principle. Heavy posts are set up in the ground without any other kind of foundation. To these the beams are nailed or dowelled according to the purpose of the building. A ground floor plan of a complete compound reveals this very clearly by showing no walls at all but only posts.

The roof construction is based on a grid of beams fixed to the top of the posts by pins or carved in the posts. The ridge pole is supported either by extended posts in the gables or by king posts from the crossing beams over the rooms. The ridge pole has normally a rhomboid section following the slope of the roof. For each bay there is a principal rafter supporting a number of horizontal purlins and the secondary rafters. A fine-meshed grid of battens gives the support for the roofing, which was originally made of wooden shingles or the characteristic thatch where sections of straw or grass bound to a bamboo stick are fixed to the roof-construction in sections overlapping each other to form a fairly waterproof roofing. The straw mats are also used to cover the gables. All the wooden parts of the construction, e.g. the posts, the beams, the shingles, and so forth, reveal clearly that they are locally cut and worked up with simple tools. The posts for instance are simply the barked logs coming directly from the woods around the village. They are one piece from top to bottom, only worked up to form a tenon on the top to meet the purlins. The buildings are erected by the family members themselves, sometimes assisted by friends or neighbours in a natural collaboration necessitated by the more complex tasks.

It is not a very unique construction and it is in fact rather surprising that the Thai tradition never seems to have employed the diagonal strut in combination with the posts to form a static triangle. This is surprising because most vernacular architecture normally meets such functional needs in a superb way. The reason for this might be found in the easy access to timber in heavy dimensions. But many houses show the lack quite clearly.

The most characteristic thing about the house in North Thailand is the large covered area. At first the houses with their many joined roofs look more like a casual cluster of small houses. However, these roofs cover a clearly defined floorage

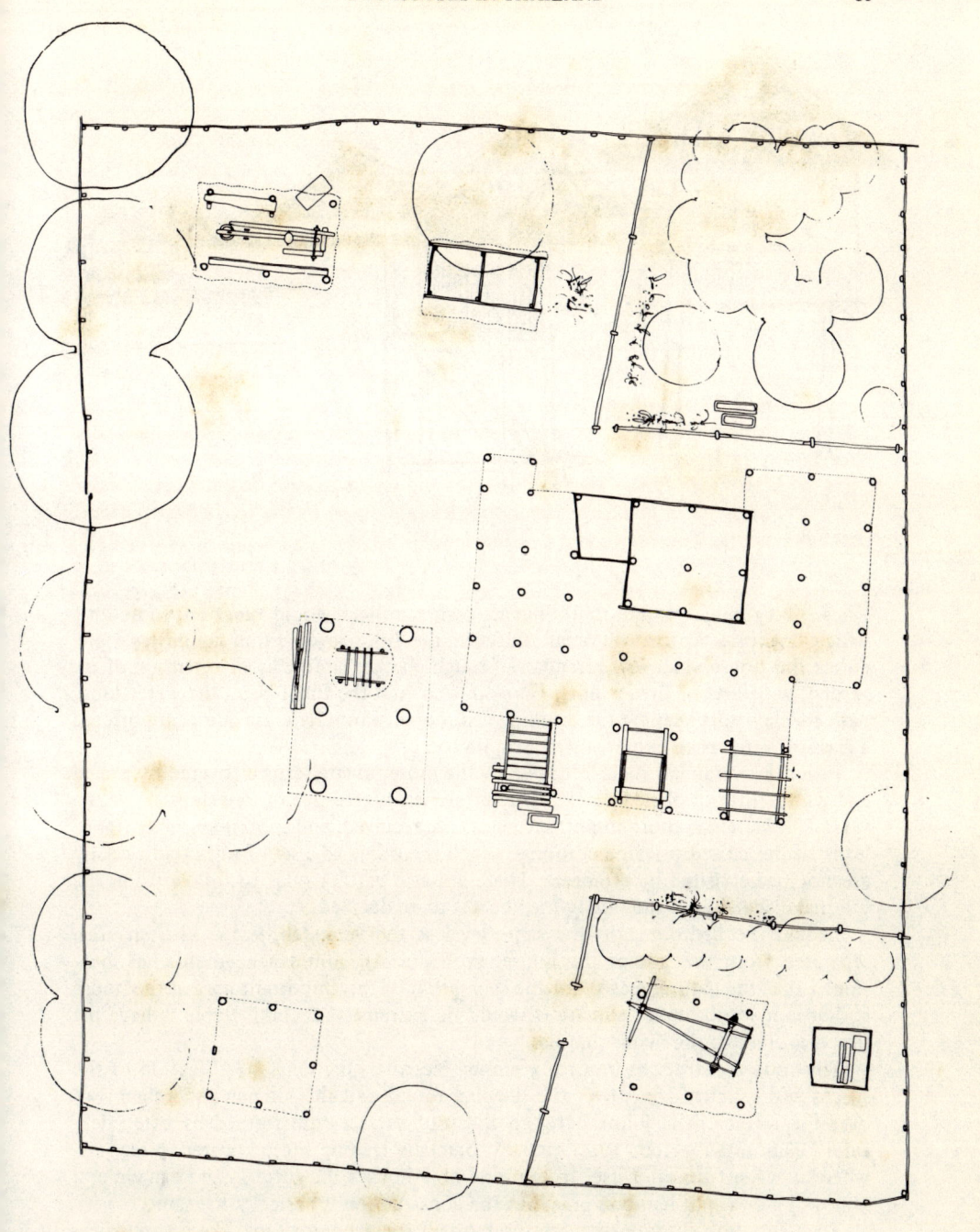

Ban Mae Mai. Groundplan of compound No. 23. Measured drawing in scale 1:200.

where every single square metre has its own significance and function, something which is expressed through small shifts in the floor level. From gound level one enters the house via a low verandah of rough planks, almost as an extension of the garden, with lots of flower pots. Here we also find the Ruan Nam, the waterstand, with its clay pots keeping the drinking water cool. From here the guests are offered a glass of water as an expression of hospitality.

From the verandah there is access to the more private terrace covered by a shed and with a floor of planed planks. The terrace is situated one or two steps above the verandah. Here the more important guests are received, and from here the entrance leads to the closed private bedrooms, which according to a set of rules traditionally are not to be visited by strangers. There are also certain rules to follow when the internal dispersion of the family members is to be decided.

Behind the bedrooms, at the same level as the verandah, is the kitchen area, separated from the rest of the house. Professor An Nimmanahaeminda has mentioned that the natural reason for the separation of this important part of the house is that in a warm humid climate it would be extremely uncomfortable to have the fireplace close to the living quarters.

The roof construction normally emphasizes the functional stratification of the spaces with pitched roofs over the sleeping rooms and the kitchen and a shed roof over the terrace. The joints between the roof surfaces are formed by often delicately elaborated gutters supported by brackets leading the rainwater to big jars, where it is kept for later use. In more humble houses the gutters can be made of a hollow log or a split bamboo pole, but the construction is basically the same.

To a functionally-trained western architect these houses look like a sophisticated building system for a dynamic and organic architecture, expressing the growth

TWO HOUSES IN THAILAND

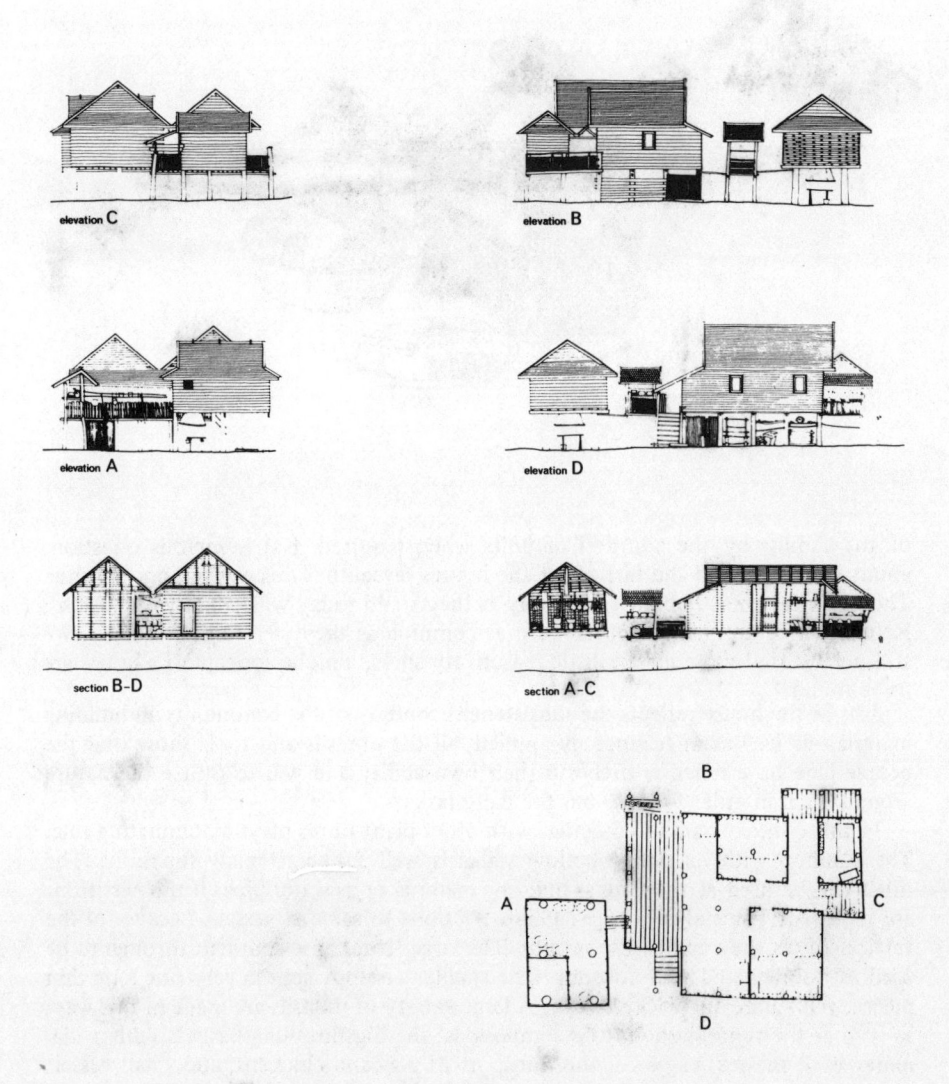

Ban Mae Mai, compound No. 23. Typical farmer's house. Measured drawing in scale 1:400.

of the family by the addition of units when required. But numerous questions about the origin and the history of the houses reveal that this was seldom the case. The houses are mostly built completely as they stand today without any extensions. References to the house spirits were as common as they were unsatisfactory. We still believe that more materialistic reasons for such a unique concept of a house are to be found.

Just as the house reflects the subsistence economy of the community in building materials as well as in technology applied, all the utensils and tools show that the people here have relied entirely on their own ability and will to utilize the nature around them in order to carry out the daily tasks.

In this context bamboo together with other plant fibres plays a dominating role. The bamboo with its strong hollow stalks is well suited to many functions. The tubes can be used as they are as building material or as water pipes if the partitions are removed. The stalks can be cut into sections to serve as vessels. Because of the vertical fibres they can easily be split. The larger trunks are split half through to be used as floorage and wall covering. The smaller ones are split in very fine long thin pieces well suited for wicker work. A large variety of utensils are made in this way, as well as the fences around the compounds, the big threshing baskets with a diameter of 2 metres, cages for the transport of pigs and chickens, and small vessels employed to keep personal belongings in. Fishing tackle is also made of wicker work, as are traps for catching birds and small animals.

Wood is used for the larger tools like ploughs and the multipurpose cart with its removable platform. Even the wheels are locally manufactured with some assistance from the local blacksmith. Also the loom with is accessories, placed under every house, is cut and assembled from pieces of wood. Here the women are busy spinning and weaving the cotton into fine striped pieces of fabric to be made into bed sheets, bags, blankets and clothing.

TWO HOUSES IN THAILAND

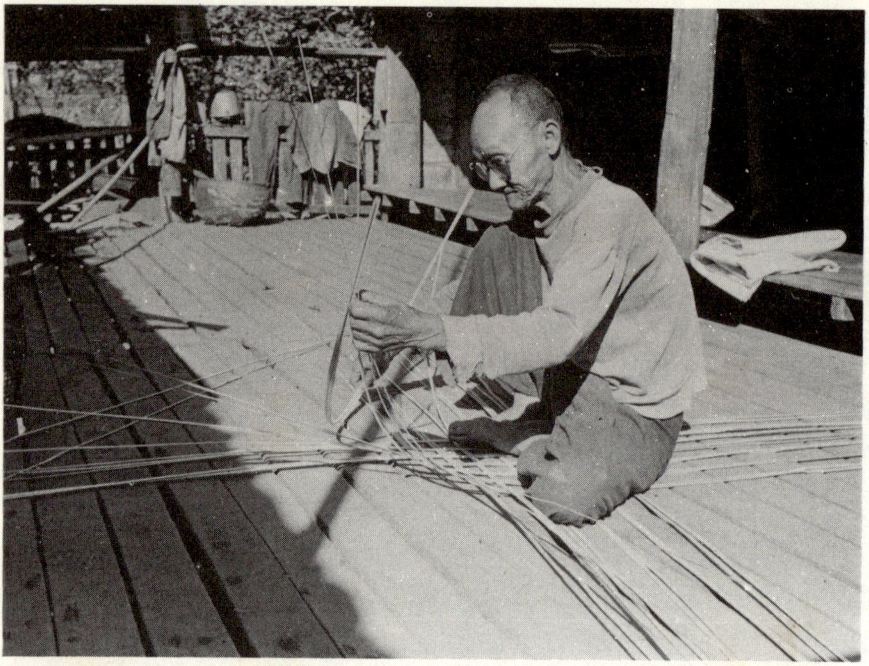

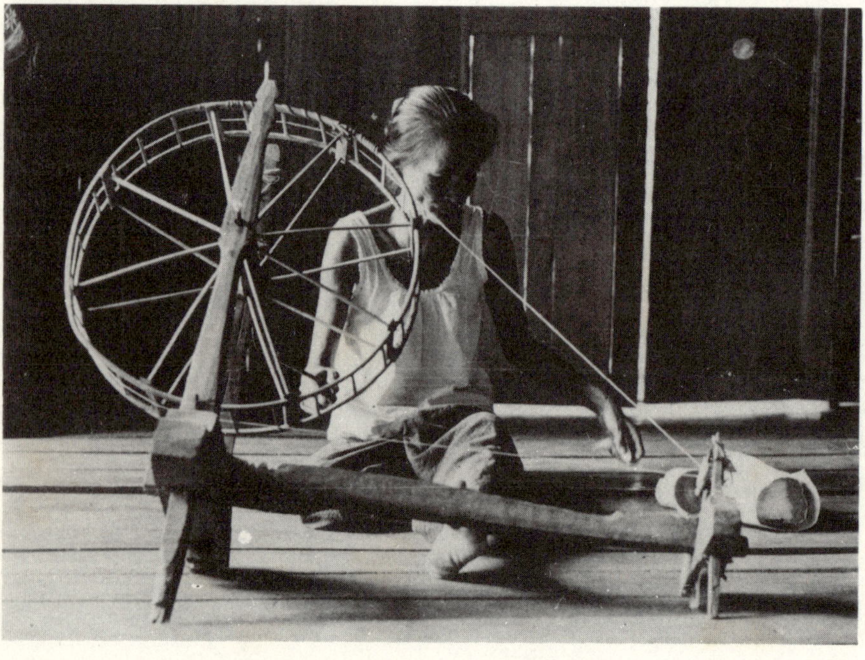

TWO HOUSES IN THAILAND

This enormous production takes place in every single family in each community, and each task has been adapted to the other activities which the family has to undertake in order to survive. Every month of the year has its special tasks to be carried out. Ploughing, sowing and harvesting of the different crops are strictly dependent on the climate and the rainfall. In the breaks between these jobs all the small tasks have to be carried out, further contributing to the family economy.

The community was traditionally self-supporting, in a proper balance with nature. But it was a sensitive balance in which child death was offset by childbirth, in which the forest was burned when more land was needed for cultivation, in which the pattern of cultivation was adapted to the family structure, and in which material needs were fulfilled by the abundance of nature.

In spite of the farmer's often extensive swiddening, the forests have played an important role in his way of life, and he seems to have been aware of his dependence on them. But this has not been the case with the other persons who have had a commercial interest in the forests—especially the exploiters of teak wood who have caused such great damage that the Thai government has found it necessary to nationalize the forests with the aim of re-establishing them. Thus it becomes impossible for the peasants to expand their landholdings, which, on the contrary, are being fragmented through inheritance. It has even become difficult to obtain wood for the various purposes mentioned above. A combination of better health conditions and an increase in the population hinders the villages in their development. The existing farm land now has to feed more people and has to be treated with fertilizers. These are expensive and have created a demand for cash crops which again influences the natural cycle of the community. The natural breaks in the yearly work disappear and with them the possibilties of producing the numerous essential things. The farmer will have to buy from others who have specialized in different poducts, so even more cash is needed. Many villagers, mostly the young people, give up and leave the villages.

The people in House No. 23 are old. Most of their children have already left Ban Mae Mai. Probably no one will take over the tasks under the present conditions. A way of life will disappear.

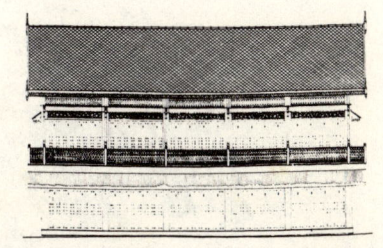

The merchant's house

Seen from a distance the town of Lampang looks just like any other town in Thailand with its scattered buildings well mixed with a tangle of electric wires so characteristic of all modern settlements in Thailand. But it would be a pity if this uninspiring view deprived the visitor of his interest in a closer study of the town as behind this uninteresting barrier you will find the charm of the ancient Lampang with its narrow and picturesque roads that follow the bends of the river, bordered by splendid one and two-storeyed houses that are enhanced by an abundance of intricate details indicating that they are not just ordinary houses.

The centre of the city has a very characteristic layout. Three main streets run parallel to the river and several smaller streets connect the main streets. The area shows a great complexity and variety in land use. All the usual city-centre functions are to be found here, but the same area also contains village-like settlements right behind the main road.

The street next to the Wang River is named Thanon Talad Kao which means the Old Market Street. Today there is nothing to indicate great hectic commercial activity in this particular street, but the name becomes easier to understand when one sees old photographs showing the buildings in Thanon Talad Kao situated right on the river bank with their backs standing on stilts in the water with jetties from which goods were unloaded into the houses to be sold from shops facing the street.

The street is made up entirely of houses which combine shops and dwellings. They can be wide buildings with the living quarters placed behind the shop premises, or they can be two-storeyed houses with the dwelling on the upper floor. One can even find buildings with a complete integration of shop and dwelling where the street facade formed of shutters will be open during the shopping hours exposing not only the commodities of the shop, but the owner's private belongings as well.

One of the houses which can be seen in old photographs is a beautiful wooden building in two storeys with a big overhanging pitched tile roof and with delicately carved details on all exposed parts of the building. The ground floor is raised 2 or 3 steps above the original street level and a landing along the entire facade leads to the row of shutters demarking the street facade. Behind the shutters is a large beautiful shop area which today has been damaged by provisional partitions. Through a large door one enters a kind of verandah at the back of the house where two smaller buildings serve as storeroom and kitchen. The verandah which today faces a wonderful garden has previously faced the river directly. From the large shop area a delicately elaborated staircase leads to the upper floor, which shows evidence of having served as the living area for the family. Around this floor runs a covered balcony which is entered through a screen of shutters similar to that on the ground floor.

Plan of the centre of Lampang, scale 1:5000.

The architecture and the craftsmanship displayed throughout the entire house give evidence of a professional hand. The wood is sawn up delicately by the hands of a skilled craftsman. This is especially evident in the richness of the carving which decorates all the prominent elements: the balcony railings, the fascias and bargeboards. Even the small gable windows have their own small roofs projecting from the gables.

On the second floor a number of private items are stored from the grand period of the house, wooden furniture, brass stands, and the family altars. Also earthenware jars and lacquer boxes for storage are found, everything excellently made and very similar to the items found in a village house, but more ornate. They are not produced in a break between other more important tasks. They have been produced by specialized craftsmen who have improved upon the village handcraft. The lacquer box for instance has a heart of bamboo, just like the village basket, but the box in the merchant's house has been coated with many layers of lacquer and has finally been decorated.

The scene has changed from that of village self-sufficiency to that of urban specialization. Busy activity has characterized this house, leaving no time for basket making, but it has left money and thereby the ability to buy products from other people.

From where did this wealth come? If we take a look at the topographic conditions of North Thailand, we will see that they are characterized by a number of mainly parallel mountain ranges which make a sharp contrast to the large areas around the river delta in the central part of the country. The mountain ranges stretching north-south form a 'comb-like' structure with relatively few reasonable passages in the east-west direction, which means that the traffic in the area seems to be forced in a north-south direction. The area is drained by a number of small rivers which are tributaries to the three main rivers Ping, Wang, and Yom.

It is interesting to compare two of these three rivers, Ping and Wang, because two of the largest towns of the area are situated on those two rivers, namely Chieng Mai on Ping and Lampang on Wang. Both rivers are parts of the great net of rivers which connects the northern area with Bangkok and other historical centres in the lowlands. The River Ping is longer and holds more water than Wang. If, however, we look at the areas drained by the Ping and the Wang, we find that on the whole the Ping creates only a connection to the valley surrounding Chieng Mai. The rest is cut off by mountains. Furthermore, the area of the reservoir created by the Yanhee Dam used to be a most difficult area for navigation because of its narrow and rocky gorges.

The course of the River Wang is not nearly that important; it is less dramatic and the bordering mountains do not form the same barrier to the areas along the river because they are lower and stretch in a much more regular north-south direction. Accordingly, nature does not in any serious way prevent a connection between the plateau around the present Lampang, Cha Hom, and the area around Chieng Rai and a great part of Burma and South China. The transportation of goods will usually follow the physically most passable routes, and therefore we can assume that the greater part of goods transported between Bangkok and the northernmost provinces have followed the River Wang and afterwards been transported over land to Chieng Rai.

It would be natural to imagine that this primarily local route has been of importance to a much larger area. If, for instance, we extend the route from Chieng Rai northwards, we will soon meet the net of caravan tracks which have served the southwestern corner of Asia, and if we look southwards it would seem plausible that Bangkok was a port of disembarkation, in connection with a considerable trade with the rest of the subcontinent. This gives a convincing reason for the localization of Lampang because the necessary change from river transport to some sort of overland transport has had to take place in this area.

From a commercial point of view the place seems almost perfect and the exchange process in itself is a strong incentive for the emergence of a town. Not only will the handling of the goods offer employment to a lot of people, but a whole net of retailers will emerge. Some of the goods might be provisionally prepared and refined, and at any rate a lot of companies in the service field are bound to emerge in a place such as this. The busy atmosphere itself will attract an increasing number of people who will settle down in the area.

It is thus natural to find the remains of a number of historical towns in this area, and archaeological excavations would probably reveal even more finds which would help to verify the importance of these locations a long way back in history. Still some of these ancient towns may be discovered in the physical structure of Lampang. This applies to the Burmese settlement dating back to the seventeenth century, the fortifications of which bear witness to the importance of the town.

TWO HOUSES IN THAILAND

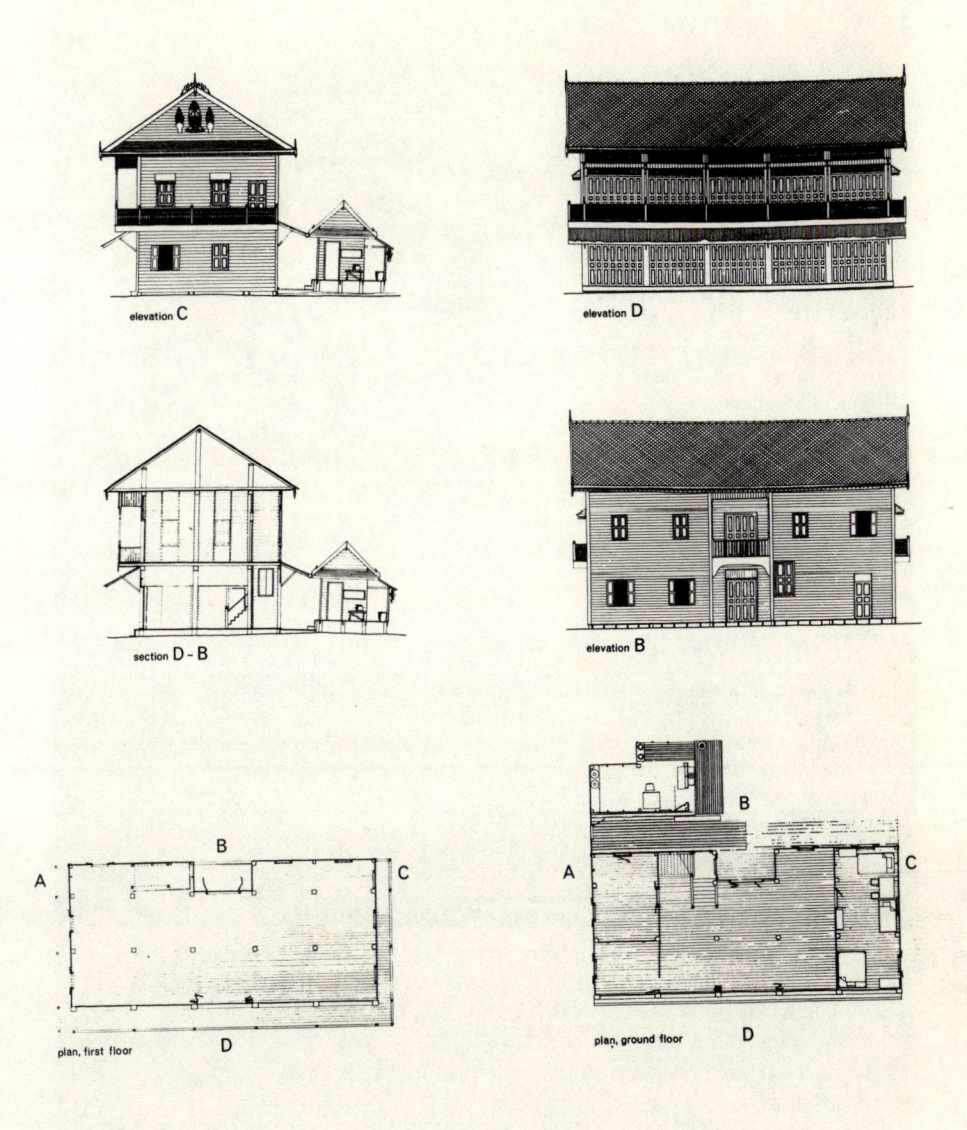

elevation C

elevation D

section D-B

elevation B

plan, first floor

plan, ground floor

Merchant's house in Thanon Talad Kao, Lampang. Combined shop and dwelling in two storeys. The house is richly ornamented with carvings. The craftmanship is excellent and the architectural standard is extraordinarily high. Measured drawing in scale 1:400.

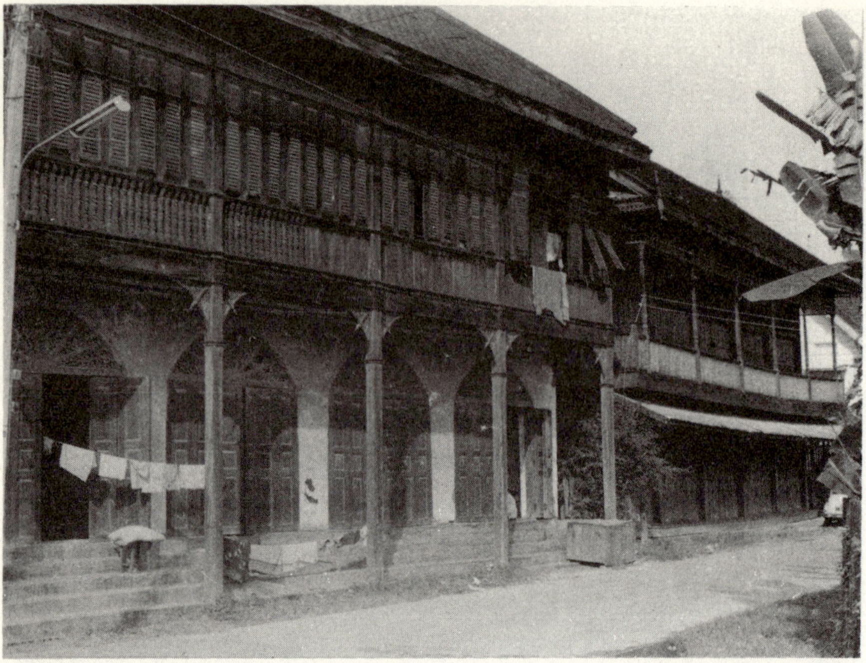

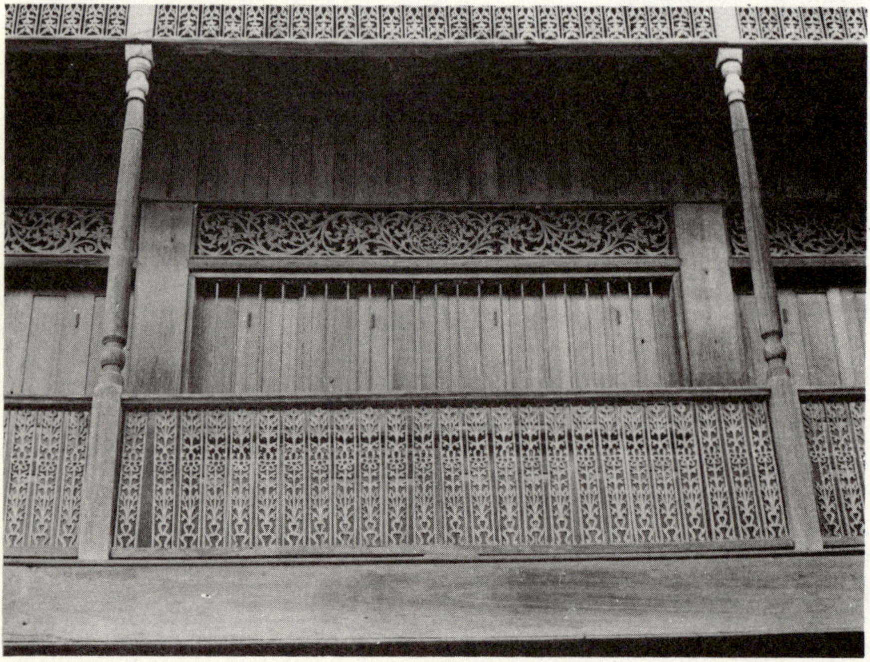

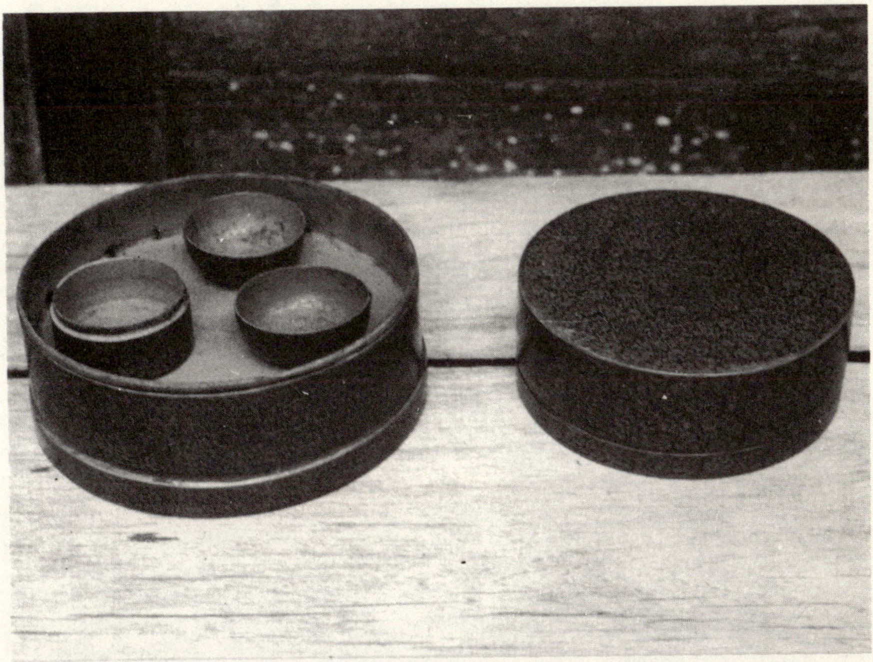

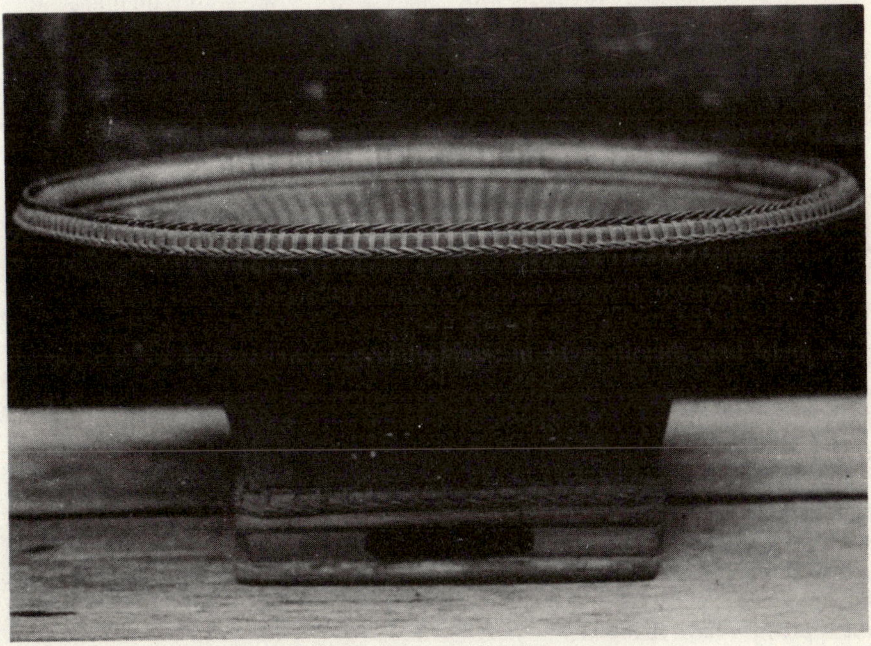

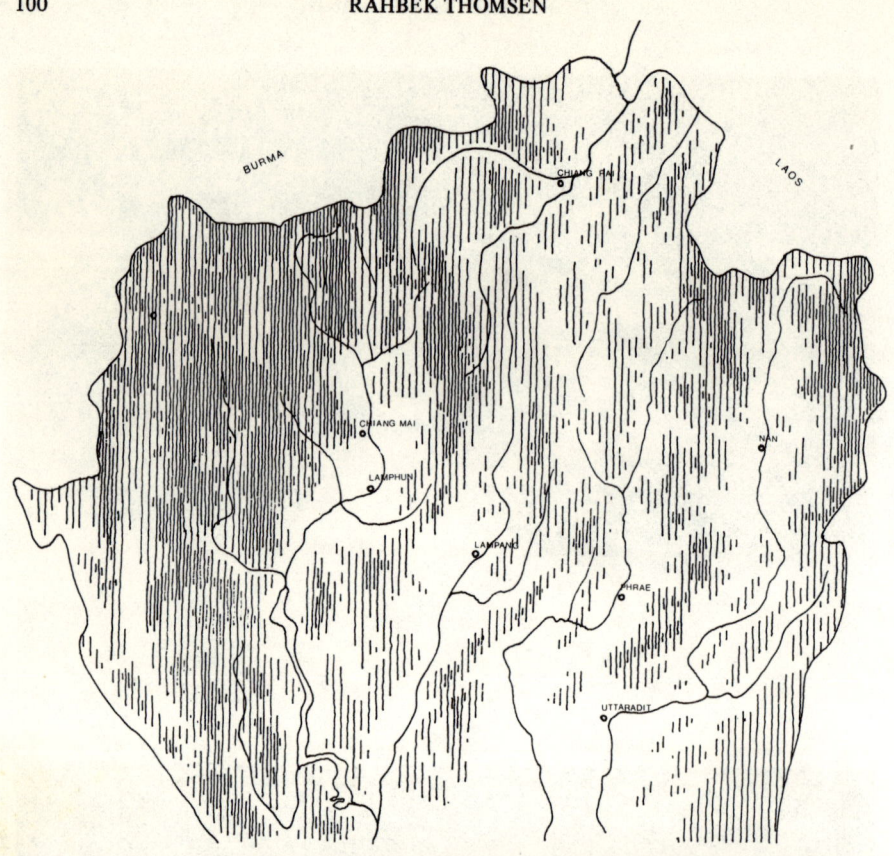

Map of North Thailand. The dark areas indicate the highest mountains, the lowlands are white. Most of the mountain ranges stretch north-south and the main rivers run south.

Which commodies were exchanged in this town? The most important was certainly teak which at a time became an essential export item but which, before that, had been a very important building material in the more sparsely wooded areas in the central part of the country. Another important commodity was tobacco which was produced in the area around Chieng Rai. During certain periods even rice would be exported although rice usually had to be imported. To the above mentioned items can be added a number of less important but nevertheless essential goods: silk and cotton fabric for which the northern provinces have a special tradition.

An article which is not very obvious but which most certainly must have brought considerable capital to Lampang was opium. The opium was smuggled from Burma via Chieng Rai to Lampang where it was shipped to Bangkok and further on to the world market. After King Rama V (1868-1910) the opium trade was prohibited, but the daily papers of Thailand state openly that this trade is still going on, though the route may have changed.

TWO HOUSES IN THAILAND

From Bangkok all sorts of goods ranging from machinery to hairpins were coming in and were distributed to this part of the country through branch offices of the Bangkok traders, whose presence give further evidence of the importance of the area.

The river transport was performed by means of small barges which were poled along, and if against the current, the voyage might last up to 3 months or more.

Today only a few, if any, barges are poled up the Wang River. The railway from Bangkok to Lampang was completed in 1911 and changed completely the economic basis for the central part of the town. The railway station was built 3 kilometres outside the city centre and attracted almost the entire wholesale trade. This was a great change for the old town, but the region maintained its importance. Nowadays, however, improved means of communication along with other developments have deprived Lampang of its importance. The big trading companies have withdrawn to Bangkok and are spinning their webs by the use of telephones and trucks, leaving only the small wholesalers in Lampang.

Today Lampang is first and foremost the seat of the provincial administration, and its commercial life is reduced to serving a minor part of North Thailand in contrast to its role during its heyday. The big house in Thanon Talad Kao is only an empty shell today, abandoned by its former inhabitants, not because it is worn out, but because its original designation does not fit in with current developments in Lampang. Its former inhabitants have found other occupations.

A Socio-Architectural Case Study in North Thailand

Hans Haagensen

Studies of foreign architecture and townscape has always been an important part of the architect's education in Denmark. Groups of students and teachers have surveyed and measured houses and towns mainly in southern Europe. Until recent years, however, studies of this sort have mainly been aimed at describing the structure and shape of the subjects rather than dealing with their origin and development. The result has been numerous publications of beautiful drawings, which only rarely explain how the houses came into existence and why they have a particular shape or pattern of organization.

In the 1960s it became apparent to many young architects that architecture could only be studied and comprehended as part of a socio-economic and functional entity, which it reflects—but also influences. Studies of architecture as *objets d'art* became irrelevant. Knowledge about the people living in a house or a town and their way of living socially and economically, became necessary if one wanted to understand the physical appearance of the man-made environment. This may be more or less obvious to most anthropologists and social scientists—but it was not so among architects.

The trend among young professionals now is to get away from the architect's traditional concept of himself as an artist above all, and instead, view himself as first and foremost a skilled technician who must apply a professional and scientific approach to his work.

As for our own studies in Nepal and Thailand, one of the main objectives has been to gain knowledge which could be applied in underdeveloped countries in the process of modernization and development. In many places "development" is based purely on imported expertise and materials, creating a vast gap between people and environment, and often causing in fact, underdevelopment contrary to the pronounced aim. The indigenous and traditional values, which should form the basis for development—or at least be taken into careful consideration—are often ignored when modernizing a society.

Houses and settlements are the most immediate reflection and physical manifestation of a culture and all its aspects. The word "reflection" is important in this context, because it implies that architecture can not be understood except in a social and economic context. The flourishing or deterioration of architecture and its function is always an expression of changes in the material basis. Thus the study of architecture must be a comprehensive, multi-disciplinary activity comprising not only physical surveys but also surveys of production patterns, economy, social life, ideological and religious features, and so forth.

This may be a very ambitious goal. Naturally such studies should accordingly be undertaken by multi-disciplinary teams. We have not had the good fortune of establishing such a team for our own studies. But even our non-specialist approach to these disciplines, has confirmed for us the value of such an objective.

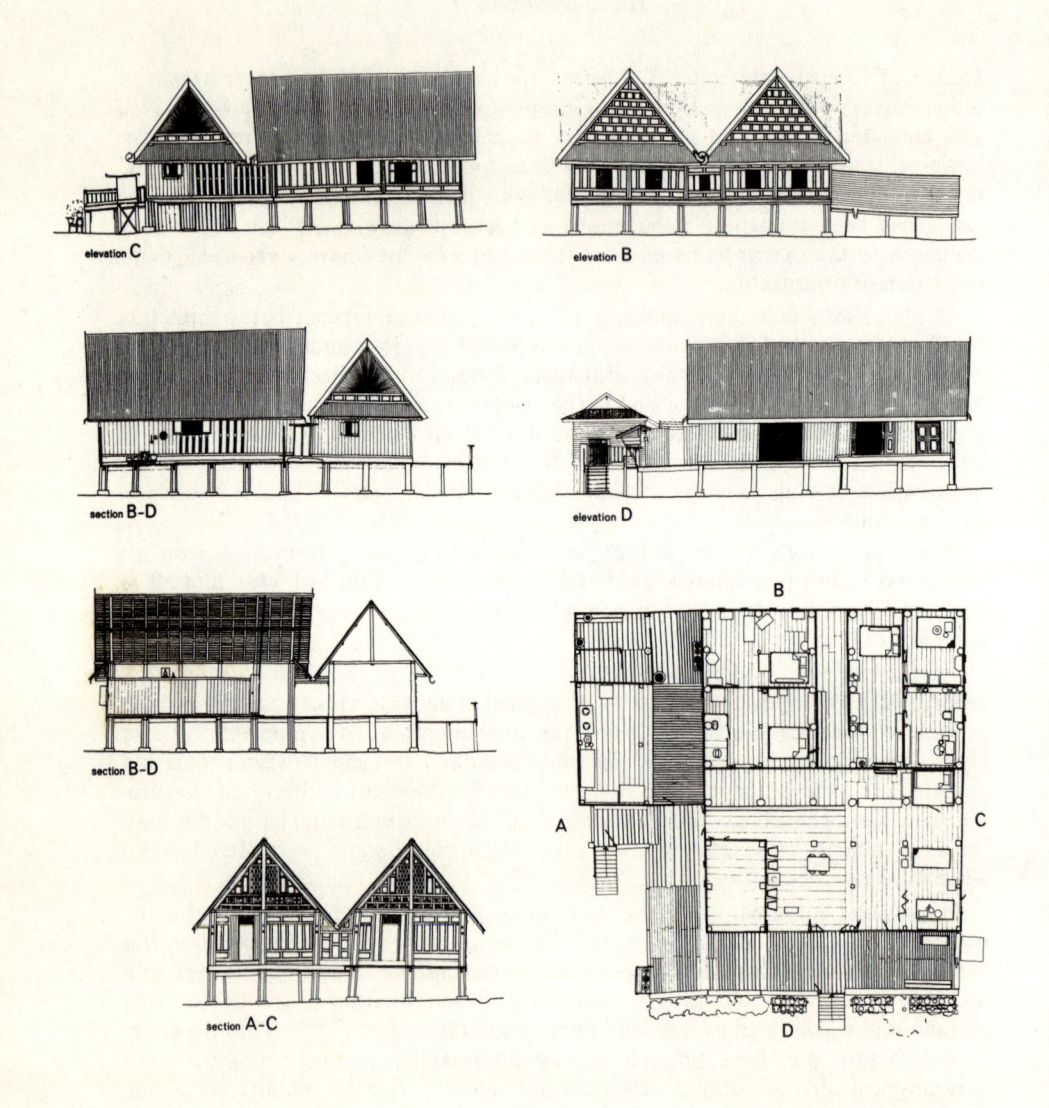

The study of architecture includes physical surveys such as this example from Lampang. Measured drawing in scale 1:400.

In our studies we have always focused on secular—or anonymous architecture—which is very often neglected by researchers. This is also the case of our North Thailand project 1972-73 which was a combined architecture and socio-economic survey of a small village hamlet, Ban Mae Mai, 40 kilometres north of Lampang. The scope of work comprised surveys within three main areas: The Physical Structure, the Functional Structure and the Socio-economic Structure.

The Physical Structure

The physical survey resulted in a map of the village and its environs, showing the pattern of fields, settlement, roads and paths and other prominent physical features in the scale 1:500. The built-up area—the village itself—was surveyed and plans and sections drawn up in the scale 1:200, showing the compounds as well as floor plans of every single house. All houses in the village were classified according to style, workmanship and maintenance. A number of houses representative of the various categories were then singled out and measured in detail, resulting in drawings of plans, sections and elevations in the scale 1:50. Finally a selection of buildings and tools used in the production were measured and drawn to scale.

This method of measuring and drawing things meticulously has several purposes. Firstly, it results in an accurate though perhaps rather theoretical picture of the subject. Secondly, it forces the person measuring to observe every structural and functional detail of the house, thus creating the basis for further investigation. And thirdly, it usually arouses interest among the inhabitants and enhances their willingness to co-operate. It is our experience that the measuring and drawing should always be the first phase of the fieldwork, as it facilitates the later phases in more than one respect. Furthermore, if one has the possibility of blueprinting the drawings for give-away purposes, it is even better.

The Functional Structure

The maps produced during the first phase are a necessity for making a survey of the functional structure. This survey included a detailed land-use map, maps showing the distribution of land according to ownership and accessibility, the location, size and nature of all public and private service facilities, an inventory of the traffic system, the population distribution, landholdings and livestock distribution. Part of this information was drawn from various official sources as well as from our own on-the-spot observations, but a large part had to be extracted from the interviews described in the following.

The Socio-economic Structure

The socio-economic survey was made in the form of extensive, standardized interviews with all family heads in the village and a number of special interviews with key persons, further supplemented by data collected from various official sources.

The standard interview form contained about fifty questions related to all aspects of material and spiritual life in the village. The interviews were conducted through interpreters, and even though it was difficult to obtain certain kinds of information —mainly concerning income, tax and land ownership, of course—the interviews give a fairly accurate picture of the socio-economic life.

The main subjects covered were demographic data, occupation, production, distribution, income, communications internally and externally, health conditions, religious and other communal activities. Special interviews were conducted inter alia with the village headman, representatives from employment sources outside the village, the senior monk of the local temple, the *wat*, and the indigenous doctor. In addition, all pertinent data available from governmental and provincial authorities were collected.

For additional documentation, besides these three surveys, the entire village was recorded photographically including most of the activities taking place there.

It is of course true that a meticulous and yet broad survey like this should be treated carefully with regard to the conclusions being drawn from it. The statistical material is very limited, and only comparative studies of other selected settlements would enable us to draw reliable conclusions.

Some of our observations, however, illustrate the close interrelationship between the socio-economic structure and the physical environment, with the former as the determinining factor.

Ban Mae Mai

Ban Mae Mai is situated on the bank of the Wang River, approximately 40 kilometres north of the provincial capital, Lampang. It is a small village with 70 houses and a little more than 400 inhabitants. The majority are peasants, but the occupational pattern is heavily influenced by land fragmentation, causing a relatively large number of villagers to seek employment outside the village and eventually to migrate.

The main crop is paddy, which amounts to approximately 70 per cent of the agricultural production and is almost entirely for local consumption. The most important cash crop is tobacco, which is grown and dried under a kind of tenancy system.

The physical shape of Ban Mae Mai reflects the family structure, which in turn reflects the more or less collectively organized agricultural work related to rice production. The traditional rural settlement is a cluster of compounds, each accommodating several generations of the same family—and often more distant relatives as well who live together in one or more dwellings. The compound usually contains a number of buildings and structures related to agricultural production besides.

This settlement pattern is now being changed basically, due to changes in the production pattern. The transition from subsistence farming into a market-oriented production and eventually into wage earning—combined with the land fragmentation—has obvious effects on the physical structure.

As pointed out above, the rice production is closely related to the joint family structure. The breaking-up of subsistence farming creates a growing number of

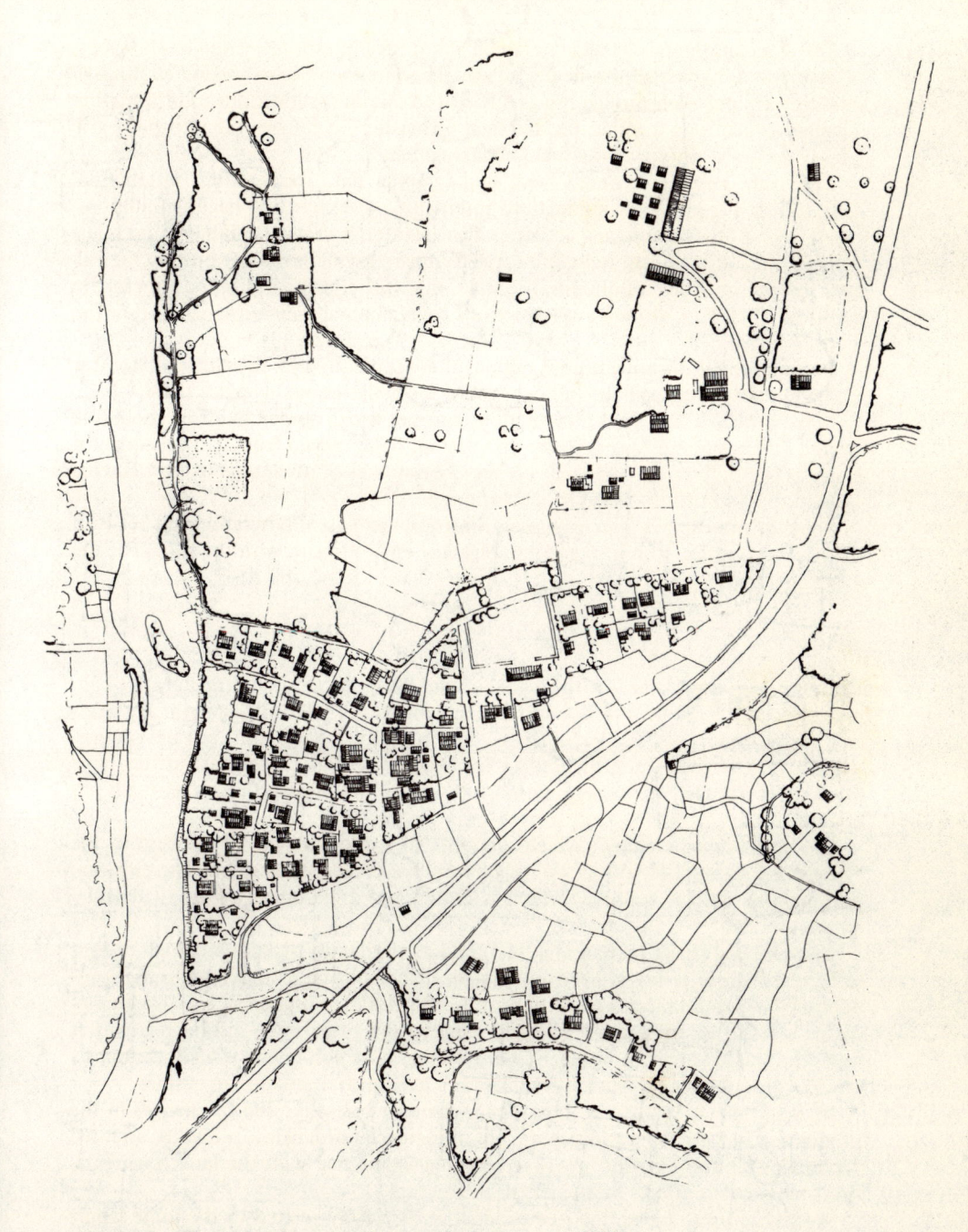

Plan of Ban Mae Mai and surrounding area. Scale approx. 1:6000.

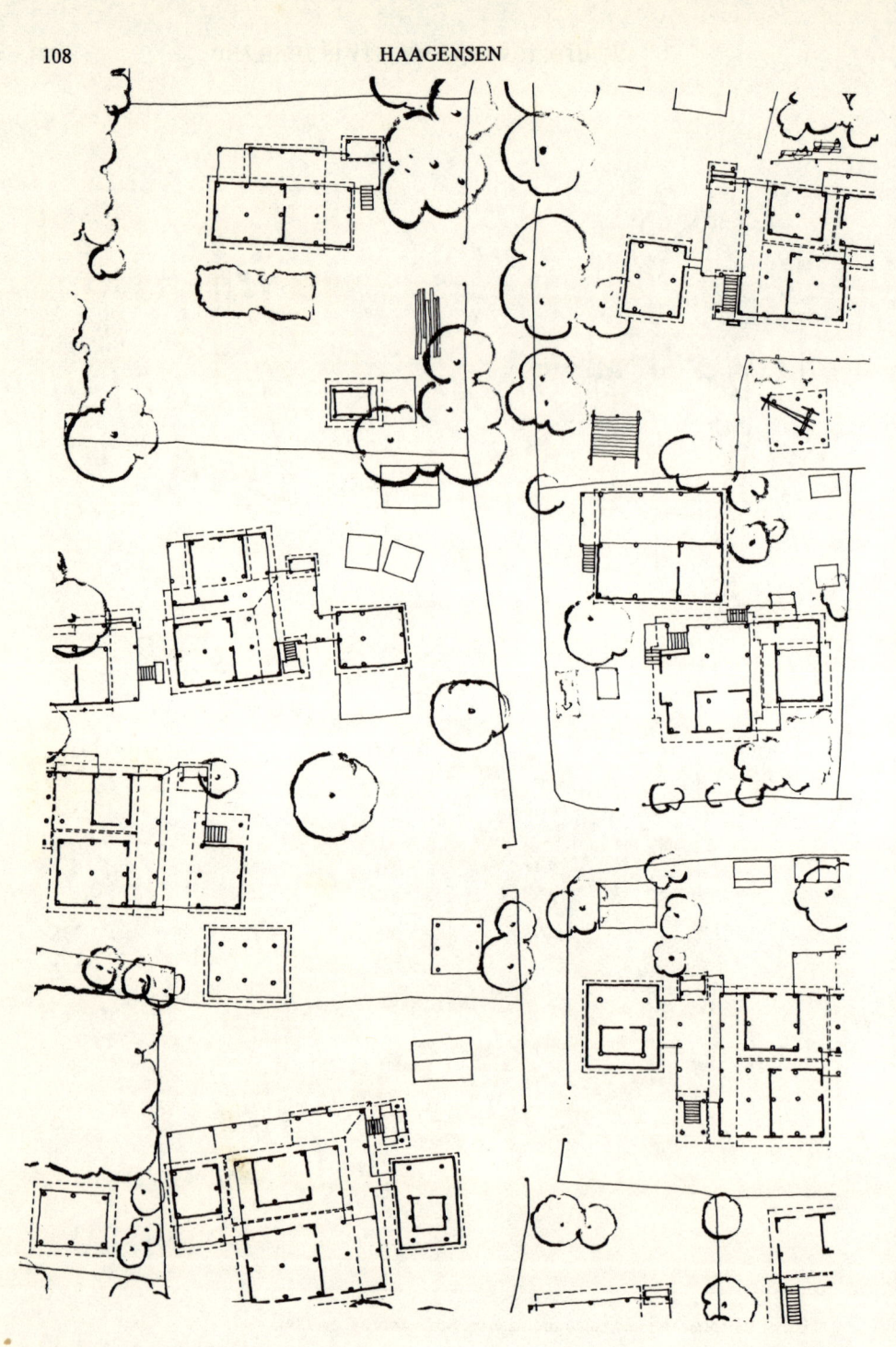

Ban Mae Mai. Example of building pattern, 1st floor. Measured drawing in scale approx. 1:400.

ARCHITECTURE AND SOCIETY IN THAILAND

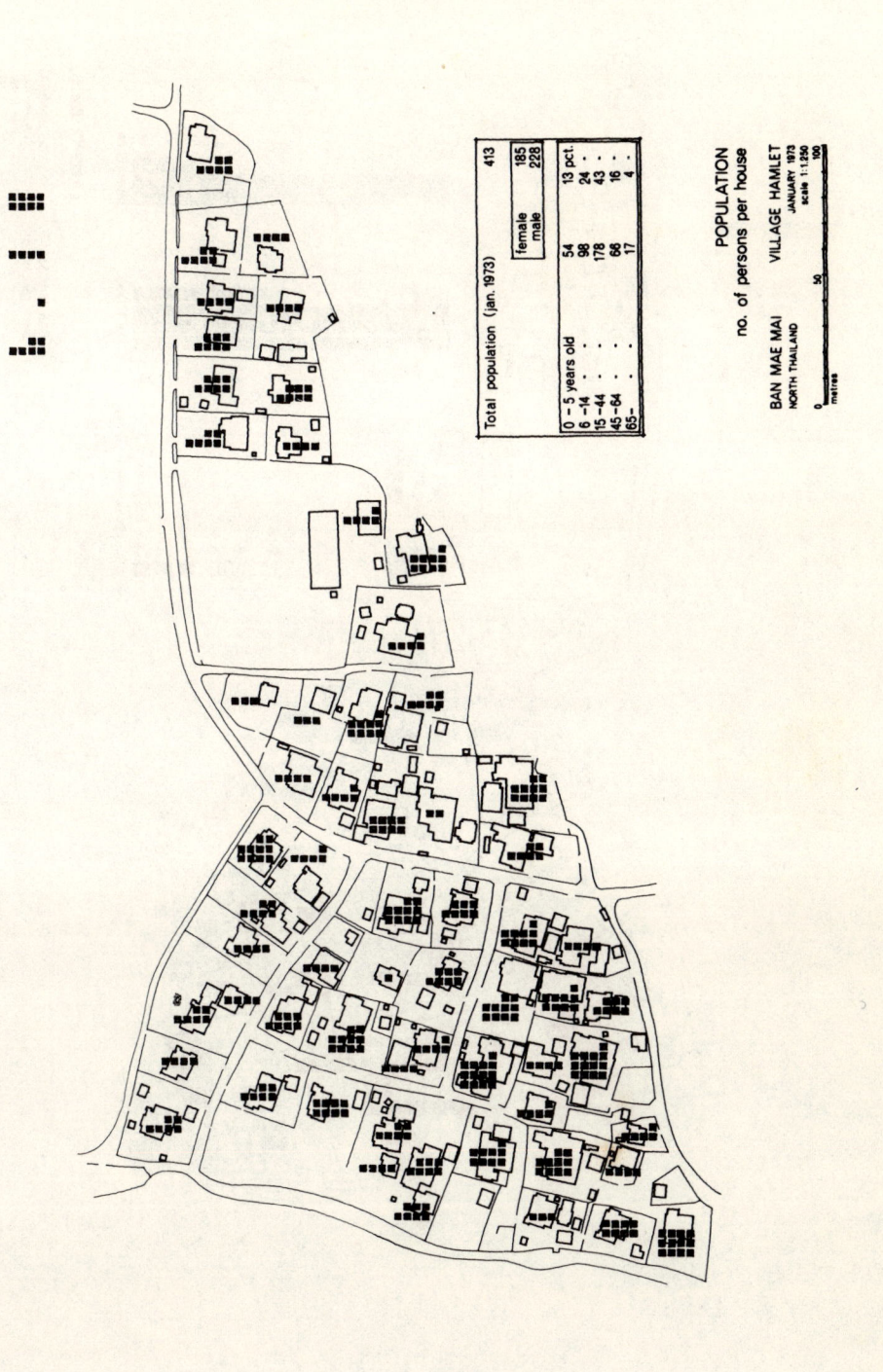

Total population (jan. 1973)	413	
	female	185
	male	228
0 – 5 years old	54	13 pct.
6 –14	98	24
15 –44	178	43
45 –64	66	16
65 –	17	4

POPULATION
no. of persons per house

BAN MAE MAI   VILLAGE HAMLET
NORTH THAILAND   JANUARY 1973
                  scale 1:1.250

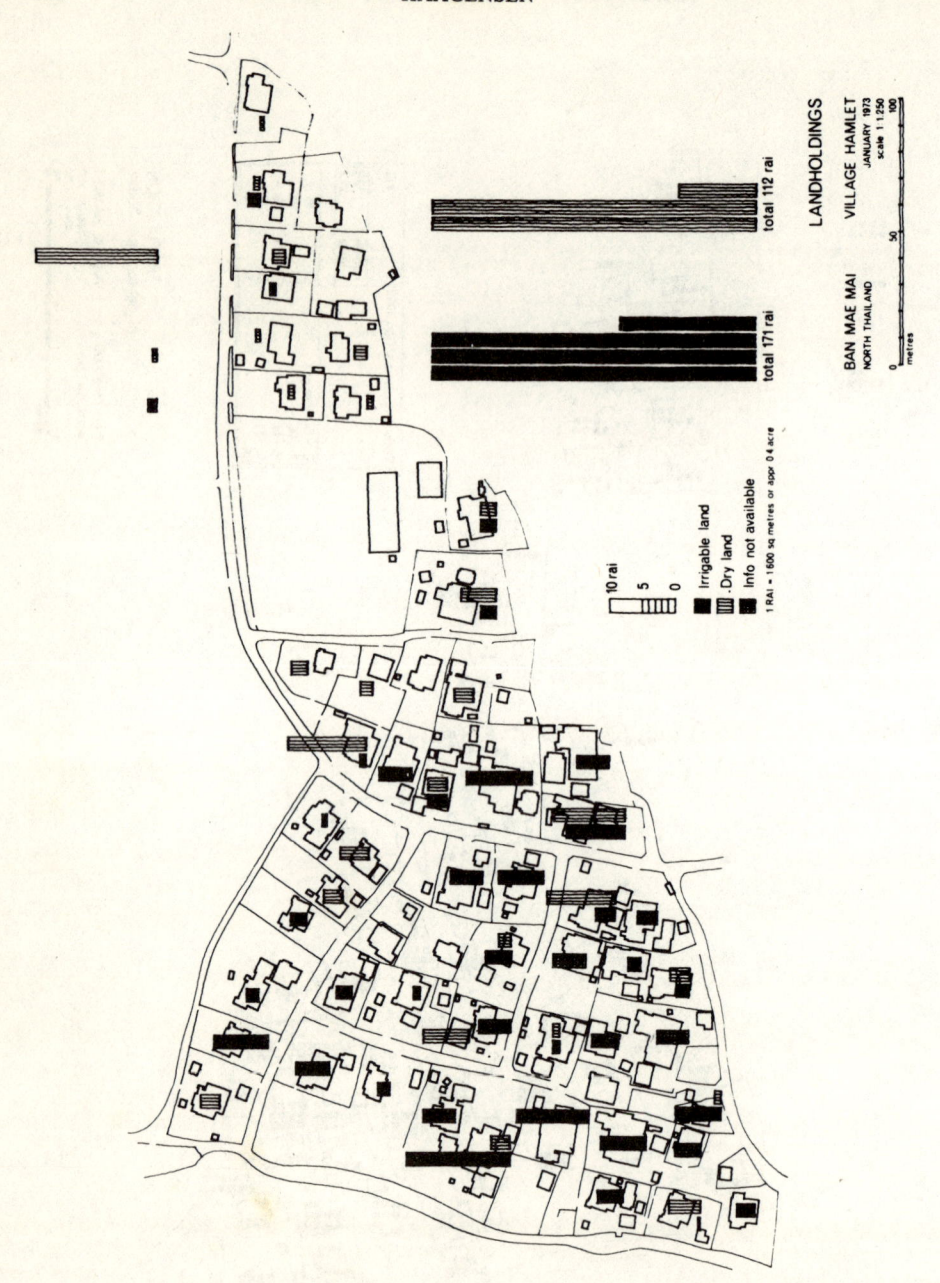

LANDHOLDINGS
VILLAGE HAMLET
BAN MAE MAI
NORTH THAILAND
JANUARY 1973
scale 1:1,250

total 112 rai
total 171 rai

10 rai
5
0

Irrigable land
Dry land
Info not available

1 RAI = 1,600 sq metres or appr 0.4 acre

PUBLIC AND COMMERCIAL FACILITIES

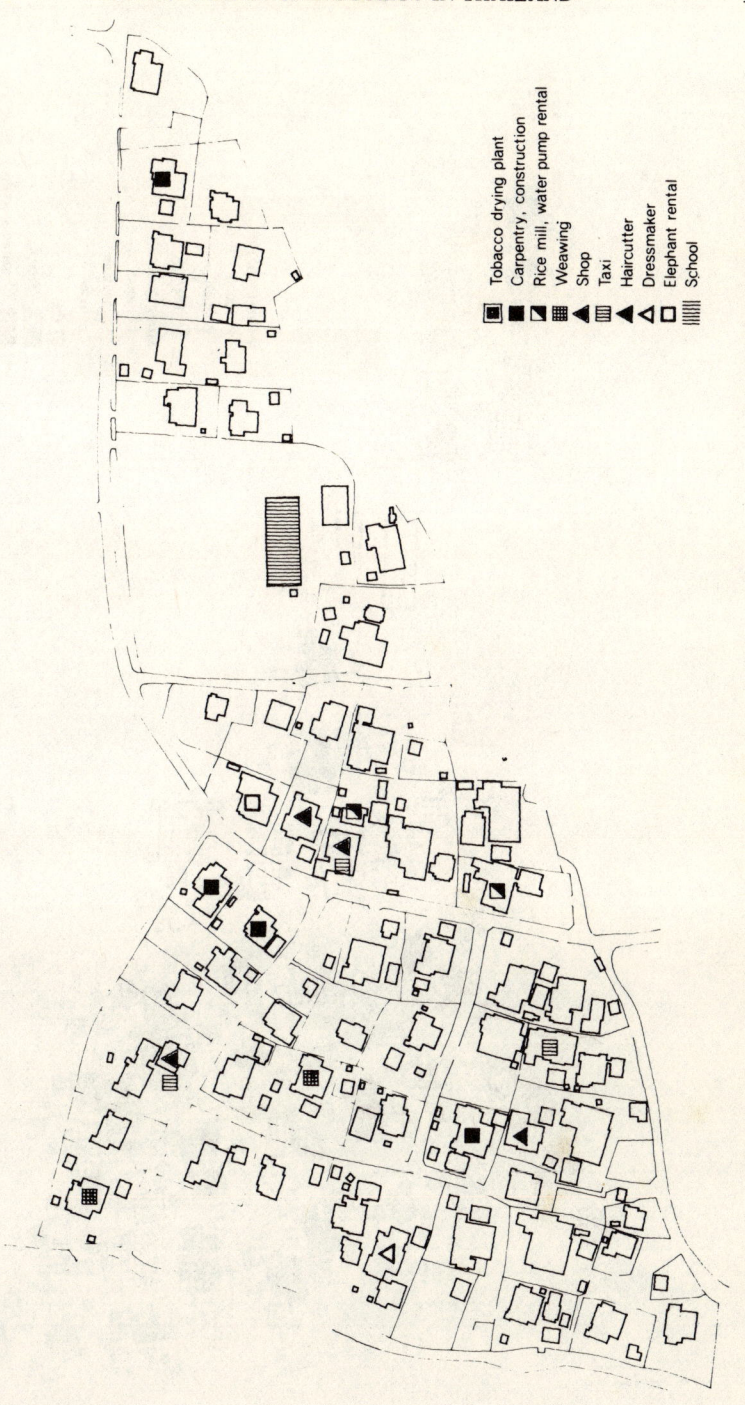

- Tobacco drying plant
- Carpentry, construction
- Rice mill, water pump rental
- Weaving
- Shop
- Taxi
- Haircutter
- Dressmaker
- Elephant rental
- School

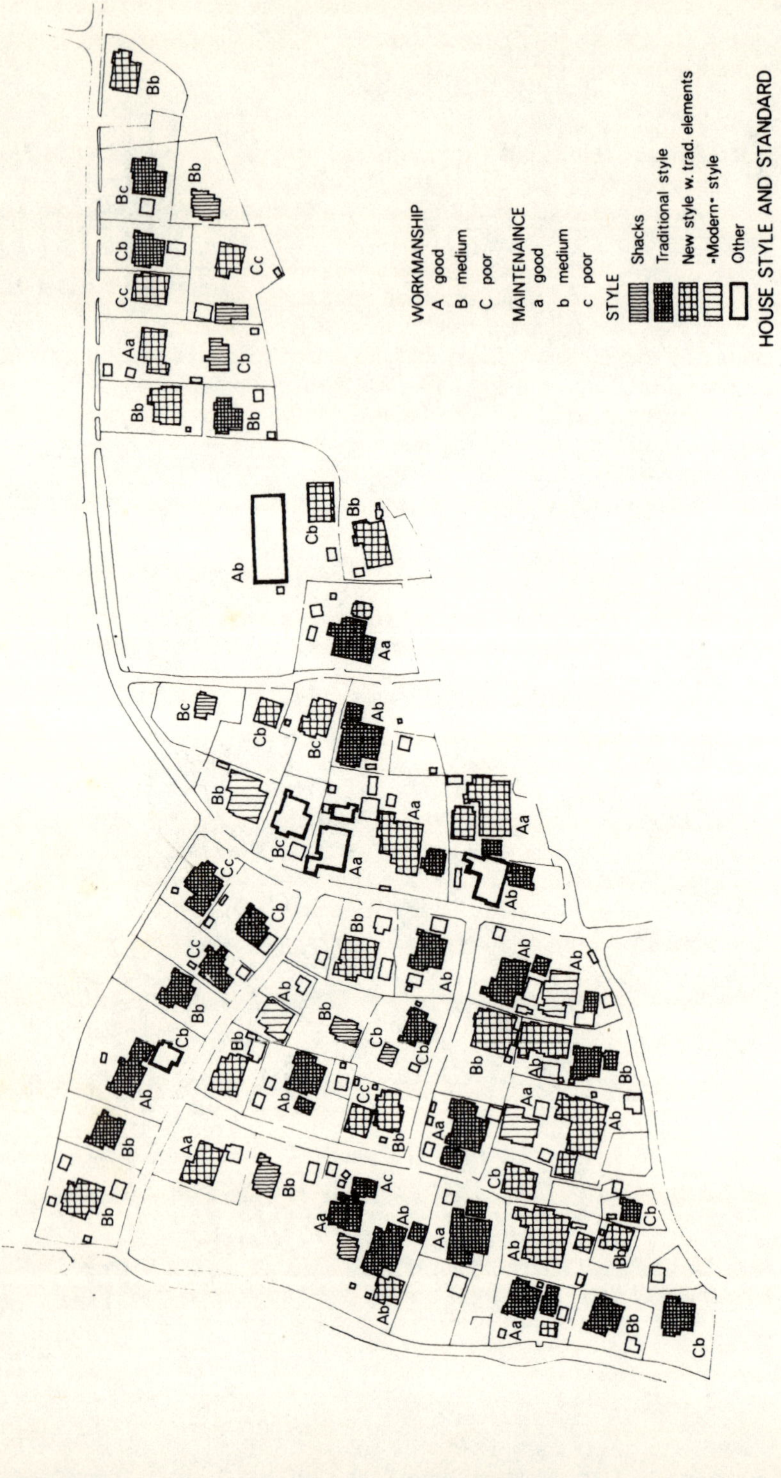
HOUSE STYLE AND STANDARD
WORKMANSHIP
A good
B medium
C poor
MAINTENAINCE
a good
b medium
c poor
STYLE
Shacks
Traditional style
New style w. trad. elements
"Modern" style
Other

nuclear families belonging to the landless wage-earning class, for whom work and habitation have become totally separated.

The immediate effect can be observed in the general lay-out of the village, in the increasing number of small plots with only a dwelling and no other buildings as opposed to the compound settlement. The new plots emerge partly as additions to the village periphery, but also through subdivision of existing compounds, changing the physical appearance of the village by introducing new proportions and raising the density.

The house is also undergoing changes in lay-out and in general appearance. The new family structure expresses itself in a more simple lay-out of the dwellings because they accommodate fewer people. It is also a characteristic of the house inhabited by the landless villager, that the shaded space underneath the house, which is a prominent feature of the traditional farmer's house serving inter alia as a work place, is being reduced to a clearance above the ground of only about fifty centimetres, solely to protect against dampness and flood.

Another change in the physical appearance of rural Thai architecture is the substitution of various materials for the traditional teak wood, which is beautiful, thoroughly tested through hundreds of years and highly functional under local climatic conditions. During the last decades teak has become a very expensive commodity, mainly because of the heavy exploitation of the Thai teak forests by foreign companies and their local affiliates. This exploitation has led to nationalization of all forests in an attempt to re-establish forestry as a source of national income. Subsequently the peasants have no longer been allowed to cut timber for their own use, and prices of wood have increased. A large part of the construction work in Northern Thai villages is nevertheless still done with wood which is often illegally procured but which becomes the legal property of the owner of the site as soon as it is turned into a building structure.

For the poor villagers who have neither the opportunity to procure wood by these means nor the cash to buy it, the weaker and less durable bamboo remains the only attainable building material. The rising price of teak wood has also resulted in more frequent use of industrial and in many cases imported building materials, which are often ill-suited to the local environment, functionally as well as aesthetically.

We do not pretend that these observations, based on a highly materialistic and functional approach to the study of architecture, can explain fully the shape of houses and settlements. We appreciate the ideological influence on architecture— whether political or religious. We are convinced, however, that the determining factor in the development of houses and settlements is the people's material life. It is with some reluctance that we have used the term 'architecture' as it is a very ill-defined term, especially as there are objects, normally labelled architecture, which have solely ideological functions—as for instance, statues and certain monuments. In most religious buildings, ideology is a dominating factor in the architectural expression. Churches have very often cross-shaped plans, gothic cathedrals are always designed to strive upwards towards a heaven, and so on. But even these structures have to fulfil certain requirements, such as accommodating a certain number of people at one time, protecting them against the weather—besides being technologically and economically attainable. In other words, the functional requirements eventually determine the over-all lay-out of a building.

Secular architecture also reflects ideology or religion to a varying extent, usually depending on the class to which the inhabitants belong. Consequently the ideological influence should be included in a comprehensive architectural survey. We regret having had to leave this aspect out of our studies due to lack of expertise, and we should welcome an opportunity to carry out studies similar to this with a multi-disciplinary team.

The Influence of the Spirit World on the Habitation of the Lao Song Dam, Thailand

Lise Rishøj Pedersen

The *Lao Song Dam* is an ethnic minority group that was transferred from Laos to Thailand some 150 years ago as prisoners of war. They now live in scattered communities from Sawankhalok in the north to the province of Chumpton in the south. Strong concentrations are found in the districts of Ratburi and Pethburi where I carried out field-work in the years of 1965/66 and 1970.

In spite of the long period that has elapsed since the settlement in the districts the *Lao Song* have succeeded in preserving much of their cultural identity. Thus they still speak their own language in the home, and the women's hairstyle and everyday dress as well as the festive dress of both sexes are particular to the *Lao Song Dam*.

Occupationally as well as with regard to material culture the *Lao Song* are broadly speaking living the lives of ordinary Thai people but in religion they differ from their Thai countrymen in that they firmly believe that the ancestors have an active influence on the life of their descendants. This belief finds its manifestation in a number of ceremonies performed with the direct view in mind of securing the favour of the ancestors.

This characteristic trait does not, however, influence their general attitude to Buddhism. Like other Thai peasants they are devoted Buddhists, attaching great importance to implicitly obeying the laws of Buddha, and they will never miss an opportunity to acquire the *bun* (i.e. merit) that is obtained through religiously meritorious acts, and which presents them with the prospect of acquiring a higher status in the next life than the one occupied in the present.

But the life of the *Lao Song* is also pervaded with the belief that the spirits, particularly those of the ancestors, have great power over the fate of every individual, and many old rites are still being performed by the members of the older generation with the purpose of establishing and/or maintaining the good relation with these powerful spirits. How much the *Lao Song* venerate their forbears is illustrated in their rituals connected with death and the spirits of the deceased.

Death and Cremation

Nowadays many *Lao Song* families choose a pure Buddhist funeral, but if a family prefers a traditional *Lao Song* funeral, the Buddhist part of the ceremony ends with the coffin containing the bones of the deceased being carried out of the temple and placed on the pyre platform erected for the cremation. The monks will then leave, and a *Lao Song* 'doctor', the *mo book thang*, i.e. 'the doctor that shows the way', takes charge of the ancient traditional *Lao Song* ritual. His function is to ensure that the ties that bound the deceased to his family are re-established, and he will also explain to the deceased the route to be taken in order to arrive at the *Lao Song Dam* paradise in Laos.

Fig. 1 The *mo book thang* on his way to the burial place. He holds in his hands the jar containing the bones of the deceased, and the thick lea of silk yarn.

When the corpse has been cremated the fire is extinguished, and some of the charred bits of bone are taken to the closest relatives who have been sitting waiting close by together with the *mo book thang*. These remains are placed on a strip of an old mat, and the relatives now proceed to perform the 'last washing' of the deceased: the sprinkling or pouring over the bones with scented water.

When the washing is over the relatives bring 'the last meal' to the deceased. Rice, fish, and a little raw pork are placed beside the bones, and one of the bereaved genuflects in front of them, inviting the dead person to eat. Then the *mo book thang* removes some bone fragments from the heap and transfers them to a small golden urn. These are the remains to be taken home to the dwelling and placed on a shelf next to the urns of the previously deceased members of the family.

Besides the urn the 'doctor' has brought along the following items for the cere-

Fig. 2 The burial plot with the house erected over the bones of the deceased.

mony: an earthen jar, a square piece of pure woven silk, and a thick lea of raw silk yarn. He now picks up as many bones as he thinks the urn will hold, and places them on the silk square, the four corners of which are lifted and tied together with the silk yarn. The bundle is then put into the jar with the free end of the lea of silk yarn hanging over the rim, and an inverted rice bowl is placed over the opening of the jar as a lid. The jar is then carried to the burial place and buried in the selected plot close enough to the surface to permit approximately 50 centimetres of the yellow lea of silk yarn to protrude. On the ground over the buried jar a small straw-thatched house on posts is erected, and the yarn will be attached to its floor. The whole construction is actually a miniature replica of an ordinary dwelling house with fenced compound.

When the last honours have been performed, graduated according to the age and sex of the deceased, the people leave the burial ground, and the family invites everybody to take part in the burial feast.

Thereafter the *mo book thang* reassumes his task, this time in his second function, that of informing the deceased's soul of the exact route to be taken to 'the old residence' in Laos. It is most important that the doctor does not omit a single ritual detail, for if he makes a single mistake the soul will return during the night and prick his shoulder, not leaving him any rest. If he has been unfortunate enough to miss something he will have to read the entire ritual text again, for the doctor and the dead person's *phi* (i.e. spirit) cannot communicate. The doctor can supply the spirit with information, the thick lea of silk yarn connected with the bones in the jar functioning as a sort of receiving aerial, but the *phi* cannot communicate with the doctor and is therefore unable to point out, e.g. which detail the doctor has missed in the ritual.

The soul of the deceased is thought to spend fifteen days on the journey to Laos and his sojourn among his namesakes in that country. At the end of this period the family will arrange a new ceremony with the two main purposes of recalling the spirit from Laos and persuading it to take residence in the family house next to the spirits of his fellow ancestors.

A special room, normally the only room of the house possible to lock, is reserved for the spirits of the dead. Strangers are normally not allowed into this room, and even the walking about under its floor is considered dangerous as such behaviour is likely to annoy the spirits, who might strike back by afflicting the living persons with weaknesses such as a stiff neck and the like. If the accident happens, the spirits can only be pacified by propitiative prayers accompanied by a special sacrifice of rice wine, betel, candles, flowers, and joss sticks placed in front of the very housepost in which the spirits are thought to reside.

Small ceremonies like the one just mentioned may be performed by the head of the family, but important rites like the one performed to call a *phi* back from Laos will always necessitate the assistance of a specialist, the *mo sen phi*, i.e. 'the doctor feeding the spirits'.

The feeding of the spirits—sen phi

A *sen phi* ceremony requires a certain period of preparation as well as a good deal of ready capital. A male pig is picked out for this ceremony and fed a special diet to make it worthy of being consumed by the ancestors, who will be offered a meal consisting of both solid food like pork (raw as well as cooked), chicken, fish, glutinous rice, vegetables, sweets, and fruit, as well as liquids like water and rice wine. Furthermore, the spirits will be offered quids of betel.

Seated in the room reserved for the spirits and holding a heron feather fan in his hand, the *mo sen phi* will intone the recitation of the ancient ritual, calling forth the ancestors from wherever they might sojourn. He informs them that the family has found the money for this feast, invites them to eat and drink, and beseeches them to protect the human beings, the livestock, and the crop. Each defunct relative is invoked by name, and everyone of them must according to the tradition be offered meat, rice, water, rice wine, and betel thrice. In a very old family this might well have the result that the ceremony goes on for several days.

The doctor seizes the food from a big plaited tray with a pair of bamboo chopsticks and eases it out through a hole in the wall or the floor. This hole is not an accidental crack in the house wall or floor, but a carefully planned detail in the construction of the house.

The *sen phi* ceremony is a necessary instrument for the recalling of the *phi* of a recently defunct person, but it has other functions as well. Every family is obliged to arrange a great *sen phi* from time to time, but since the cost is heavy, a *sen phi* may take place with intervals of years, particularly when the family is prospering financially and is in good health. But as soon as accidents begin to occur, the *Lao Song* will know with near certainty that the spirits want to impress upon them the necessity for the arrangements of another *sen phi*.

In between the great and costly ceremonies the *Lao Song* will, however, make small offerings in the afore-mentioned closed room to preserve the favour of their ancestors. The paternal or maternal head of the house kneels down in this room and invokes the family *phis*, inviting them to eat and drink what is now put before them. The food and drink will remain for a couple of minutes on the floor in front of the house-post in which the spirits have been asked to take residence. Then it is removed, and the members of the family will consume the meal of which the smell was enough to satisfy the spirits. Incidentally, a small bowl meant for the spirits' rice wine is permanently placed in front of the afore-mentioned post. Whenever rice wine or beer is ingested in the house the ancestors will be served first and informed of the occasion.

On the whole the spirits must be kept informed of everything that goes on in the family. They must know about the birth of every child, about strangers staying in the house, be it only for a visit of short duration, and they must be consulted about important decisions to be taken, as for instance the inclusion in the family of new members either by adoption or marriage, or building of a new house. Special rituals are required for their sanction and blessings on such occasions.

House-building and house-warming

The building of a house will most often start in March and preferably on a Friday, this combination being considered auspicious for the success of such an enterprise. The site of the house will be chosen by a 'doctor', as the building must on no account hinder the normal passage of spirits and more or less divine beings of the locality. Should this happen, the consequences for the family might be catastrophic, but more about this later.

When the first posts are positioned in their holes, monks are called to bless the house-building through their recitations and sprinklings of the house-posts and holes with sacred water. The more significant house-posts will also be wound with colourful materials in deference to the spirits who reside in them, and bits of cloth with cabalistic characters will be put up to ward off possible evil spirits.

Among the *Lao Song*, the inauguration of a new house will always take place

Fig. 3 Monks invited for recitation in a private house. The ceremony completed, the monks are offered as sumptuous a meal as the owner of the house can afford.

with due consideration and respect for the ancestors and the Buddhist religion. Thus the invitation the builder sends out to relations and friends has two items on the programme: a *sen phi* ancestral ceremony and a *tham bun ban*, i.e. 'merit making in the house' with a *liang phra*, i.e. 'feeding of the monks'.

The inauguration will commence early in the morning with a *mo sen phi* performing the feeding of the family's departed members while informing them the donator has arranged this ceremony in their honour, hoping that they will like the new dwelling and enjoy the meal they are now being offered, and that in return they will protect and bless his home and family, fields and animals.

In the evening the monks invited will enter the house. An altar with Buddha figures is erected in a corner of the largest room in the house. The *sai sin*, the holy white thread, is strung from the ancestors' room to the Buddha figures and from these to each of the monks who hold the thread between their hands throughout

Fig. 4   The family with the 'sick' banana plant holding a strong female spirit.

the ceremony. During the recitations from the holy scripture and the blessings the abbot holds a dripping wax candle over a vessel with water, thus consecrating the water. The ceremony completed, the abbot sprinkles the assembly and the posts, floor, and walls with this water, whereupon the monks are offered tobacco, betel, and tea but no food, the monastic order not permitting them to eat in the period between midday and sunrise on the following day.

The actual *liang phra* (the feeding of the monks) will therefore take place the next morning when the monks return to the house for a short recital and benediction ceremony and a subsequent treat consisting of the best the house can offer in the way of food. The more monks the house-owner is able to feed, and the more money he can donate to the *wat* and monks through his *tham bun ban*, the more *bun* he will obtain, and part of this *bun* is transferred to the ancestors. The transfer is effected partly through the white thread leading into the closed room (it is a *bun*-giving act to listen to the holy script), and partly through the house-owner's ritual pouring of water from one vessel to another during the last blessings, whereby the merit he acquires is shared with the ancestors.

As mentioned, the selection of the right site for a new house is all-important, for in spite of the holding of an inaugural *sen phi* in deference to the ancestors and a *liang phra* in honour of the monks, the owner is still not absolutely safe. In addition to the ancestral spirits there are many other categories of spirits and divinities who might have an influence on the family's existence. I will illustrate this by an example.

One of the more wealthy families in a village in Ratburi province was suddenly struck by a series of inexplicable accidents. The daughter of the house fell ill, the harvest failed, the cattle died, and domestic disagreements and quarrels soon became the order of the day. Moreover, the banana plantation surrounding the compound began to wilt quite suddenly. Only one of the bananas blossomed, but the flower was a very peculiar one. Instead of protruding from the leaf rosette on a long, curved pedicel, the flower's head appeared on the very stalk of the plant.

Devoted Buddhists as they were, the despairing and terrified family sought advice from the local monks, who suggested that a *liang phra* be performed in the house. The ceremony was duly arranged, a sumptuous repast was given and donations made to the temple and monks, and the guests as well as the banana plants were sprinkled with holy water to drive off any evil spirits.

After the ceremony I went to see the plantation and its only flowering plant. The daughter of the house told me that the plant held a very strong female *phi* in whose honour it was dressed up in the most beautiful woman's clothes the family possessed. The banana flower itself was the head and decorated with coloured silk scarves, plastic garlands, bank notes, and silver and gold chains. Around 'her' neck were silk scarves in red, yellow, and green colours, and her sarong was held up by a solid silver belt. In front of her on the ground was a bowl with flowers, candles, and joss sticks (offerings to the female spirit), and the daughter explained that the family itself did not benefit from the recently held *tham bun ban*, as the *bun* obtained had been transferred to the bananas.

For some time I did not see the family, but one day one of the relations told me that the family was about to rebuild the home. The news surprised me, for the house was really a good one and not very old. At my next visit I found the family in the kitchen. The main building had been pulled down, and for the past four weeks the whole household had been living, sleeping, and eating in the small kitchen.

The reason for this drastic step was that the *liang phra* ceremony had been of no avail: the bananas continued to languish and so the family had consulted a *mo* who had found the cause of the trouble. According to the doctor, the withering of the banana plants, the failure of the harvest, and the bad luck that seemed to adhere to every member of the family, were all due to the fact that the 'Proprietress' of the land on which the family lived was annoyed because the house was in the way of her coming and going on the place. They had tried to mollify her by erecting yet another spirit house at the compound for her alone, and by 'sacrificing' themselves in the shape of miniature human figures of clay. As this, too, proved to be without avail, the doctor had convinced them that the only thing left for them to do was to pull down the main building and move it to another site on their land where it would not impede the wanderings of the divinity.

Consequently the house was pulled-down, but not until the ancestral spirits had been persuaded to leave the closed room and take up their temporary abode in a bottle of rice wine, which for the present was reposing on a platform in the barn.

The most propitious moment to start the reconstruction and the most favourable site had been carefully worked out by the doctor, and he was there in person when the first posts were erected. Five monks had been called in to bless the place and sprinkle it with consecrated water. The doctor had also ordered the erection of a two-storeyed bamboo structure, the platforms of which were shaded from the sun by a parasol. Each platform displayed a cushion and some materials in attractive colours. The doctor explained that he had invited the divinity or *phi* (he was unable to define the exact nature of the supernatural powers belonging to the locality) to take up residence there and protect the family.

To complete the story I shall add that when I returned four years later it was evident that all the efforts and expenses the family had undertaken had proved to be fruitless. The family was now living in poverty. The daughter's health had deteriorated; she was now a permanent resident in a nunnery, and distant relatives paid for her keep. The mother was alone on the farm with her youngest daughter and the latter's three small children. As they had no domestic animals left they were not able to cultivate the few rice fields still in their possession, and the son-in-law had been obliged to take up work as a car driver in Ratburi in order to provide the money for the sustenance of the family.

In another *Lao Song* village a woman's failing health gave rise to a corresponding series of rituals and ceremonies, even though the physicians had explained to her that her illness was caused by her entering the menopause. The medicine prescribed by the physicians did not bring about an immediate improvement of her condition, so instead she went to a local doctor for help and advice. In quick succession, a very big *sen phi* for the ancestors' spirits as well as a *tham bun ban* with no less than eleven monks invited to recite in the house, were arranged. In the eventuality that her illness might have been caused by some wandering evil spirit (*phi daj hong*), the woman herself made a propitiative offering whereby she placed banana and fish rolled into a banana leaf at the junction of three roads.

The woman's husband had previously been a very enterprising farmer. Ten years earlier he had made a clearing in the wood on an unreclaimed mountain slope at a distance from the village and had planted kapok and jackfruit trees there. Ever since then he had arranged an annual shadow play as a thank-offering to *cao khaw*, the 'Lord of the Mountain'. This year was to be the last time he arranged the play, and the performance would this time be dedicated also to *cao pha*, the 'Lord of the Forest'. The reason was that in the first place he had made the clearing without asking permission from the Lord of the Forest and, secondly, that he had felled a very large tree to get timber for the construction of his house without making a sacrifice to the spirit of this very tree. These sins of omission, combined with the mistake of putting up his house without making sure that the site was an appropriate one, were according to the local doctor the causes of the illness in the house. So the doctor had strongly advised him to move the house closer to the highway, as in its present

Fig. 5 Children gathered around the habitation of the guardian spirits of the village. After the ceremony the hens offered are distributed among the children present.

position it was a hindrance to the comings and goings of the spirits hovering about the place.

The man had resolved to follow the doctor's instructions, and he would invoke the ancestral spirits asking them to enter a can containing a piece of paper inscribed with all their names and wait there while the house was pulled down, moved, and re-erected.

Sacrifices to the guardian spirits of the village and of the house

Just before the new rice season starts the guardian spirits of the village, who are considered the original owners of the land, will receive a sacrifice from every family in the village. These spirits have a dwelling of their own, a miniature house erected on posts with a platform in front and a room at the rear. In the latter a multitude of small clay figures is heaped, representing animals, human beings, dancers, etc. They are the spirits' servants and draught animals. Such figures are from time to time donated by the various villagers.

Early in the morning of the sacrifice, a representative of each family will set out for the spirits' abode carrying a tray of offerings. The tray will usually hold such presents as rice, fried bananas, eggs, cigarettes, betel, rice wine, water, candles and joss sticks. The kinds vary from one family to another, but pork will always be

Fig. 6 Offering to the spirits of the family's own land.

absent from the trays as, contrary to the ancestral spirits, the guardian spirits dislike pork. Some families will donate a whole boiled hen. The sacrifice of a hen is agreed upon by the villagers who take turns providing this rather important sacrifice.

When all the offerings are piled up inside the house, a candle and some joss sticks will be lit, and the doctor kneels down to pray. He asks the guardian spirits to condescend to accept the presents, to protect the village and its inhabitants and animals during the year to come, and to let the rice in the fields grow abundantly.

Fig. 7　Woman preparing offerings to the Rice Goddess on the threshing ground of the family.

While the invocation and prayer are going on, the water in the vessel is consecrated by dripping wax from candles, and subsequently small lumps of cooked rice are passed through the cracks between the floorboards and dumped over the edge of the platform as food for the servants of the spirits.

The consecrated water is brought back to the family compound where the household will drink from it; the residue (including the wax drippings) is poured into the large ceramic vessels containing rain water for drinking.

In addition to their participation in the sacrifice to the guardian spirits common to the village, the individual family will make an offering at the spirits' house or houses, i.e. the *san phra phum* on the family's own land. Candles and joss sticks are lit, and the tray of offerings (a hen, rice, rice wine, sweets, cigarettes, betel, etc.) is put down on the ground in front of the spirits' abode. Usually it will be the father who kneels down, and facing north he invokes *nang phra thorani*, the Earth Goddess, and her father and mother, addressing them with the following words:

> Today is a happy day, and I invite the three of you to accept my offerings as a token of my respect and honour. May you give us all happiness and good fortune, all of us who are living in this house.

These words are directed mainly to the Earth Goddess, but the sacrifice encompasses all the spirits and divinities of the place. Their collective name is *cao thi*, i.e., the spirits or lords of the locality.

The sacrifice to the guardian spirits of the village is the last big communal ceremony to take place during the dry season. The individual families are now free to commence the planting at their leisure; that is, if the natural conditions for the resumption of the field-work are met, i.e., if the monsoon rains have come.

Rice and religion

Rice and religion are the two most important factors in the life of the *Lao Song* farmer. However, as they are so highly interconnected, it is not easy to decide which of the two factors is *the* more important.

The growing of rice is the *Lao Song* farmer's principal occupation and the economic basis for his own existence and that of his family. Without rice, no food. Therefore he devotes all his efforts and all of his skill to get a good crop.

Yet it does happen that the work he has done is out of proportion to the result obtained. Forces more powerful than his own are decisive. Too little rain, or too much at the wrong time, attacks from crabs, worms, birds, wild animals, etc.–and the crop will become poor. This is why he performs all the ritual sacrifices that are supposed to create good will among those spirits and divine beings who have the power to decide whether or not he will be able to safely gather in his rice with the grains intact, whether or not his animals will thrive, and whether or not he and his family will be happy, prospering and in good health.

To the religious activities already mentioned, the aim of which is to establish or uphold the good relations with the spiritual world, I shall add just one connected with *mae poosup*, i.e., the Rice Goddess or Rice Mother.

The cycle of *mae poosup* and the cycle of woman have many traits in common, e.g., when the rice plants seed, *mae poosup* is pregnant, and the rice grains that are reaped from the fields are her children. Her *khwan*, i.e., her soul or vital principle, is contained in the rice grains, so it is imperative that the *khwan* goes with the rice from the fields and into the barns, to be preserved in next year's seed.

The offerings to the Rice Goddess may vary, but they always consist of dishes she is supposed to like, such as chicken, rice, soups, sweets, and a little rice wine. Some of the *Lao Song* women will take the offerings to the reaped fields and kneel down with their lit candles and joss sticks, inviting *mae poosup* to come and eat. Later they ask her to accompany them to their homes and stay there until the next season when she can return to the fields and make them fertile again and give a good crop.

Then the offerings are put in a basket and taken back to the compound. On her way home the woman, for as a rule it is the mistress of the house who performs this ritual, is not allowed to speak to anyone. When spoken to she will not reply; if she does, *mae poosup* may follow, not her but the one addressing her.

When at home she arranges the presents on a tray with fresh candles and joss sticks and takes it to the family's threshing floor. Again she kneels in prayer to the Rice Goddess, asking her forgiveness for the ill-treatment of her 'children', i.e., the cutting of the rice straws and the threshing. Then the tray is made to rest for a short time on the full rice containers in the barn, and this act completes the thanksgiving and atonement sacrifice to the Rice Goddess. *Mae poosup's khwan* is now present in the rice containers, and when the sowing begins it will be returned to the rice fields together with the seed, so that a good harvest may be obtained.

But the very fact that the *khwan* of *mae poosup* is present in the rice containers explains why you will find when entering a *Lao Song* house that in token of reverence to *mae poosup*, the floor of the barn is raised to a higher level than the floors of the ordinary dwelling rooms. It would not be decent for ordinary people to reside above or on a level with a divine being such as *mae poosup*.

The Group of People Living in a House

Wil Lundström

The material presented in this paper is the result of field research carried out from March 1974 to April 1975 in two villages in the countryside of Minahasa. Minahasa is a region at the tip of the northeastern arm of Celebes (Indonesia). The present culture has resulted from intensive contact with the West. The contacts first recorded date as far back as 1560 (Godee Molsbergen, 1928). Originally the Minahasans were shifting cultivators, in small autonomous tribes with kin groups as their major social units. Contact with the West has brought about dramatic changes. The inhabitants have become settled peasants, with an economy based primarily on cash crop cultivation (coconut, coffee, clove) and with a highly Westernized culture. Dutch influence has been profound, resulting in, among other things, virtually complete Christianization. About 1850, 90% of the population were Christians. The mission and the Dutch colonial government founded many schools. By virtue of education, a large number of Minahasans were employed in the civil services before independence (1949).

As the title suggests, I will deal with the spatial organization of society. The spatial dimension is not a primary factor for the formation of social relations and activities. Closeness in space need not imply a certain pattern of relations and activities. If presence in space can be expressed in more than just physical terms, for example kinship or common interests, then the spatial dimension will also influence the social relations and activities. Membership in a dwelling group is defined according to certain princples. For example, the kinship system often provides the basis for group dwelling, its members being recruited on the strength of ties of consanguinity and affinity. Though kinsmen as well as non-kinsmen may constitute the occupants of a dwelling, the nucleus is often formed by a kinship constellation. In many societies the handling of property and rights in time is regulated by kinship. This is hardly amazing, as one of the most common uses of kinship is recruitment.

The topic dealt with in this paper is often labelled domestic group or household. Meyer Fortes, in his introduction to *The Developmental Cycle in Domestic Groups* (Goody, 1958, p.8), states that:

> '... the domestic group is essentially a householding and housekeeping unit organized to provide the material and cultural resources needed to maintain and bring up its members.'

He clearly recognizes the development factor as intrinsic to domestic organization. Fortes (ibid. pp.4-5) distinguishes three phases in the developmental cycle of the domestic group: expansion, fission, succession. Expansion lasts from the marriage of two people until the completion of their family of procreation. Fission begins with the marriage of the oldest child and continues until all the children are married. Succession ends with the death of the parents and the replacement in the social structure of the family they founded by the families of their children. This cyclical sequence is characterized by a continuous replacement by the members of the domestic unit. Upon completion of these sequences, new individuals come to occupy already established roles which fit the domestic activities.

In a working paper from The Department of Social Anthropology, University of Gothenburg, 1975, Göran Aijmer argues that he finds it necessary for analytical purposes to distinguish the vague notion of domestic activities into: sleeping, eating, cooking, and production. In congruence with this he suggests (ibid. p.2) considering people who habitually sleep together as a shelter group, people who habitually share meals as an eating group, people who are dependant on one particular hearth as a hearth or stove group, and people who pool their efforts in providing food for the various cooking hearths as a production group. The distinctions are analytical ones and the different groups may be identical. This is often the case in the constellation of people we call household or domestic group. In this paper I will incorporate Aijmer's analysis of core activities of shelter, eating, cooking and production, into Fortes' paradigm which he describes in *The Developmental Cycle in Domestic Groups* (Goody, 1958) and *Social Structure* (Fortes, 1949). I think that this can be done in two ways. One is to focus on the domestic groups in terms of their development and of their age-specific characters. Studies by Raymond Smith: *The Negro Family in British Guyana* (1956), and Jack Stauder: *The Majangir* (1971) form convincing examples. Another way is to consider a person's life cycle in the context of the domestic group, or more precisely the shelter, eating, hearth and production group. I intend to employ the latter method and will distinguish the phases from birth to old age.

In the village of Tara tara situated in the countryside of Minahasa, houses are raised on high poles, and are built with plank walls and thatch roof. Formerly they might contain apartments for 12 to 15 families. The storage is underneath and the kitchen is separate on the ground (Graafland, 1898, part I, p.266).

Today a dwelling may be occupied by a married couple with their children, a married couple with their children and one of the parents of one of the spouses, a married couple with their children and other adult relatives, an elderly couple whose children have moved away, a single person, widowed or divorced. The most common composition is a married couple with their children and one of the spouses' aged parents or relatives.

An individual's relations with other persons, his shared membership in the shelter, eating, hearth and production group, are patterned by his position at various stages of life from birth to old age.

Birth

During her last weeks of pregnancy, the woman calls in help from her relatives, preferably her mother or sisters. They are expected to help with the cooking and care of the other children. During this time as well as in cases of illness the number of dwelling occupants has obviously increased. Some days after delivery, there is an open house for guests, both kinsmen and non-kinsmen; they bring presents which are carefully recorded. Reciprocal equivalents are expected at corresponding occasions. The guests are offered refreshments and sweets. The costs are covered by close kinsmen on both sides and voluntary private associations. These associations pool together fixed contributions in money or kind, for the members at certain occasions, such as childbirth, marriage, death. Those who help in the preparation of refreshments and sweets are considered *tuan rumah* (literally: man of the house). Participation in the preparation of food serves here as well as in other celebrations and ceremonies as a distinction between *tuan rumah* and *tamu* (guest).

Childhood

During the first five years the children are indulged by everyone and they remain primarily with the parents and siblings. Only in cases of frequent illness is the child *buang* or 'thrown away' whereupon a kinsman 'picks him up', he is given another name and will stay with that family and in their house till he is recovered. Those kinsmen that 'pick him up' are in most cases a childless couple or grandparents whose mature children have already left the house, people who no longer or never have had a child-rearing function. As an occupant of their dwelling, the child receives food from their stove and his parents have no obligations to provide that stove with food or cover any additional costs of the child. When the child returns to his parents' house at a later age, he continues to have special relations with the family that 'picked him up' and has domestic duties towards them until adolescence. At the age of six, children begin school and are assigned more domestic tasks. The girls' activities are centred around the house, except perhaps their sale of snacks in the streets of the village. The boys have their activities centred in a wider field, such as gathering fruit in the gardens or bathing the cattle in the dams, etc.

The village is divided into *diatas* (above) and *dibawah* (below). This territorial division corresponds to the division between protestants and catholics. Connected to each church there is an elementary school with a six year course. Adherents to the protestant church will send their children to the protestant school, and the catholics to the catholic school. In this way they limit the number of potential playmates for their children. At school the children start to join separate play groups.

The group of girls consists in most cases of nieces and neighbours, who play their games close to the dwellings. The boys form slightly wider groups which have their activities in a more extended area, though in most cases these groups of age-mates are neighbourhood bands. They commonly cluster together under and around the house, in the streets, on their way to school and in the fields. Around the age of ten to twelve years, they often sleep together in the various houses. They sleep freely in each other's house and get refreshments and snacks, though seldom or never cooked food. They are never invited to cooked meals, as adults are, who always hear the invitation or rather salutation when passing by: 'come and join us for eating.' But they are not supposed to accept the invitation, not even when repeated several times. Adults let the children carry out all kinds of small services: 'go and buy me a package of cigarettes,' or 'carry this for me.' But the community has no claims on them yet.

At the age of twelve, the vast majority of the children start a four-year course at secondary school. There is just one secondary school in the village, the one connected to the protestant church. The catholic parents used to send their children to the neighbouring village of Woloan at a distance of 4 km. Nowadays more and more parents send their children to the secondary school in Tara tara on advice of their new priest, a Dutchman. He teaches the course in religion for catholic children at the school. The other courses they attend together with the protestant children. The protestant and catholic children still form separate play groups and the boys and girls from Tara tara who attend the school in Woloan do not form play groups with their classmates from Woloan.

The boys and girls continue to join separate play groups. Immediately after they have finished school, they can join official mixed groupings. It seems that age forms a more decisive criterion in group formation for boys than for girls. Girls interact more frequently with younger and older people. Kinship and residence are more decisive than age in the composition of their play groups. Both groups lack formal organization and shift in size and composition. These amorphous groups first become corporate groups when the members stop going to school and start to work regularly in the gardens.

Boys and girls who do not attend secondary school, or who do not finish it for some reason, often economic, start agrarian activities and form corporate groups at an earlier age.

Adolescence

Once out of school, their needs and the demands on them get stronger. For example, they will seldom work for relatives without payment. They get formally organized by the church and by arrangements for labour. They are now labelled *pemuda protestant* (protestant youngsters) and *pemuda katolik* (catholic youngsters) by the church. The collectivity of *pemudas* is subdivided into about twelve units, corresponding to neighbourhoods. Each unit of both boys and girls has a leader who is in charge of calling them together for learning to sing and dance. They have the rehearsals in the evening after work. These form the first occasions at which girls may go out after sunset without the company of some adult.

In addition to the singing and dancing and learning how to act as dedicated members of the church, these groups are engaged in sports and other recreational activities. Under the guise of *pemudas* all kinds of activities are accepted by the adults. For example, an adolescent boy and girl are not permitted to go together to the gardens to work, but are allowed to spend a whole day with the *pemudas* at the beach at a distance of 30 km. These groups, marked by leadership and closed membership, show noticeable coherence in singing and dancing contests as well as during ceremonies and festivities. There have been efforts made to get both groups of *pemudas* together during activities, but these failed. The only occasion at which they get together is at wedding parties. Whether the bridal couple is protestant or catholic does not matter.

In the labour situation they are also formally organized. The organizations of work named *mapalus* have leadership and show solidarity. The principles of recruitment are several: age, neighbourhood, friendship, common objectives and sometimes sex. But the separation between protestant and catholic persists in most cases. They themselves will not conceive of religion as something that separates people in work situations. They will just say, it happened to be so, it was easier to get people from *diatas* or *dibawah* thus underlining another principle. The number of participants in a *mapalus* range from five to forty. With an increase in number, they get more formalized and regimented. A *mapalus* often coincides with other ways of grouping like neighbourhood or age. In a *mapalus* consisting of *pemudas*, the members work each other's land, or more correctly their parents' land. In some cases the youngsters rent land though they seldom own land. The amount of work each member is entitled to is measured in time, or in space or in number of people who have to work the land, all measurements being transferable with each other.

There are *mapalus* consisting of only boys, or both boys and girls, but never only girls. Often the girls get more thoroughly domestic tasks, thus enabling their mothers to work in the gardens to a larger extent. Work groups of mature women do exist. We may say that both boys and girls get more regular work; the girls partly in domestic duties and partly in farming, the boys mainly in farming. The boys do all the different elements of farming, the girls just some elements. They learn to master the adult way of life in groups, such as previously described for production and religion.

Eventually, parents and close kinsmen cannot have the same demands on them, but nevertheless they remain as members of the same hearth and eating group as their parents. The parents are losing control over the method of production as well as their way of spending part of their income. Concerning sleeping, they continue to sleep together in the various houses. Also, boys may accompany one of their friends to sleep under or in front of the house of the girl he is in love with. They get more freedom for participation in village life, especially the boys. This is exemplified by their permission to chat, smoke, drink and play cards in the small shops during the evenings.

The community makes regular demands on them; the boys have to participate in *kerja bakti*. This is a system of services to the community, which consists of participation in village projects and routine obligations. The system affects the whole village and is very regimented and formalized, as well. The male population between 16 and 55 has to participate once a week in *kerja bakti*. Those men who are of higher age or who are hindered in participating, have to contribute with food and cigarettes.

These examples suggest that the adolescents are directed in various ways by the normative values of self-reliance. Not all the youngsters are directed towards the end of working their own farmland. An increasing number of the young have their attention directed outside the village, aspiring to white-collar jobs. The bureaucracy cannot absorb their increasing number and quite a number of them have to return to the village and start farming. They are often restless, spend time and money on jobs which do not have very bright prospects. Losing their incentives, it takes some time before they feel motivated to work the farmland regularly.

Adolescence can be characterized by more formal grouping, some lumping together of both boys and girls, regular participation in farming and housekeeping aiming at self-reliance, and learning the adult way of life in groups.

Marriage

After marriage the spouses withdraw from their groups of age mates. They are expected to spend more time and effort contributing to the family resources. Usually they move to the house of one of the spouses' parents. Economic considerations are most important in the choice of residence such as the number of unmarried children in the parental houses. The newly married couple start with some capital in the form of dry farmland, wet rice fields, coconut trees, clove trees. These are part of the *harta* (brideprice). The proportions depend on the economic capacity of the two families; in most cases this will not be enough to live on. They will try to get an additional income by working as farmhands on other persons' properties, or by sharecropping activities that should provide them with money in order to buy land and build a house, in short, activities directed towards their becoming more self-sufficient. By marriage they form a *rumah tangga* (household or family). They are treated formally as a *rumah tangga* in certain activities like village administration, tax payment and membership of the church. But otherwise they are not. This is due, in my opinion, to the fact that they do not yet have a cooking hearth which they fully control. By marriage they do in principle form a *rumah tangga*, but conceptionally this seems to be connected with the full control of a hearth, in the eyes of the villagers. (In former times, when the houses were inhabited by several married siblings and their offspring, the houses had several hearths. Then, the villagers used to talk in terms of how many hearths there were in the house and not how many households.)

If we turn first to the production sphere, we notice that part of their resources they pool together with the parents whose dwelling they share. As such, they can be considered members of their parents' production group but on their way to establishing one for themselves. They may spend the rest of their resources in their own way. For example, they are free to choose how many associations they want to join, and how much money they want to save in these associations or to borrow from them.

They sleep under the same roof as their parents. They are given a separate room, as their privacy is highly recognized. Habitually they share meals with the parents, they can thus be considered as members of the same eating group as their parents. They eat food prepared on the same hearth which they help to provide with foodstuff. It is mainly in this sense that they are not considered to be an independent unit. They have no separate hearth which they fully control; they share one which they only partially provide with food. This is clearly noticeable in the treatment by the community; there may be several *rumah tangga* sharing the same dwelling, but in cases of celebrations they never get separate invitations. The invitations are directed to the *tuan rumah* conceived as the owner of the house and the hearth. There are cases where the newly married couple have moved to a house of their own, on the compound of the parents, often of a semi-permanent character such as bamboo construction. They still lack a hearth of their own and do not get separate invitations. As stated earlier, it is highly valued that they should provide for themselves, but as long as they are dependent on the parents' cooking hearth they lack the full recognition of a *rumah tangaa* by the community, although in economic transactions, like loans and sales, they act independently.

Maturity and old age

From the time the children are born till they come of age, the married couple steadily increase their independence and power, becoming a *rumah tangga* in its full sense. Either they have built a house of their own, containing a hearth which they control, or they stay in the house of the parents.

Mature men and women may work together in groups. More often men will work regularly in groups of a more institutional character which have a name, leadership, fixed work-schedule, etc. These organizations of work, which also function as aid institutions during the great family occasions are always connected with a rotating credit association. Apart from these very regulated groups, there are several smaller groups. These are less formalized, have no leadership or a firm work schedule. The women usually join these smaller groups, which consist of four to five members. They work their gardens at irregular intervals and for varying lengths of time. The women have more difficulties in following a fixed working schedule, for it is often interrupted by their domestic and trade activities. Those who regularly visit the market in a nearby town for buying and selling, are women. One could say that the market is dominated by women.

Both men and women join several voluntary private associations. These are institutions for saving, which is done either in money or kind. The money is used to cover the costs of the great family celebrations of the members, or to buy collectively eggs, sugar, flour and other necessities for the preparation of food, during the celebration of Christmas and New Year. Saving ranges from that of durable goods like rice to the raising of animals, especially pigs. Many efforts in these associations are directed towards the covering of costs, mainly food, for celebrations and ceremonies. By then, the hearth group and the eating group expand dramatically. Principles of recruitment to the voluntary private associations are several. These discrete social entities are patterned by one or a combination of the following criteria: religion, kinship, sex, territorial division, occupation, interests and age.

When the grandparents get old, they can no longer produce enough to live on. More and more they have to rely for goods and services on their mature children and kinsmen, who may take them into their houses. In cases where their mature children never left the parental home, there is a shift of centre from the grandparents to their mature children. Of course this happens very gradually and there are individual and situational differences.

The old people are honoured, they have authority, but they do not have much real power left. They withdraw from decisive roles, and decisions are left in the hands of their mature children. In questions concerning *adat* (customary law), however, they are always consulted. In sum, they are wise people, who are entitled to honour and authority but have no power.

They still possess farmland and also owns the house and its surrounding compound, which will be inherited immediately after their death, but they no longer contribute in any active way to the family resources, which suggests dependence on their children's cooking hearth. Although there are personal and situational variations, they do not get separate invitations any longer and this demonstrates that they, in the eyes of the villagers, are a dependent unit.

Bibliography

Aijmer, Göran, 1975, *What is a Household?* Working paper, Dept. of Soc. Anthropol. Univ. Gothenburg. Gothenburg.
Goody, Jack (ed.), 1958, *The Developmental Cycle in Domestic Groups.* Cambridge Univ. Press. Cambridge.
Fortes, Meyer (ed.), 1949, *Social Structure: Studies presented to A. R. Radcliffe-Brown.* Clarendon Press. Oxford.
Godee Molsbergen, E. E., 1928, *Geschiedenis van de Minahassa tot 1829.* Landsdrukkerij. Weltevereden (Bogor).
Graafland, N., 1898, *De Minahassa. Haar verleden en haar tegenwoordige toestans.* De Erven F. Bohn. Haarlem.
Smith, Raymond T., 1956, *The Negro Family in British Guyana. Family Structure and Social Status in the Villages.* Routledge & Kegan Paul. London.
Stauder, Jack, 1971, *The Majangir. Ecology and Society of a Southwest Ethiopian People.* Cambridge Univ. Press. Cambridge.

Habitation Among the Yakan, a Muslim People in the Southern Philippines[1]

Inger Wulff

Whereas mainland Southeast Asia, apart from Malaysia, is predominantly Buddhist, and Malaysia and Indonesia are predominantly Muslim, more than 90 per cent of the inhabitants of the Philippines are Christians, mostly Catholics. This is a consequence of the Philippines having been colonized by the Spanish. Right from the beginning of the colonization in the second half of the sixteenth century it was the purpose of the Spaniards to Christianize the archipelago, and on the whole they succeeded. In the south, however, in the Sulu Islands and in parts of Mindanao, Islam was already firmly established, and the Muslim peoples there, called Moros by the Spaniards, resisted all efforts to be converted by them. Today there are some 3 million Moros, by far the largest minority group in the Philippines.

Actually the Muslim Filipinos do not comprise one single minority group, but are divided into several groups, differing in language and culture.

One of the minor Muslim groups is the Yakan which lives on the island of Basilan, just off the southwestern point of Mindanao. The Yakan live mainly in the interior of the island. Their number is estimated at about 70,000.

Although the Yakan are Muslims, and probably have been so for a long time, many of their older traditions have survived the introduction of Islam. Not a few rituals are of pre-Islamic origin, though the Yakan themselves consider such rites part of Islam. It is also characteristic that the introduction of Islam never brought about a segregation of the Yakan women.

The Yakan are agriculturists. Their main crop—at least the one that they themselves value the most—is upland rice, but only a few Yakan can harvest enough rice to last them for a whole year. To supplement the rice, they grow various other crops, the most important one being camote (sweet potato), but they also grow cassava, maize, vegetables and various sorts of fruits. Coconuts are of increasing importance, as the Yakan have taken up the making of copra for sale, thus making a cash income.

The rice is cultivated in non-irrigated fields. After one crop of rice a field may be planted with camote or cassava, or it may be left for a couple of years, while rice is planted in another field. After two or three years, however, rice can once more be planted in the former rice field. This rotation of the crops makes it possible for the Yakan to be sedentary. The fields are privately owned.

The Yakan have no compact villages; the houses are scattered among the fields, and as a rule it is difficult to see where one settlement ends and the next one begins. The centre of the community is the *langgal*, i.e., the mosque, which is quite a simple building. The head of the *langgal*, the *imam*, is not only the religious, but also the secular head of the community, in the last capacity in cooperation with three elders. Usually the house of the *imam* stands next to the *langgal*. Most often the houses in the neighbourhood of a *langgal* are attached to that *langgal*, but this is not necessarily the case. During my field work I was staying in a place called

Fig. 1 The *langgal* of Sabana. Like the house walls, the walls of the *langgal* may be made of plaited bamboo or reed, or of horizontal boards.

Bohebessey. However, although the house in which I was staying was situated nearly in the centre of Bohebessey and not far from the *langgal* of Bohebessey, it belonged to the parish of Sabana *langgal*. This was due to special circumstances. Originally there had been only one *langgal*, the *langgal* of Bohebessey, covering also what was to become Sabana. But because of some quarrels, the congregation became divided, and the *langgal* of Sabana was established at the eastern end of Bohebessey. Most of the houses of Sabana were near the *langgal*, but a few of them were situated right in Bohebessey, and some members of the congregation lived even farther away. The parish of Bohebessey was by far the largest one, comprising 31 houses, whereas only eight houses belonged to Sabana.

The houses are family dwellings, usually occupied by a single family: husband,

Fig. 2 Yakan house on rather low piles. To the left an open porch, in the middle the main building with a covered porch in front, to the right the kitchen. The walls of the main building as well as the walls of the kitchen are of reed. In front of the house is the rice mortar.

wife, and unmarried children. Sometimes also a sibling of husband or wife may join the household, especially if the person in question is not married. Also, a newly married young couple will live with the parents of either husband or wife. Later, however, the young couple will build their own house. Whether on the land of the husband or of the wife, is up to their own choice. But in case of a divorce, the one on whose land the house is situated, will keep the house, while the spouse must leave.

As already mentioned the Yakan houses lie scattered among the fields, and like these are privately owned. Around the house vegetables as well as various fruit trees are grown. Near the house may be some small building; very common is a building in which copra is made. In a few cases two or even three houses may be close to one

Fig. 3 A house under construction. The floor has been laid, one side of the roof is thatched, and the owner of the house has started making the walls. Bohebessey, 1961.

another. They will then most probably belong to parents and children.

The houses are rectangular pile buildings of varying size, and also the elevation of the floor is varying. The elevation has a practical purpose in that during the rainy season it is extremely muddy. Besides, in former times, when fighting was not uncommon, the elevation gave protection against enemies. The space under the house is seldom used. The roof usually is steep. It is thatched with either cogon grass or leaves of the nipa palm. There are two kinds of walls: either they are made of plaited bamboo or reed, or they are of horizontally placed wooden boards. The wooden walls are the more esteemed, but actually the plaited walls are the more pleasant, because they make the room more airy, while especially a smaller room with wooden walls may be hot and stuffy. The floor is made of split bamboo poles with the convex side upwards, or it, too, may be of wooden boards, but in this case either a small part of the floor is made of bamboo, or at least there will be a hole in

Fig. 4 The same house in 1966.

the wooden floor to spit through, not only because the Yakan are fond of betel chewing, but also because they are used to rinse the mouth after eating. In former fighting days the bamboo floor might be dangerous, as an enemy might try getting under the floor to thrust his spear through it between the bamboo poles.

The first stage in the building of a house is the erecting of a wooden framework, after which the floor is laid. Then comes the making of the walls and the thatching; these two works may be done simultaneously. Sometimes a family will move into a new house, before it is completely finished. When the family is moving in, the very first time the owner brings some of their belongings into the house, he will suspend a small bamboo tube from the roof inside the house. This bamboo tube contains rice, oil, water, and fish to ensure that there will always be food in the house, and water as well, and besides, it contains all the ingredients for the betel quid, to make sure that desirable guests will come to visit the house. Furthermore, when the

Fig. 5 House in Bohebessey. The main building (to the left) has wooden walls, the kitchen reed walls. Between the main room and the kitchen is a covered porch.

family has moved in, an *imam* will be called to perform a prayer for the blessing of the house.

In the course of time the house may undergo some changes. It may be necessary to add to the house if more people are to live in it, e.g., if a son or a daughter marries and the young couple stays in the house. And an enlargement of the porch, at least, may be required if many guests are expected for some celebration in the house, e.g., a wedding.

A house is expected to stand for ten to fifteen years. Then a new house will have to be built, but still usable materials from the old house may be employed for the construction of the new one.

As a rule a Yakan house consists of three parts: the main building, the kitchen, and the porch. Sometimes the hearth may be placed in the house proper, but most often it is in a separate kitchen, built together with the house, but usually on a

Fig. 6   The kitchen of the house shown in figs. 3 and 4.

somewhat lower level. Whichever kind of floor and walling the main part of the house may have, the floor of the kitchen is always of bamboo, so that waste can be thrown through it, and the walls are plaited making it possible for the smoke to escape. In the kitchen there are pots and pans, and some pottery, as well as long bamboo containers for water, ladles, rice measures, and so forth. Over the hearth there may be a frame made of bamboo for drying fish and remnants of the meal. Under the house is the rice mortar.

A house will always have a porch, sometimes between the main room and the kitchen, sometimes along one side of the house. It may be covered or open. More often it is made of bamboo. The house is entered from the porch. Access to the porch usually is by steps made of long bamboo poles or a bamboo ladder, or merely by a wooden or bamboo pole with steps cut into it.

When it comes to the main part of the house one feature is noteworthy: considering that the Yakan are Muslims, one would expect a division of the house so that there was a special closed part for the women. This, however, is not the case. Usually the main building consists of one room only, which is used by men as well as women, not only residents but guests as well. Recently some people have made one or a few small rooms by putting up low bamboo walls, but this is rare, and does not really change the pattern, as the greater part of the building will still be taken up by one big room where people—men and women—may gather. Traditionally the house has no windows, but these, too, have made their appearance. There is no ceiling. It is said that there is sometimes a sort of attic under the roof, mainly used for storage, though it may also be used for sleeping. However, I have never seen this.

Along one side wall of the room are chests for storing clothes, metal trays for the serving of food, bronze boxes for betel, and other bronze receptacles. There are

Fig. 7 Interior of a house prepared for a wedding. Mattresses and mats are rolled out for the guests, who have not yet arrived.

also rolled-up mats, and most often mattresses, too, to be rolled out at night for sleeping on, or at parties to sit upon. And there are pillows, the more the better. Pillows and mattresses are stuffed with kapok, grown by the Yakan. In the room a backstrap loom is often seen, maybe even more than one, as many women, though not all, are expert weavers.

During daytime the room is not very much in use, except in case a woman is weaving there. Much more important is the porch. This is where the dwellers of the house will sit whenever they are not doing work that cannot be done on the porch. And on the porch neighbours may drop in for a talk, and are at once offered betel or cigarettes. Only at feasts does the room play a more important part during daytime. Then guests may be served in the room, sometimes also on the porch, whereas everyday meals are eaten in the kitchen. At night, and that means already from

Fig. 8 Wedding guests on the porch.

Fig. 9 The 'mosquito net' inside which the bride is sitting.

about 7 o'clock, the house is closed, the mattresses and mats are rolled out, and people lie down in the big room to sleep, perhaps after talking a little. About 5.30 the next morning they arise.

In one house, however, there will still be some activity during the evening and part of the night. This is the house where the children are taught to read the Koran. The teaching will take place in the room of the house of the teacher, most often a woman. Her pupils will come to the house after sundown and spend the night there, reading for some three hours before going to sleep, and starting again a couple of hours before sunrise which marks the time for them to go home.

There are times, however, when also in other houses the main room is used during daytime, namely, when there is some celebration in the house, e.g., the big celebration held when a boy or girl has finished the Koran study, or for a wedding. During a celebration the room is decorated, the mattresses and mats are rolled out,

Fig. 10 The celebration marking the end of the Koran study. Along the walls are pillows and metal trays. Clothes are hanging on a cord above.

clothes are hung on a cord along one of the walls, usually the back wall. And if it is a wedding, the 'mosquito net' is hanging down, and the bride is sitting inside it most of the time, only coming out for the final ceremony. During daytime, guests may sit on the mats; if the celebration is during the night, the guests may lie down to sleep if they get tired, and they will be given a pillow, maybe also a blanket. There is a good reason for this. The Yakan very seldom leave a house during the evening or night. Consequently, if there is some celebration during evening and part of the night, the guests will stay there till the next morning.

Most of the celebrations held in the house are family celebrations, whereas the religious festivals usually take place in the *langgal*. This was always the case in Bohebessey, but in Sabana, if many people were attending, some of the bigger religious celebrations were transferred to a big house next to the *langgal*, which belonged to the father of the *hatib*, one of the assistants of the *imam*. There was more room

Fig. 11 Modern Yakan house. Next to it is a traditional house. Bohebessey, 1966.

in the house than in the comparatively small *langgal*, which was moreover already rather old and dilapidated. When the house was used instead of the *langgal*, a cloth that covered the walls of the *langgal* during service was brought to the house and hung up there.

The traditional house as described above was the common Yakan house at the time of my stay in Basilan. However, a new type of house had made its appearance. Its main features were the same as in the traditional house: one big room, a porch, and a separate kitchen. But it was better built. One example was in Bohebessey. This house was built on very high piles, the floor and walls were of finely made wooden planks, the roof of corrugated iron, covering also the porch, and the house could be safely locked up during the night. It was under construction when I came to Bohebessey, and was finished during my stay. Some chairs were bought for it when a feast was to be held. Later on the space under the house was also walled in to make an extra room downstairs. In this house lived a husband and wife and their son who studied in another part of Basilan, and therefore was seldom at home. In a traditional house next to the new house lived a daughter with husband and children. Two other families had started building such houses, and in the following years they became much more common. It seemed that they were to be the future Yakan house.

This, however, was not to be. At least for the time being this development has been suspended. During recent years there has been an insurrection in the southern Philippines, many Muslims having rebelled against the government. On the whole the Yakan have tried to keep neutral, but there has been heavy fighting in Basilan,

Fig. 12 Houses of Yakan evacuees in Zamboanga, 1975.

Fig. 13 Houses of Yakan evacuees in Basilan, 1975.

also in the area around Bohebessey, and most of the population had to be evacuated, some to the small towns of Basilan, some to Zamboanga in Mindanao. Most of them are now back in the interior of Basilan, though they have not yet been able to settle in their homes, but are still living together in a resettlement camp. A few families are still staying on the outskirts of Zamboanga City. The Yakan houses in these places are small, mostly poorly built, and with only a slight eleveation above the ground. And one of the characteristics of the Yakan settlement has disappeared: whereas typically Yakan houses were scattered among the fields rather far apart, they now are close together. It is to be hoped that the Yakan will soon be able to return home and continue the development that was broken.[2]

Notes

1. Thanks to grants from the Carlsberg Foundation I was able to do ethnographical field research among the Yakan during two periods: from December 1960 to April 1961, and from April 1964 to February 1965, with a further short visit in April 1965. Both times I was staying in the eastern part of the island. I paid two short visits to Bohebessey, where my main field work had been done, in 1966 and 1970. During a brief stay in Zamboanga City in 1975, I went to Basilan for two days, and visited the Yakans in Zamboanga a couple of times.
2. Since this was written (1975) the Yakans from Bohebessey have been able to return to their homes. At first they were living in miserable huts—one family e.g. living in the small building used for making copra—but later on they have been able to build better houses. As the situation is still far from safe, some families have preferred to stay in Calarian on the outskirts of Zamboanga, though transferred to a smaller lot. Here they are making a living through weaving and selling their products mostly to tourists visiting the settlement.

Certain Aspects of Housing in Nepal

Camille Milliet-Mondon

The land of Nepal, whose surface area is 148,000 square kilometres, is spread in a rectangular shape from East to West with China to the North and hemmed in by India on the other three sides. This Himalayan country is composed of five main regions spread in natural parallel bonds between the north and the south boundaries, each region forming a different geographical unit. From the south to the north they are as follows (fig. 1): 1) the flat country of the Terai, 2) the range of Siwalik and Mahabarat, 3) the middle hills, 4) main Himalaya, 5) inner Himalaya. Deep valleys cross these regions from north to south.

Nepal as a whole has a monsoon climate, with summer rains from June to September, and a rather dry period of nine months. The range of mountains forms a natural wall against the monsoon winds which blow from the southeast. Thus precipitation is heavier on the southern slopes and gradually decreases from the Terai to the Himalaya (fig. 2). There are three main types of climate from south to north: sub-tropical, temperate, and alpine. In addition to these three main types and according to the topography of each region there are several micro-climates.

Because of the vertical structure of the country, the altitude of which ranges from 100 m to over 8,800 m, and because of the monsoon influence, the population is mainly located in the southeast and mostly in the middle hills. Few people live in the inner and main Himalaya and rarely over 4,400 m. Ninety three per cent of the population of Nepal live in rural areas, and the different types of housing are adapted to an agricultural economy. The greater majority of country people are grouped together in villages. Isolated houses, which are rare, are to be found mainly in the eastern part of the country.

The Nepal villages are divided into three different types of habitat:
1. Grouped in lax order: the houses are placed far from one another and are separated by cultivated fileds. This type of housing is characteristic of the humid regions of the Himalayas (northeast Nepal).
2. Grouped close together: the houses are arranged around a central axis, or staggered on a slope. The fields are spread out around the cluster. This kind of housing is found in central Nepal and in west Terai.
3. Closed-in villages: the houses are built side by side and form a compact cluster. The fields are grouped near the river and can be far from the village. This kind of housing is found in the inner Himalaya.

In central Nepal there are at least twelve different ethnic groups which speak Tibeto-Burmese languages, each with its own territory. Inner Himalaya is inhabited by people of Tibetan stock, who speak a Tibetan dialect, and the Terai by people originating from India, with their own dialects.

The following is a general survey of housing in five specific regions: 1) west Terai, Dang Valley (Tharu people), 2) central middle hills, Siklis region (Gurung people), 3) east middle hills, Timalbesi region (Tamang people), 4) east inner Himalaya, Khumbu region (Sherpa people), and 5) central inner Himalaya, Thak region (Thakali people) (fig. 1).

Fig. 1 Nepal.

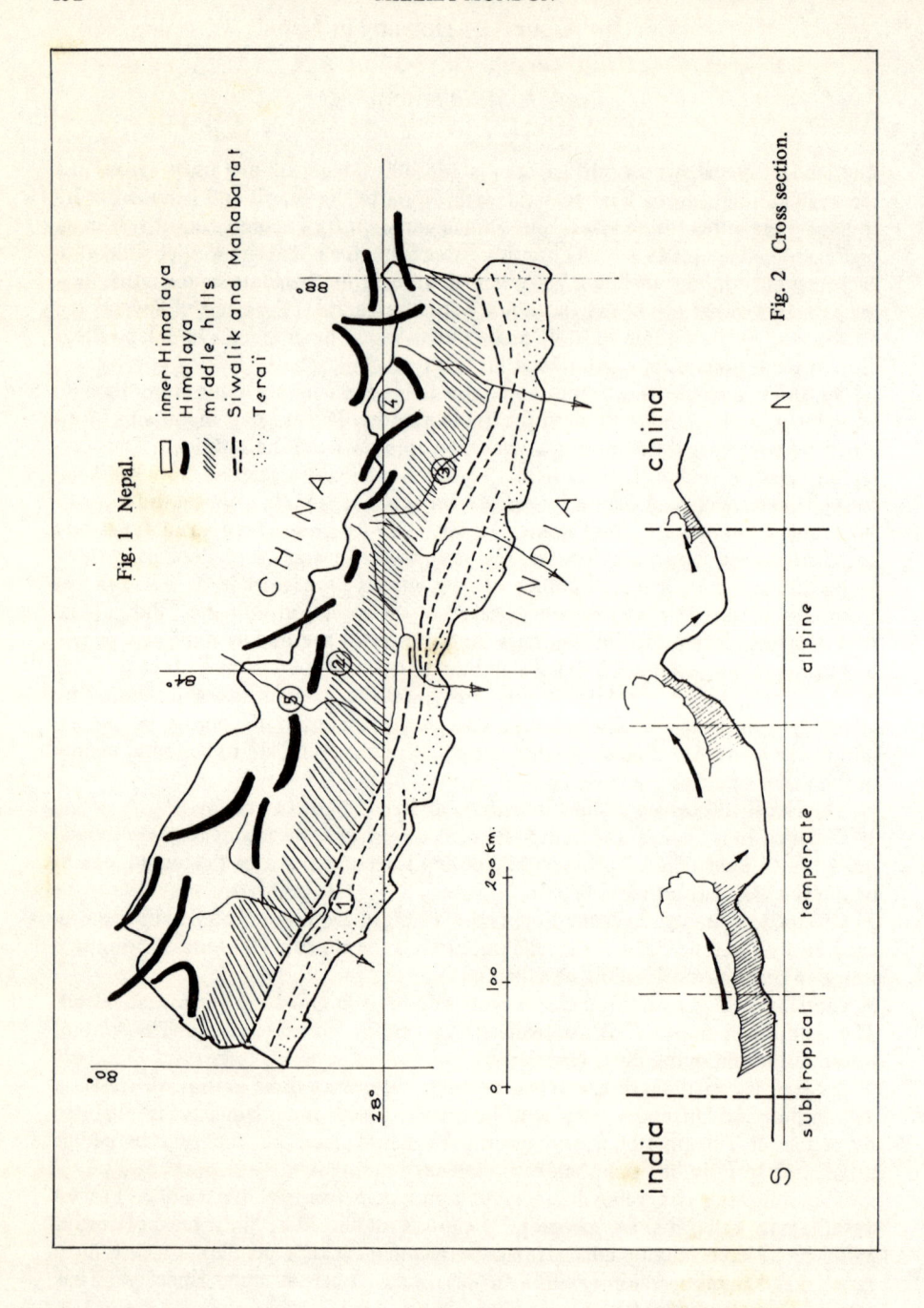

inner Himalaya
Himalaya
middle hills
Siwalik and Mahabarat
Teraï

Fig. 2 Cross section.

1. Tharu Housing in the Dang Valley

The Dang Valley is situated in the western part of the Terai, at an altitude no higher than 600 m. This is a flat valley completely deforested over an area of more than 200 square kilometres. A tropical forest occupies the surrounding mountains. It is watered by the summer monsoon, but is less humid than the rest of Terai.

The Tharus are peasants and stock-breeders, and work as share-croppers on land belonging to rich landlords. Mainly rice growers, they also cultivate corn, wheat and mustard. The herds consist of cows which produce milk and cow dung (the latter being used for domestic fires), as well as of sheep and pigs which provide meat.

The valley is dotted with villages which are tradiionally oriented north-south, as are also the houses. The villages are situated at about a twenty-minute walk from each other, and have from 150 to 250 inhabitants. They are surrounded by bamboo, banana and mango trees (fig. 3). Cultivated fields are laid out between the oases made by the village areas.

The houses of the village face one another on opposite sides of the main street which traditionally runs through the whole agglomeration in length from north to south. In front of each house there is an open space where the animals stay on their return from the pastures. A pig-sty and a shed may be built there. Behind the house there is a small yard used for domestic work (weaving, basket-making, and rice-alcohol making), and the family's kitchen garden. The dwelling and the open spaces which surround it form a whole unit, identical for each family. Each unit is separated laterally by a hedge of cactus and are closed in by bamboos planted at the bottom of the garden (fig. 4).

The Tharu houses are long, rectangular, and single-storeyed, and they are covered with a thick, steeply sloping (45 degree) thatched roof descending to within a metre from the ground, and supported by a wooden structure composed of several rows of seven posts arranged along the length of the building. The walls are built in cob, i.e. bamboo framework and mud (fig. 6). The roof rests on wooden beams held by posts. It is slightly convex from the ridge to the brim. The thatch is kept in place by bamboo sticks laid out lengthwise on the roof. There are a few openings to the outside: one door in the front wall for animals, and two doors, a front one and a back one, for the people. They both open into the hall and face each other. Light enters the habitation through round openings in the walls.

The inside is cool and dark, and is composed of three distinctive parts: the cow-house, the hall and the habitation itself (fig. 6). The stable, which shelters the animals during the night, is separated from the hall by a bamboo partition. The platform over the animals serves as a storage area for fodder. If the hall serves as a room which links the different parts of the house, it is also the privileged area for social occasions. It is around the central fire-place that the master receives his visitors. The living quarters are the private area of the house. A partition separates it from the hall and access to it is through a double hanging door. The different cells of the dwelling are separated by partitions going half-way to the ceiling and made up of containers shaped like large, flattened bottles (fig. 5). The cells have various functions. One serves as a workroom in which is placed a husking-pounder, another is used for storage of water and rice-wine. The kitchen is equipped with an earthen-

Fig. 3 Tharu village in Dang valley.

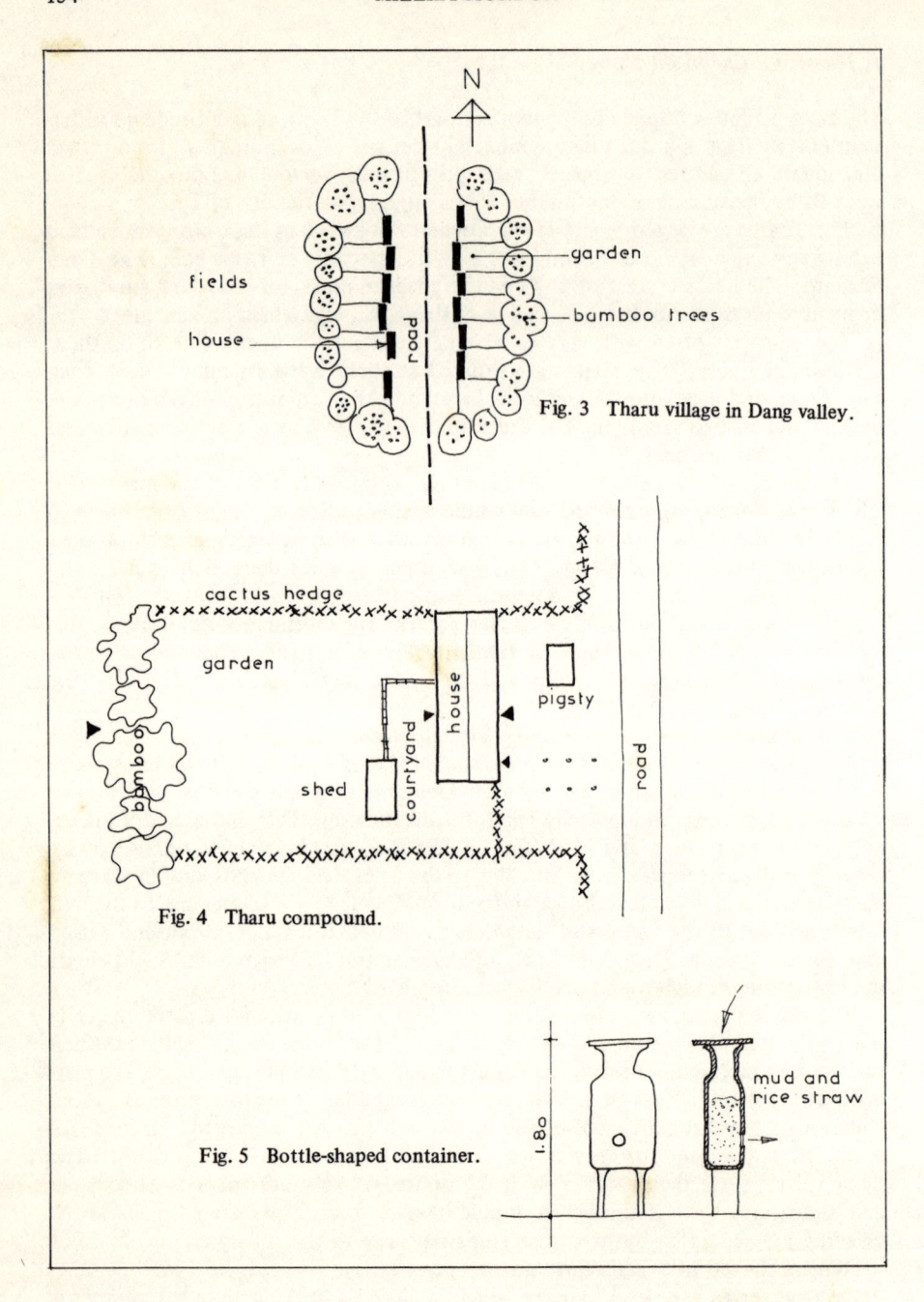

Fig. 4 Tharu compound.

Fig. 5 Bottle-shaped container.

CERTAIN ASPECTS OF HOUSING IN NEPAL 155

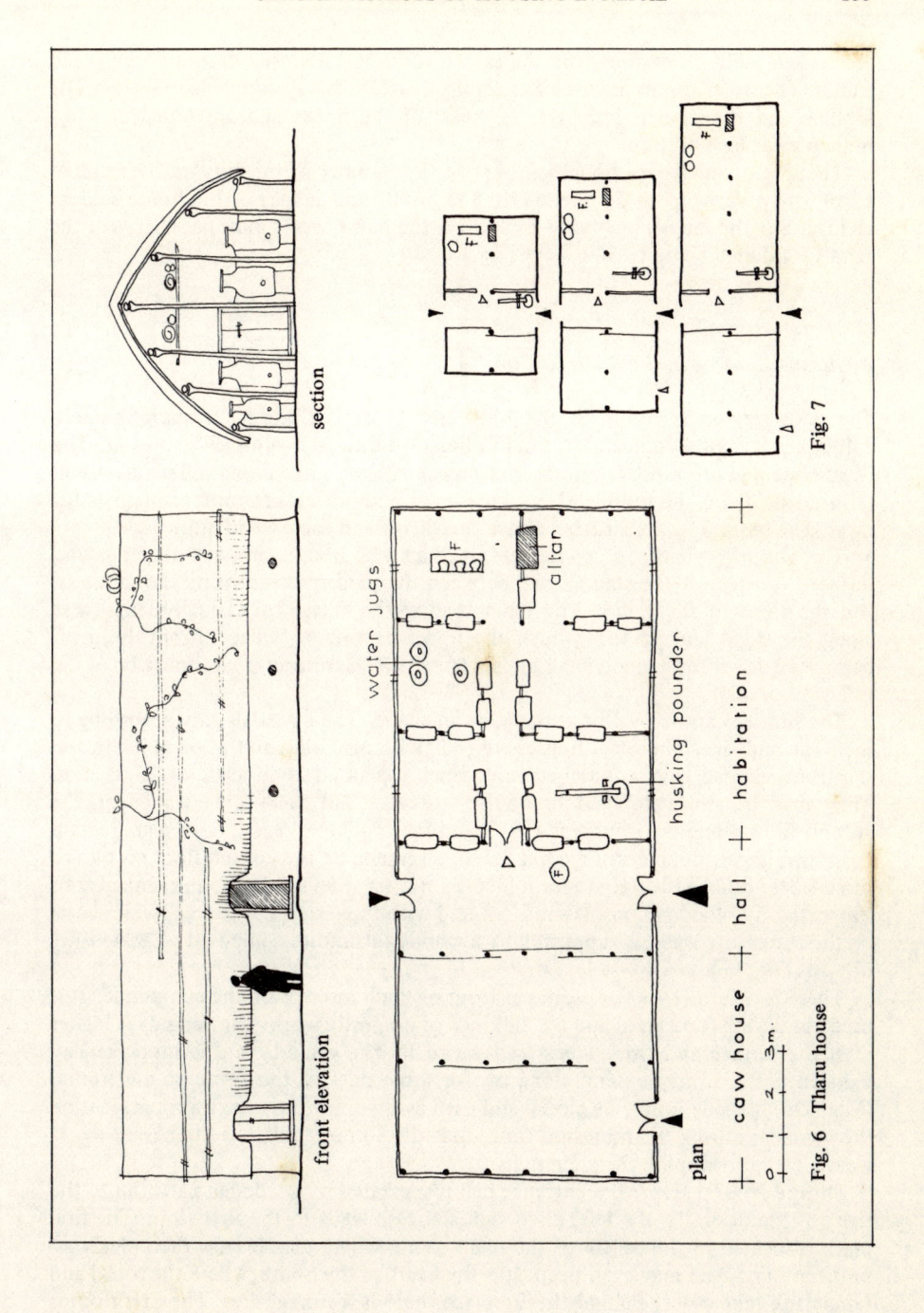

Fig. 6 Tharu house

Fig. 7

ware stove with three fires, and the sacred room is where the decorated holy silo stands. The other rooms are used as sleeping quarters. Every couple has a room. The kitchen and the sacred room are the heart of the house and are sometimes forbidden areas by tradition.

The size of the Tharu house varies with the number of inhabitants. The united family may have up to 25 members. The width and height of the house seldom change, but the length may vary to contain the number of rooms necessary for the family, and may be up to 54 m long (fig. 7).

2. Gurung Housing in the Siklis Region

The Siklis region is found in the hilly area of central Nepal, at approximately 2,400 m. It has a temperate, humid climate during the summer monsoon. The Gurung people are mostly farmers and breeders. They grow corn, millet and rice in terraced fields on the hillside. They raise cows and buffalos for milk, and goats for meat. The pasturages are situated above the village and can extend quite high.

The Gurung village can contain more than 100 houses grouped together and terraced on steep deforested slopes, between the preserved forests on the summits, and the floor of the valley. The main road to the village runs usually lengthwise along the slope and passes through the upper part of the village. From the road, paths lead down to the individual houses (fig. 8). The front of every house faces the valley.

The houses can be oval or rectangular in shape. The materials vary according to their age and size. The older houses are oval, with pisé walls and wooden boards on the front, capped with a thatched roof which is slanted at an angle of 35 degrees. They may be single-storeyed or double-storeyed, and there is a veranda on the ground floor along the front wall (fig. 9 and fig. 10). More recent houses are rectangular and larger, double-storeyed and with a veranda on the ground floor on two or three sides. Built with flat stones joined by mortar, they have a double-sloped roof supported by wooden consoles and covered with fixed slates. The roof, which rests on the top of the walls, is supported by a wooden structure composed of three rows of posts (fig. 11).

There is a terrace of flat stones in front of the house within the compound. It is used for drying food grain and for all kinds of domestic work. The veranda is higher than the terrace and three steps lead up to it. The veranda roof is supported by wooden posts. It may extend along two or three sides of the house on the ground floor. On one side it may be closed and used as a wood store or extra room. It is on the veranda, during the monsoon time, that the Gurang talk, rest, do basket-work, weave, and also employ the grain mills.

On the ground floor, the entrance hall is separated by a wooden partition to the right of the door. To the left, a wooden staircase leads to the first floor. The fireplace is located in the centre of the main room, where people have their meals, sit in the evening, and may even sleep. It is the heart of the house, where the social and family life take place. Behind the fireplace there is a storage area. The first floor is

Fig. 8 Gurung village.

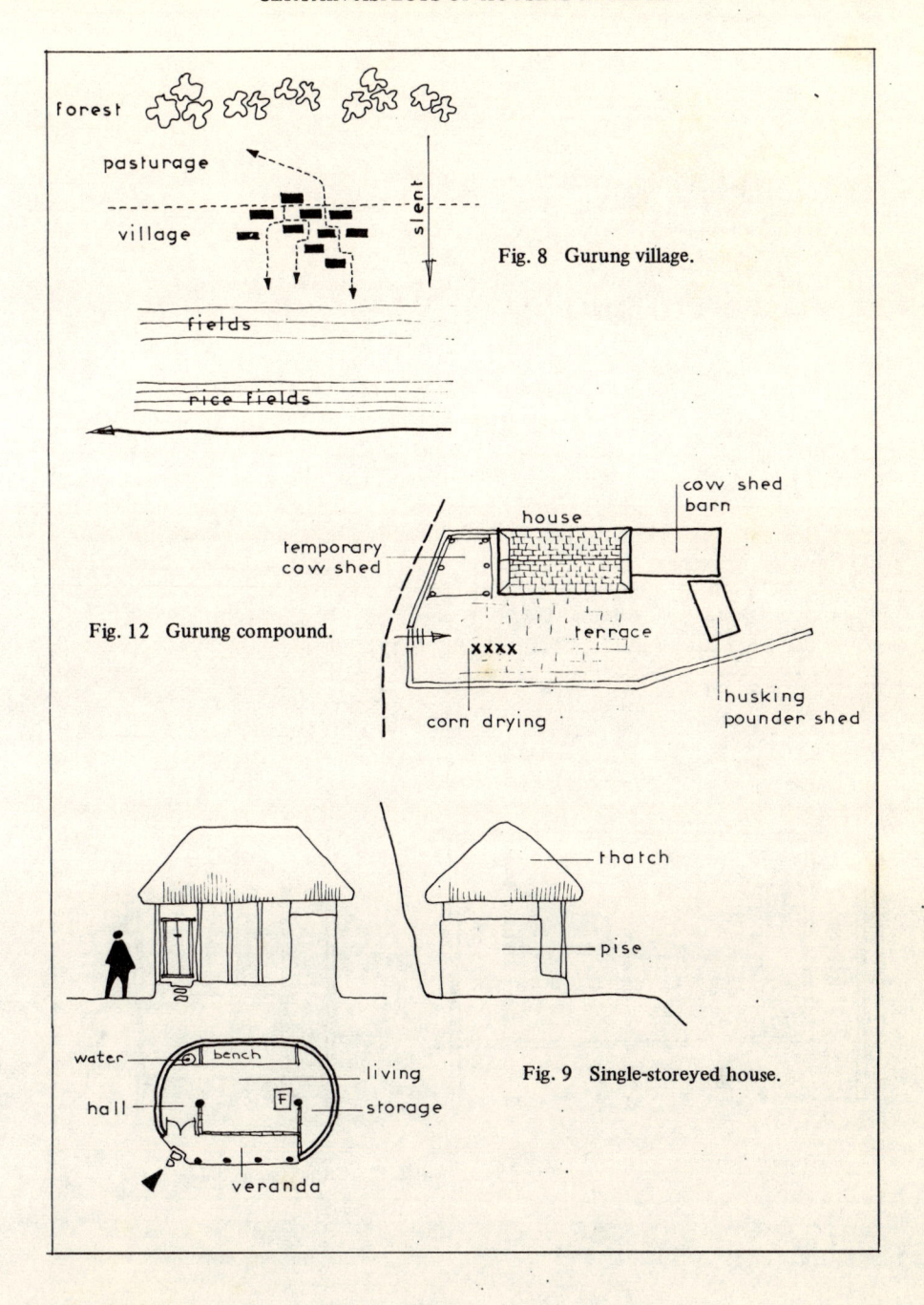

Fig. 12 Gurung compound.

Fig. 9 Single-storeyed house.

Fig. 10 Two-storeyed house.

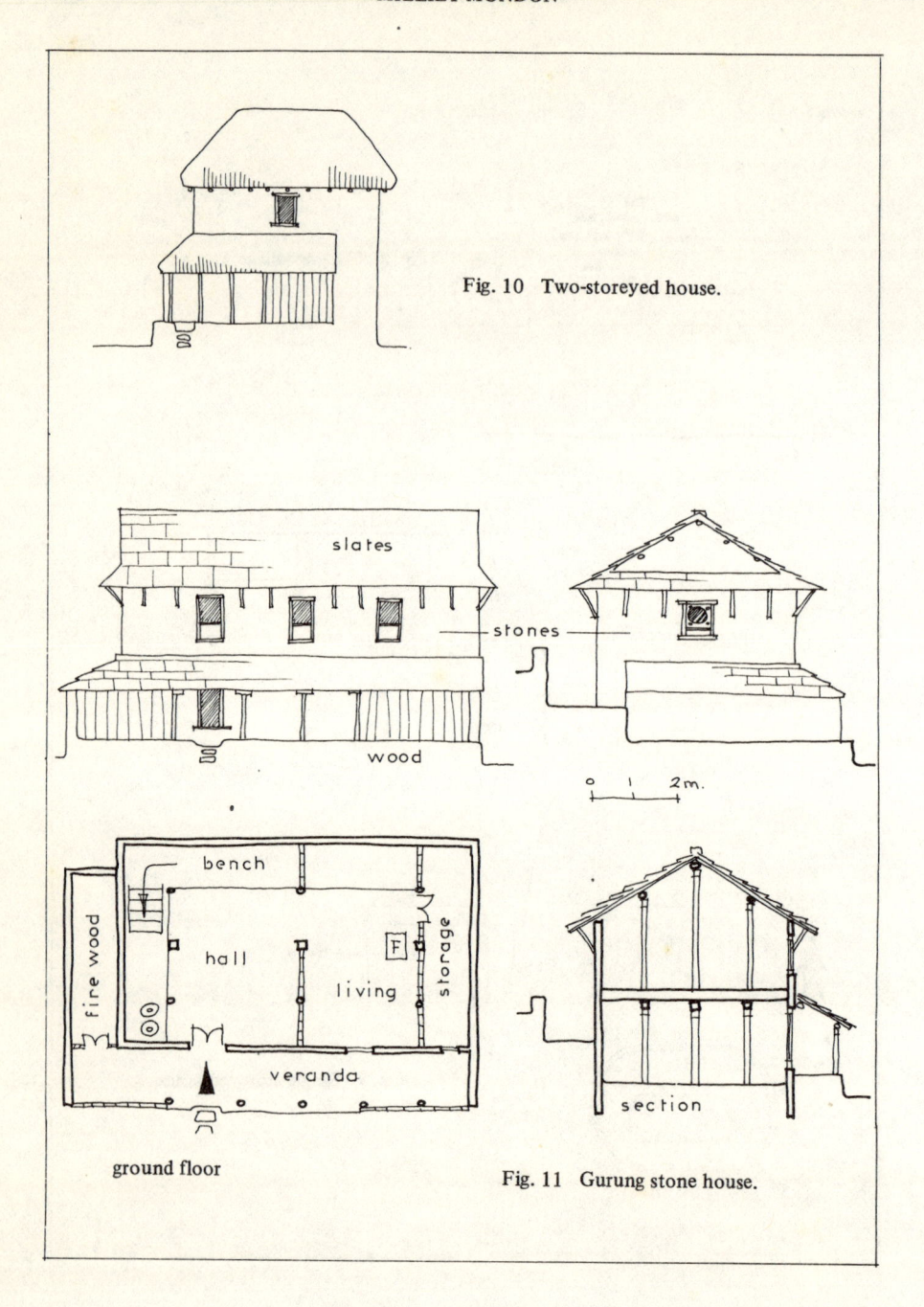

Fig. 11 Gurung stone house.

not lived in, but is used as a granary, a barn, and a store-room. It is lit by three similarly shaped small windows in the front wall.

An annex similar to the house is often added. It will have a cow-house on the ground floor opening on to the terrace. On the first floor there will be a barn and a room for keeping tools. A husking-pounder can be either in the cow-house or in an independent shed. A temporary shelter made of wood and bamboo mats may be built next to the house (fig. 12).

In larger villages there are often semi-detached houses along a common terrace.

3. Tamang Housing in the Timalbesi Region

The Timalbesi region is situated in middle Nepal between the Mahabarat range and the Sun Kosi Valley at approximately 1,400 m. It has a temperate climate with quite a wet summer, and a dry winter.

The Tamang people choose to build their villages near the summit of the hills in sheltered vales. Partly destroyed forests are found in the valleys. As farmers and breeders, they cultivate corn, wheat and mustard, and the fairly hot climate also allow them to produce cotton and peanuts. Every family breeds two or three cows, buffalos for milk and a small herd of goats for meat. The surface of the cultivated land is inferior to the land of the Gurung. The village is composed of several groups of five to ten houses placed side by side on terraces beside their cultivated fields (fig. 13).

The Tamang house is a small rectangular building whose longitudinal axis is always perpendicular to the slope. Built on a narrow terrace of beaten earth surrounded by a low stone wall, this terrace is used for grain and vegetable drying and for the cattle (fig. 14).

The walls are made of pisé, stone and mortar. The upper part is whitewashed, while the lower part is painted red. A door and three windows overlook the valley, the other three walls are blind. The window frames are carved and blackened with soot, and new ones may be painted blue (fig. 15). The four-fold thatched roof, the eaves of which stick out over the walls, rests on three posts situated in the longitudinal axis of the house, and the floors are sustained by two poles.

The houses have three storeys. The ground floor is divided into two distinct parts: the goat-house and the living area. In front of the entrance door there is a ladder which leads to the first floor. The living area is occupied by the family fireplace and the water jars. The open fireplace is on the floor, and is always at the far, opposite corner to the door (fig. 16). The living area is where all the household activities take place: the preparing and eating of meals, the evening get-together, and the receiving of visitors. The oldest man in the family sleeps on the ground floor and the other members of the family sleep on the first floor. The first floor is divided into two parts by a wooden partition. The hall is a storage area for grain, alcohol, and baskets, and has a ladder leading the second floor. The other part is the bedroom. The third floor is used as a barn and a granary. The Tamang house is occupied by two to twelve people. It may have a veranda on the front side of the ground floor and sometimes on the first floor.

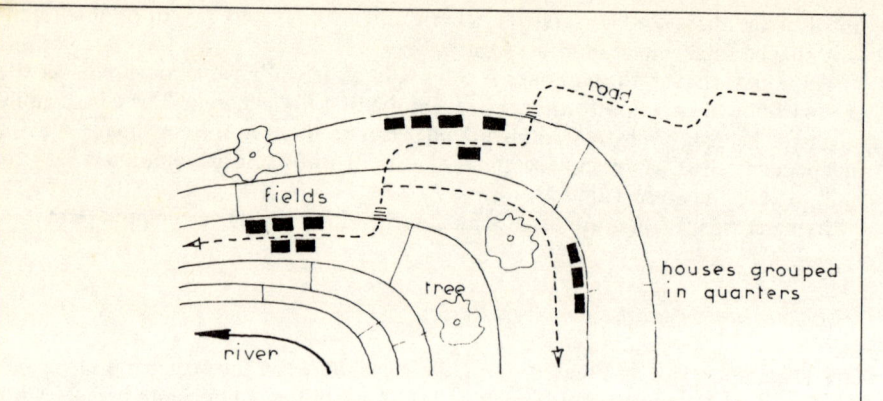

Fig. 13 Tamang village in Timalbesi.

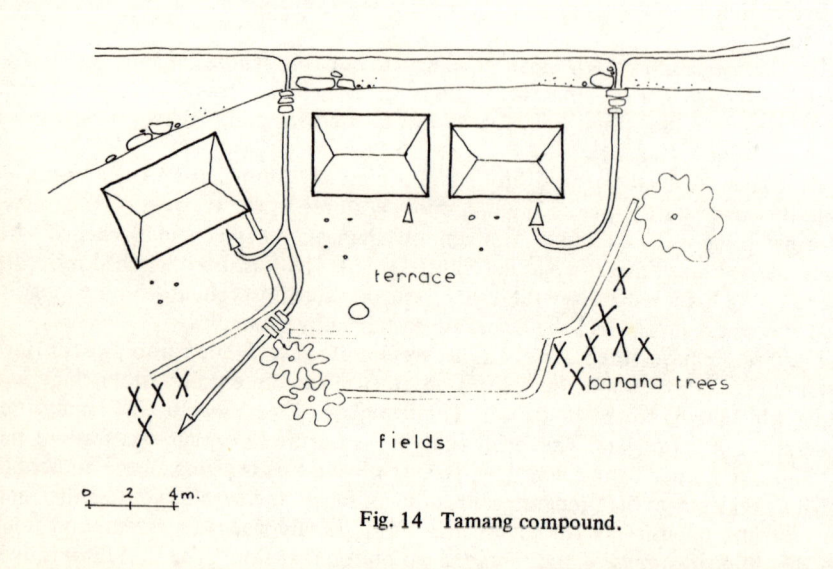

Fig. 14 Tamang compound.

CERTAIN ASPECTS OF HOUSING IN NEPAL 161

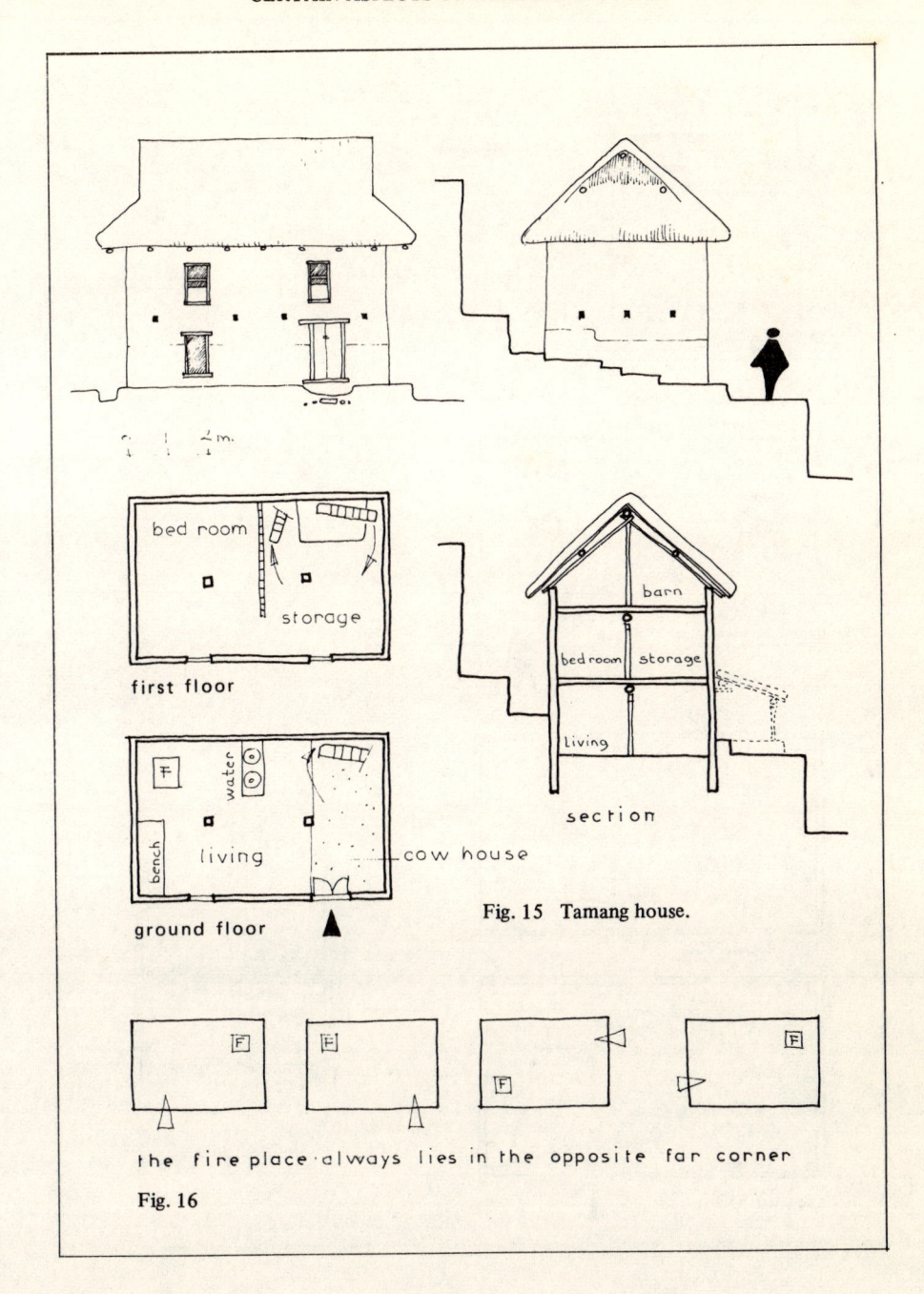

bed room

storage

first floor

water

bench

living

cow house

ground floor

barn

bed room storage

living

section

Fig. 15 Tamang house.

the fire place always lies in the opposite far corner

Fig. 16

Fig. 17 Sherpa village.

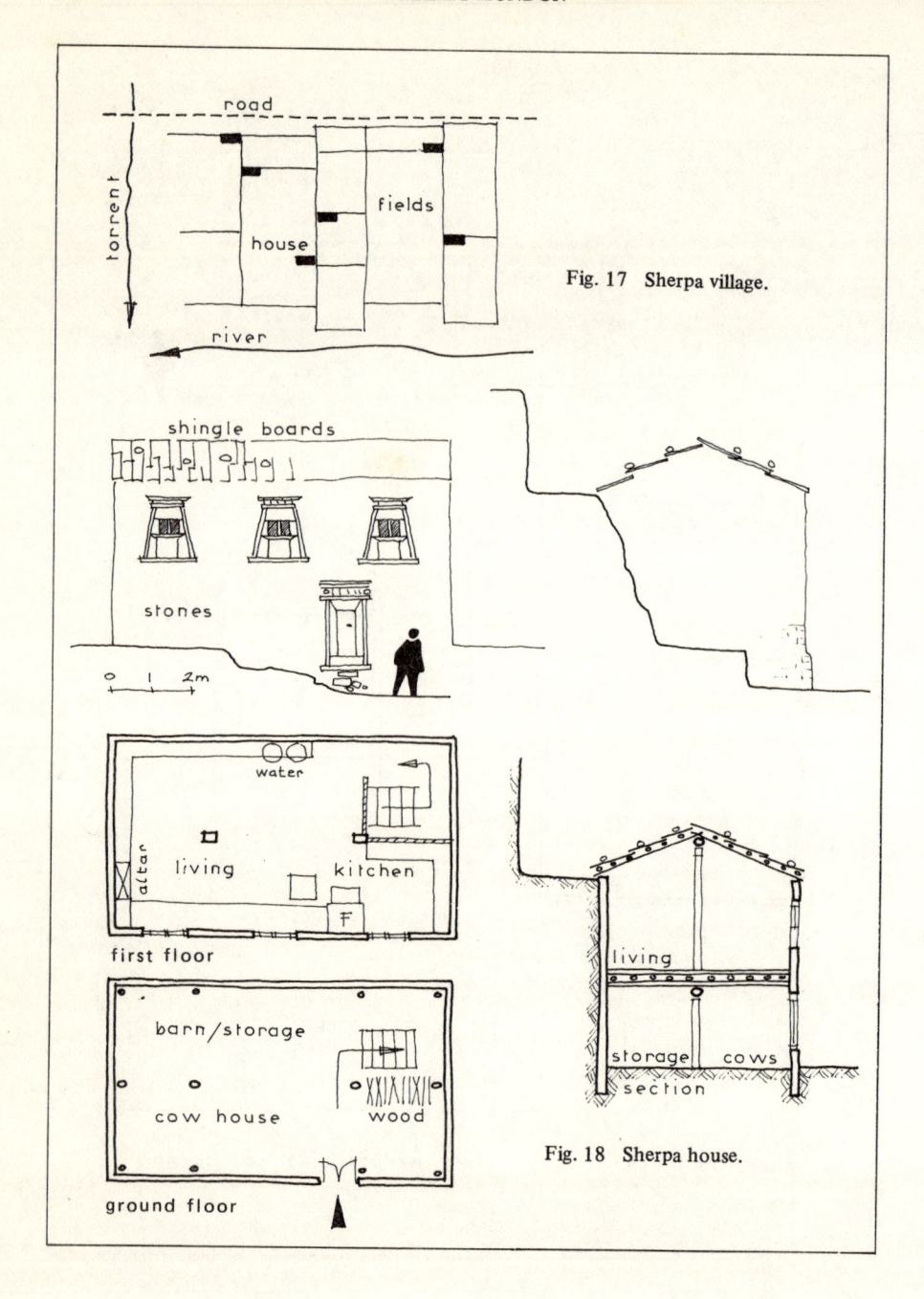

Fig. 18 Sherpa house.

4. Sherpa Housing in the Khumbu Region:

The Sherpa, settled in the high mountainous Khumbu region, located in the east Himalaya, are mostly breeders, because of the severe climate and a six months' winter. The wet summer enables them to have one crop a year. Potatoes and buckwheat are planted in April and harvested in October. They breed and cross-breed yaks for carting and for meat. The cattle stay in the high pasture half of the year. The only natural vegetation growing over 5,000 m consists of juniper trees and short grass. Below this altitude are forests of evergreens.

The highest village lies below an altitude of 4,400 m. Houses are scattered in the vales slightly above glacial valleys. They are separated by cultivated fields fenced in by low, dry stone walls (fig. 17).

The dwellings are rectangular and two-storeyed, and occupied by two to seven people. Their four walls are of dry stone. The back wall often leans against the mountain slope. A door in the ground floor and three windows in the first floor are found in the front wall. The window frames are solid and often decorated with carvings. A roof with double slants of 20°, made of shingle boards is sustained by walls and by two wooden posts in the longitudinal axis of the house (fig. 18).

The ground floor is never inhabited, but is used for wood and potato storage, or as a barn and a cattle shed. To reach the first floor, the Sherpas must go through the cow-shed and up a seven-stepped wooden staircase at the right end of the house. The first floor is a large room covered with wide boards. Inisde it, to the right of the entrance, we find water jars. The kitchen is separated by a partition and wooden shelves for cooking utensils. A pisé stove is situated against the front wall. Between the fireplace and the west wall, where the family altar is found, a long bench runs along the wall under the window. The bench serves as the men's resting place, as a seat for the visitors and as a bed for the couple and their children. The other walls of the room are occupied by wooden shelves containing the household stores and clothing.

The *gunsa* houses just described, which are situated in the village, are not lived in for more than six months of the year, from spring to autumn. At the end of the winter and after spring planting they climb with their herds to the high pastures. There, the majority of the families own a *yersa* which is a shelter built with one room only where they prepare milk products. It also serves as a storage area for tools, fodder, etc., and as the living quarters. Around the *yersa*, buckwheat and potatoes are grown, and the animals are fenced in.

5. Thakali Housing in the Thak Region:

The Thak region is located in the northwest of Nepal. This region of the upper Kali-Gandaki valley has a dry and windy climate and is only slightly influenced by the monsoon. It is the driest region in Nepal. The vegetation on the flat bottom of the valley is composed of scanty bushes. Evergreen forests cover the upper part of the slopes.

The economy of Thakali people differs from the other populations of Nepal. If

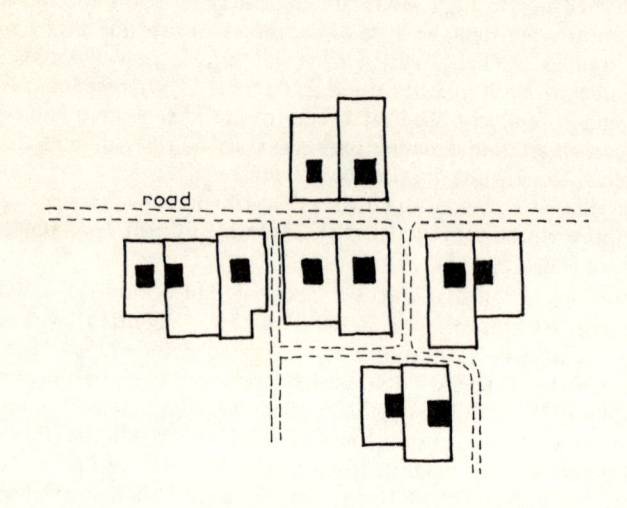

Fig. 19 Thakali village.

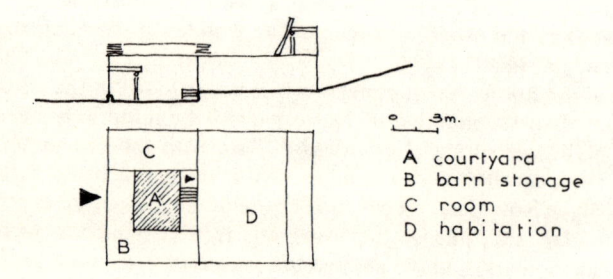

Fig. 20 Thakali compound.

A courtyard
B barn storage
C room
D habitation

they are farmers and breeders, they were also traders for more than a century, during which period they had the monopoly of the exchanging of products between Tibet and central Nepal. Since the closing of the Chinese border this activity has diminished and many of them have left their villages to establish themselves in the south.

The population lives in closed-in villages with the houses placed side by side (fig. 19). The villages are spaced out on the bottom of the valley, and hang from the side of the mountain in tiers. The fields are few and are grouped by the river bank.

The houses are mostly rectangular with one or two storeys: each inhabited by two to seven people. They are very big in comparison to the other Nepal houses. They are composed of many parts arranged around an inner courtyard and united by a common flat terraced roof. The whole construction is built of large blocks of stone bound together by mortar. The walls serve only to close in the living quarters. They do not support the roof which is held up by several rows of wooden poles placed inside the walls. The terrace roof made of stone and mud, is stamped smooth, and used for drying and pounding the grain. Stored firewood makes a parapet around the terrace. A house consists of four main parts: 1) An inner courtyard used to hold the animals (fig. 20A), 2) a barn, a storage area for wood, and a stable, all open to the courtyard (fig. 20B), 3) the family bedroom which is closed in and has a door and three similar windows looking out into the yard (fig. 20C), 4) the habitation itself (fig. 20D).

The habitation is always above the level of the courtyard even if it is single-storeyed. Access to it is by stone steps. The front of the habitation faces the courtyard and has one door and one large window with three openings. It is composed of several rooms separated by stone walls or wooden partitions (fig. 21). Every room has a specific use. The first rooms at the entrance are reserved for family life and the social occasions. They are composed of a hall, a space for water storage and a large living-room incorporating a small kitchen. The living area is where all the activities take place: eating of meals, commercial transactions and receiving of visitors. In this room is an earth stove and wooden shelves which contain various copper plates arranged in a decorative way. The meals are prepared in the kitchen. Another room or summer kitchen contains the stove for alcohol making. It may be placed inside the habitation or down in the courtyard.

The inner rooms are reserved for traditional festivities. There are three storage rooms surrounding the sacred room and containing grain and flour, family goods and religious objects. Inside the sacred room the central pillar stands as the symbolic support of the construction. The altar which is also the stove, is placed beside wooden shelves where the ceremonial plates are displayed. All the inner rooms of the habitation are lighted and ventilated by openings in the flat roof.

Because of the great geographical and ethnic diversities, houses in Nepal take various forms. If the traditional house is adapted to the climate, the topography and the natural resources used for construction, it is also a concrete example of the behaviour of each social group. The shape of the building, the organisation of its living space, the techniques of construction show their physical and psycological traits and needs.

In choosing these five house produced by five different cultural and social

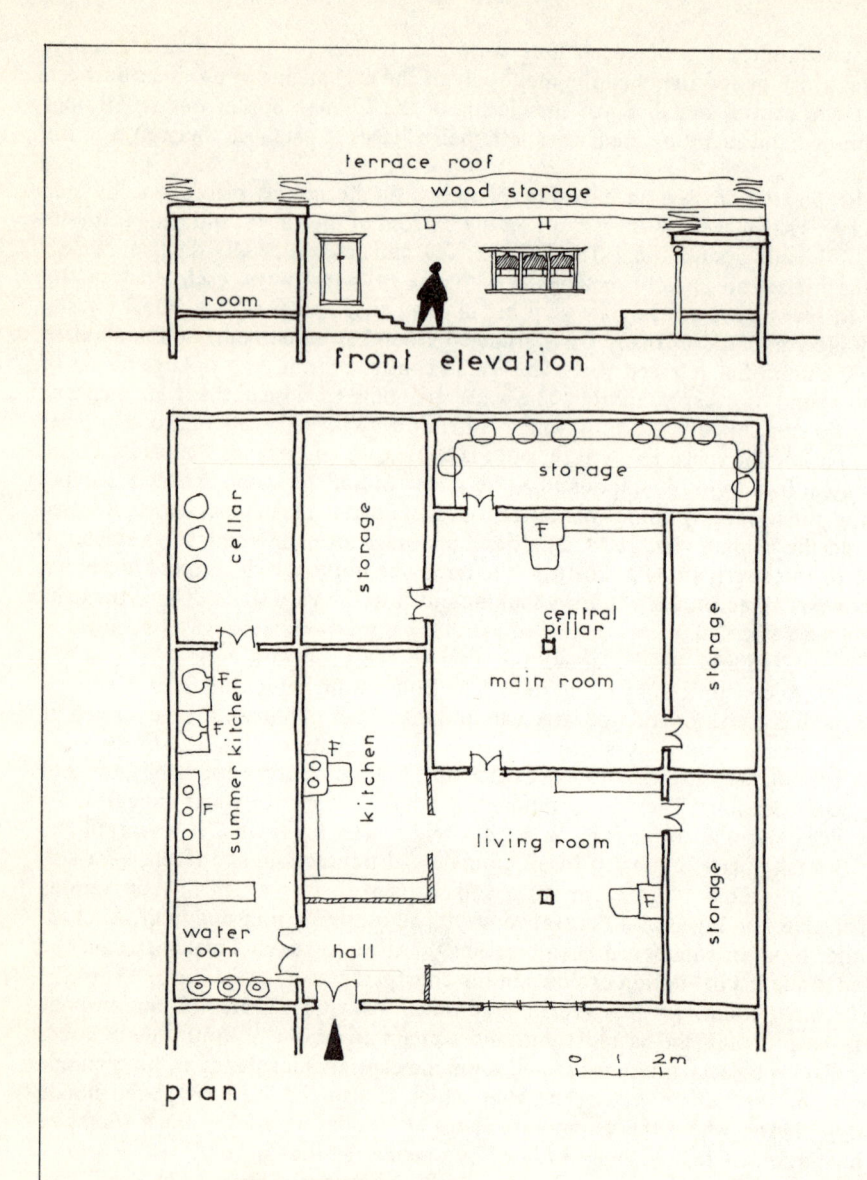

Fig. 21 Thakali habitation.

groups, and located in distinct regions in the most representative parts of the country, we have only presented a limited survey of Nepal housing.

Bibliography

Bista, D. B., 1967, *People of Nepal*, Department of Publicity, His Majesty's Government, Kathmandu.
Dupuis, J., 1972, *L'Himalaya*, Col. Que Sais-je? No. 1470, Presses Universitaires de France, Paris.
Hagen, T., 1960, *Nepal, royaume de l'Himalaya*. Kummerly and Frey, Berne.
Jest, C., 1964–65, Les Thakali: Note Préliminaire concernant une ethnie du Nord-Ouest du Népal. *L'etnographie*, pp.26–49.
Karan, P. P., 1960, *Nepal, a cultural and physical geography*. Lexington, University of Kentucky Press.
Kleinert, Ch., 1973, *Haus- und Siedlungsformen im Nepal Himalaya unter Berücksichtigung Klimatischer Faktoren*. Universitätsverlag Wagner, Innsbruck/München.
MacDonald, A. W., 1969, Notes sur deux fêtés chez les Tharu de Dang. *Objects et mondes*. Tome IX, Fasc. 1, pp.69–89.
Pignede, B., 1966, *Les Gurungs, une population himalayenne du Nepal*. Mouton & Cie., Paris/La Haye.
Srivastava, S. K., 1958, *The Tharus*. Agra University Press.
The physical development plan for Kathmandu valley. 1969. His Majesty's Government of Nepal, Kathmandu, Department of Housing and physical planning.

Housing in the Upper Kali-Gandaki Valley: Its Adaptation to the Environment

Camille Milliet-Mondon

The upper Kali-Gandaki Valley is populated by a people of Tibetan origin which differs from the other populations of inner Himalaya by its language and culture. They can be divided into two distinct groups: the original Thakali people, living in the Thak country, in the southern part of the region, and the Panchgaonle, living in Panchgaon, which is a group of five villages located in the northern part of the valley.

The Kali-Gandaki Valley is a natural route between Tibet and central Nepal. The Thak region is a transit area between the north where salt and wool are produced and the south where wheat and rice are grown. At the beginning of this country trade became the basic economy of the Thakali, and the villages of Thak expanded until 1962. Tukche, a salt-trading town, became the regional capital. During the same period the Panchgaonle continued to uphold their traditional way of life, based on agriculture and animal breeding in a barren region having a very dry and cold climate in winter. The lack of fertile land makes life difficult.

The whole population is grouped in villages spread along the upper valley between two villages about 40 km apart, village Ghasa in the south, at an altitude of 2,012 m, and village Jomosom in the north, at an altitude of 2,800 m. The river Kali-Gandaki flows southwards in a deep valley which goes through the Himalayan range. The region concerned spreads out along this north-south axis and can be divided into two distinct geographical areas with the village Dhampu separating them (fig. 1).

To the south of Dhampu the valley is deep and narrow, only 350 m wide, with a rather steep slope having a gradient of 8.3 per cent. The river bed is strewn with large rocks. There is rain during the monsoon and some showers in winter. The land is quite fertile. There are fir tree forests on the hillsides and in the valley proper.

To the north of Dhampu there is a wide open valley with a flat bottom covered with alluvium and a slope with a gradient of only 1.7 per cent. The climate is dry. During the monsoon the rain is very scarce, and in the winter there is a strong wind blowing from the south with some rain and snow. The land is barren and may be called a kind of steppe with some fir trees on the higher slopes.

The Thakali and the Panchgaonle houses are based on the same conception and show the influence of Tibetan architecture: blind outer walls, a terraced roof, and several rooms for living or for storage, opening into an inner courtyard. The size of the houses and their distance from one another vary with their situation in the valley and depend on the wealth of the people and their way of life. It is necessary to make a difference between the two groups on account of their housing systems. Generally the rather loosely clustered houses in the Thakali villages are located at the side of the road which leads to Tibet, in the flat bottom of the valley or on the lower part of the rocky slopes.

The Thakali, made prosperous by trading, live in large houses with one or two

Fig. 1 High Kali Gandaki

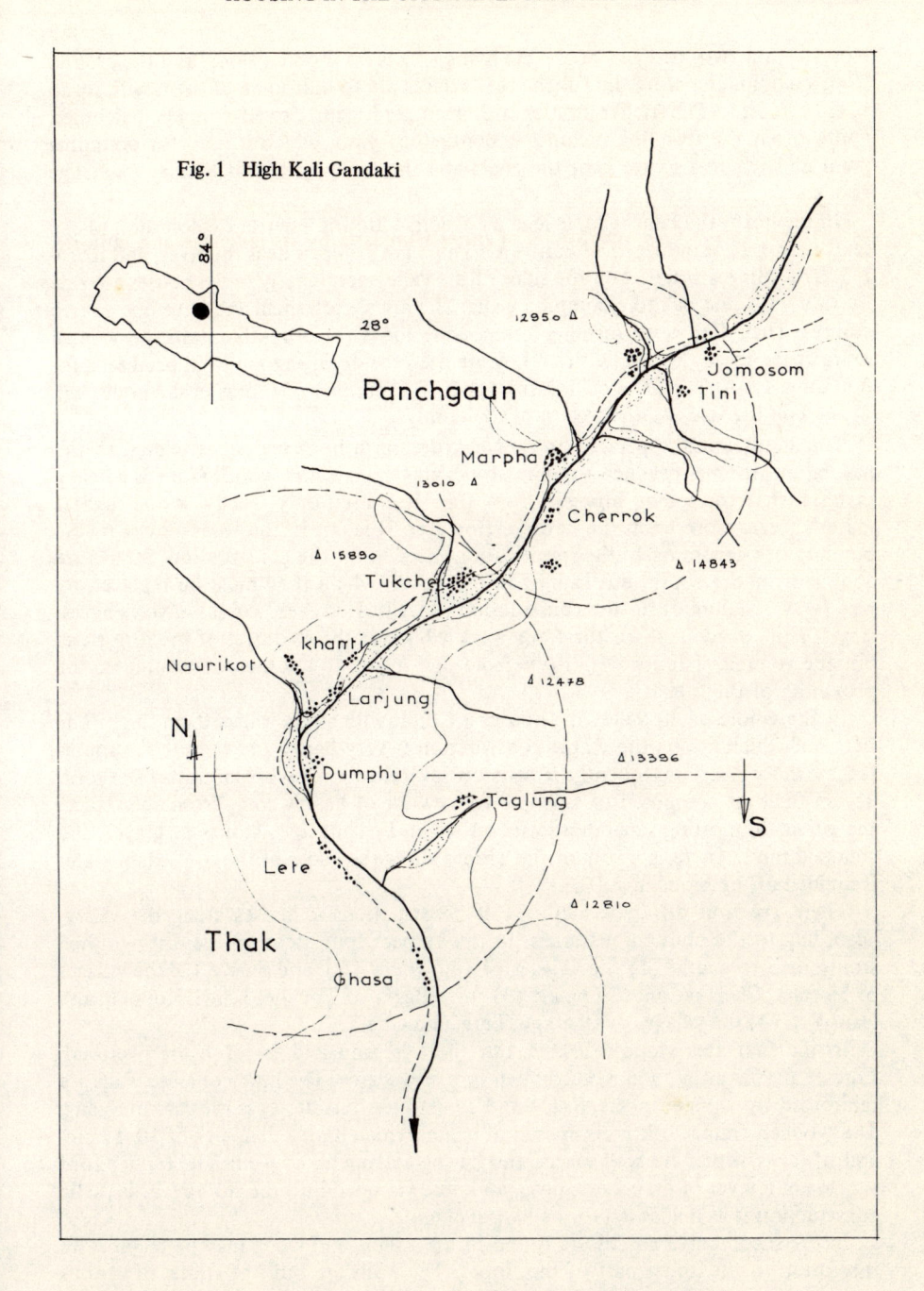

storeys. In a two-storeyed house the living area is on the first floor, and the ground floor contains the store. In Tukche real palaces are found, some of them with up to twenty rooms. The richer houses are decorated with carved wooden balconies. Quite often the dwelling includes a contiguous yard, which is used for pounding grain and where also are kept the goats and the mule flock which carry exchange goods.

In the north the Panchgaonle lead a collective life for a better exploitation of the scarce natural resources. The cultivated lands are grouped near the river, and irrigated. The villages situated on the sides of the valley are densely built, houses are side by side with one or more common walls. The houses are small and have one or two storeys. Their flat roofs, forming terraces one above the other like stairs, provide an extra space for various activities. They are used for drying agricultural products, for pounding grain, and for stocking firewood. The number of rooms in the house will depend on the size and the wealth of the family.

The architectural aspect of house construction in both regions is related to the natural environment, which supplies stone, gravel, clay, and wood. Stone is a heavy material that cannot be brought from afar. It is used only locally. Wood, lighter material, can more easily be carried. However, it is cut in the forests next to the building site according to the specifications needed for the construction. Stones are abundant in the south, but lacking in the north, where they must be replaced by pisé (gravel and mud) for the construction of walls. However, wood is always necessary for the inside and for the framework whatever the resources of the forest are, but the volume of timbering differs from one region to another, depending on the proximity of the forest.

In the whole of the valley the houses are built with stone walls 50 cm thick. The flat roof which covers the whole construction is very heavy and cannot be supported by the walls. Consequently it rests on several rows of wooden posts. The roof, 35 cm thick, is composed of a simple framework of beams going from one wall to the other, supporting separated joists on which lie split logs, stones or gravel, and stamped mud. There is a row of flat stones along the edges of the roof. Rain water is drained off by wooden gutters.

There are four different methods of construction of houses along the valley, according to the building materials. In this respect four areas can be distinguished from north to south: (1) the villages of Jomosom, Tini, and Syang, (2) the villages of Marpha, Cherrok, and Chimang, (3) the villages of Tukche, Kanti, Kopong, and Naurikot, (4) the villages of Dhampu, Lete, and Ghasa.

In the first area stone is scarce, but there is sand and gravel in the river bed. Forests are far away, and wood is therefore also scarce. The mud-concrete walls are reinforced by wooden posts, inside and sometimes outside, as is the case in Syang. The wooden framework is composed of beams which have a diameter of 10–12 cm, and of joists which are well spaced and having a diameter of 8 cm. The terrace roof is made of a layer of branches, gravel, and mud stamped into the surface. This rustic construction is well adapted to the barren climate.

In the second area stones are found in the valley, and wood may be taken from the forest on the upper part of the slopes. The walls are built of stones of various sizes, and mortar. Beams are set in the walls to make them stronger. The beams of

Fig. 2 Terrace Roof

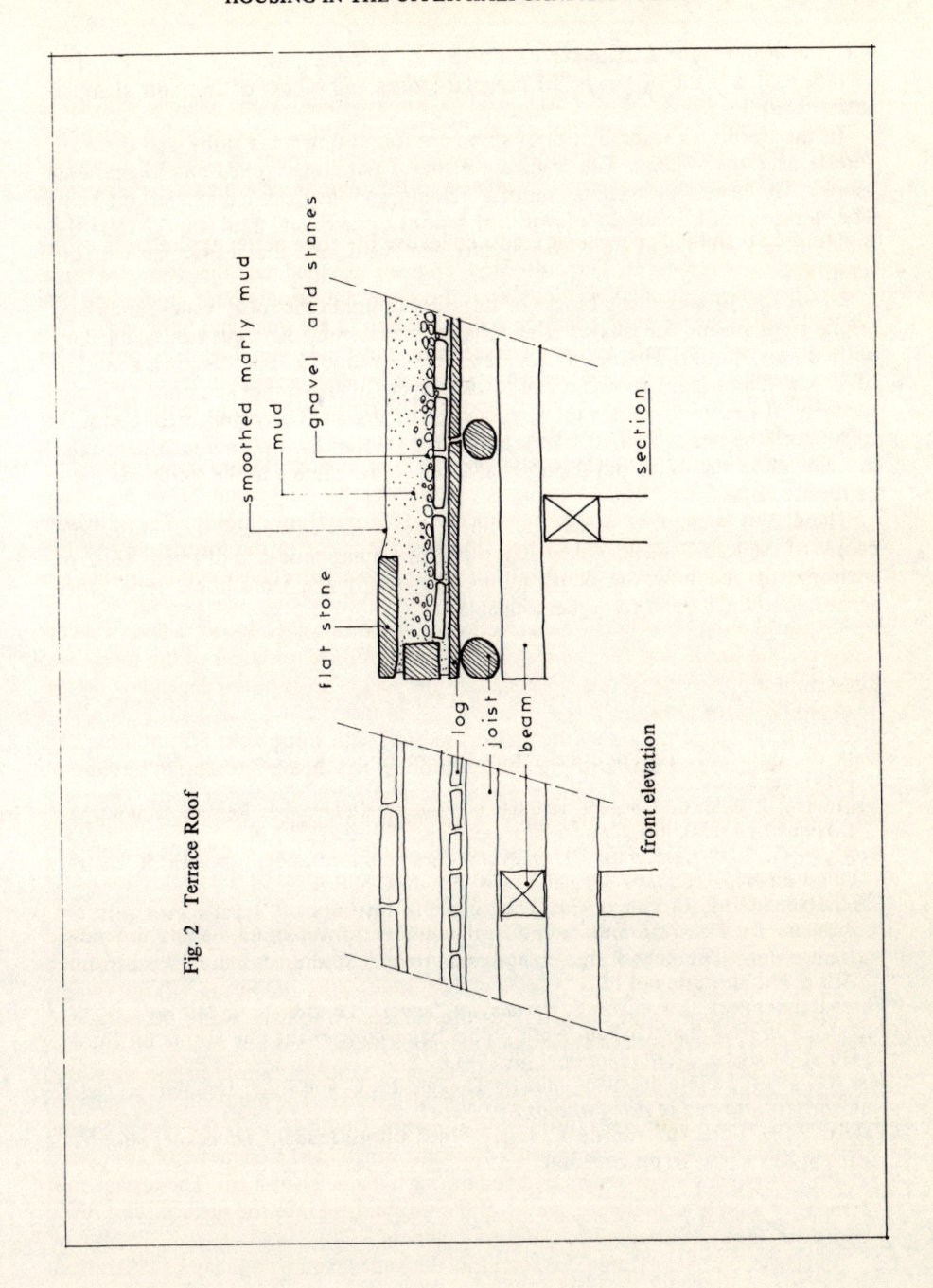

the framework have a diameter of 12-15 cm, and the joists one of 10 cm. The terrace roof is made of a layer of irregular stones and blocks of dry mud, stamped into the surface.

In the third area some blocks of stone are found down the slope, and there are forests near the villages. The walls are made of flat stones, piled and joined with mortar. The beams have a diameter of 15-20 cm, and the joists a diameter of 12 cm. The terrace roof is made of a layer of flat stones, gravel, and mud (fig. 2). Here the buildings are solid and hold out against the wind and the scanty rains of the monsoon.

In the fourth area many blocks of stone are found in the rocky valley, and there are fir trees around the villages. The walls are made of regularly cut stones, piled up without any mortar. The beams have a square section of 20 cm, the joists a section of 12 cm. The terrace roof is made of two layers of flat stones and mud. Here the quantity of timber permits a thick wooden structure and framework strong enough to support the heavy roof. It is interesting to note that the flat roof is suited to the dry climate in the north but is poorly adapted to the climate in the south and must be repaired often.

These four examples, briefly described, show how different sections of the people of the Kali-Gandaki Valley adapt the same house model to different kinds of environment and how the construction of basically the same house type varies according to the natural resources available.

Bibliography

Bista, D. B., 1971, The political innovators of upper Kali-Gandaki. *Man*, vol. 6, No. 1, pp.52-60.

Dobremez, J. F. & C. Jest, 1971, Carte écologique du Népal 1. Region Annapurna-Dhaulagiri, 1/250,000, *Cahiers népalais*. Paris, Ed. du C.N.R.S.

Dollfuss, O. & P. Usselman, 1971, Recherches géomorphologiques dans le centre-Ouest du Népal. *Cahiers népalais*. Paris, Ed. du C.N.R.S.

Fürer-Haimendorf, C. von, 1974, The changing fortunes of Nepal's high altitude dwellers. In: *Contributions to the Anthropology of Nepal*. Ed. by C. von Fürer-Haimendorf. The School of Oriental and African Studies, London, Warminster, Aris & Phillips, pp.98-113.

Fürer-Haimendorf, C. von, 1975, *Himalayan Traders*. London, John Murray.

Jest, C., 1964-65, Les Thakali. Note préliminaire concernant une ethnie du Nord-Ouest du Népal. *L'ethnographie*, pp.26-49.

Jest, C., 1974, La fête des clans chez les Thakali. In: C. von Fürer-Haimendorf (ed.) *Contributions to the Anthropology of Nepal*.

Valeix, P., M. Fort, Ph. Alirol & C. Jest, 1974, La Kali-Gandaki, *Objects et mondes*, Tome XIV, Fasc. 4, pp.269-306.

The Organization of Space in a Tibetan Refugee Settlement

Claes Corlin

In this paper I will deal with the house as studied from an anthropologists's point of view—as a representation of the culture of its inhabitants. Basically, a house might be described as a limitation of space, attained through certain techniques (that is, 'architecture' in a narrow sense), and this building will then provide shelter for its residents, storage for food and property, and a space for various activities.

But the house is shaped not only by materials and tools, but also out of ideas, values and norms—notions about how to be and behave when entering or leaving, or performing works or being social inside the building. Thus the house can clearly not be regarded simply as a utilitarian implement designed for physical existence, but as a 'microcosm', a design for living. The study of all this, which demands knowledge of such areas as kinship, group relations, etiquette, and ritual, would be called the study of 'architecture' in a wider sense of the word.

Bearing these points in mind, I will now introduce a Tibetan refugee settlement, situated in the district of Rasuwa (upper Trisuli river valley, at an altitude of about 2,000 m), northern Nepal. My data were gathered during seven months of field work in 1973. Rasuwa district contains about 500 Tibetan refugees, all of whom originate from the Tibetan district of Kyirong, immediately north of the border. It might be useful to summarize the traditional village and house plans of Kyirong, before we proceed to discuss the Rasuwa settlement.[1]

Kyirong district consisted of a district centre (*Kyirong Dzong*) with its marketplace and some thirty villages and hamlets dispersed along the valley, connected by footpaths. Each village (sizes varied from about ten to more than a hundred domestic units) was a tight cluster of houses, often around a central square where the village sanctuary was placed. There were usually no kinship or status divisions to be seen in the village plan (with the exception of the *yawa* households, mentioned below). The houses seem to have been fairly uniform in layout and size, although richer families may own several houses.

Houses were usually two-storeyed (except for the very poorest families, who dwelt in a single-storeyed kitchen-*cum*-stable shack) and were built of dry stone with a slightly sloping shingle roof resting on wooden beams, the butts of which were let into the stone walls. Chimneys were not used—the smoke from the kitchen hearth pouring out through a hole in the roof or through the fissures in the walls. The inside of the walls was plastered with clay and whitewashed. The ground floor consisted of compressed clay, the upper floor of broad planed planks on a framing of heavy logs. Windows were few and small, often with carved frames, not glazed but always provided with heavy shutters and bolts.

A side view of a typical Kyirong house is reproduced in fig. 1. From the stables at ground level, a staircase or notched tree trunk leads up to the kitchen, also living room and bedroom for the entire family. Beside the stone hearth there are benches fixed to the walls, shelves, wooden chests and lockers, baskets for food, etc. The chapel is adorned with *thangka* (paintings on cloth), and has a carved wooden altar

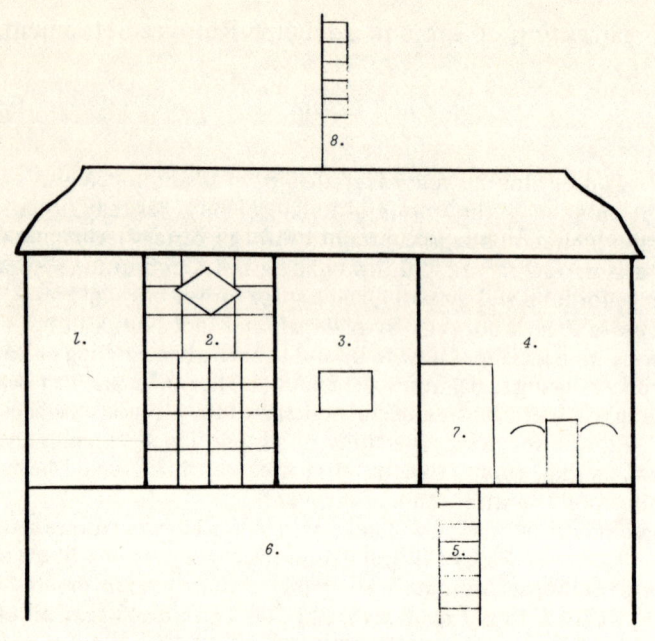

After a sketch by an old carpenter.
1. Storage
2. Chapel with carved windows
3. Empty room or Passage
4. Kitchen
5. Staircase
6. Stables
7. Entrance door
8. Prayer flag

Fig. 1 Kyirong house (side view).

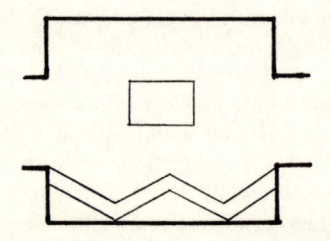

Fig. 2 Elaborated 'empty room' passage (side view).

with images and pictures of the Dalai Lama, butter-lamps, water-bowls, sacred books, etc. The chapel is not only a ceremonial room, but also a guest room for honourable guests. Between the kitchen and the chapel there is often an empty room or passage with a window but no furniture. In the houses of well-to-do families, this passage is even made longer by means of small flights of steps leading up and down (fig. 2). No informant has been able to explain this peculiar custom.

With the Chinese annexation of Tibet in the 1950s, many Kyirong Tibetans chose to go into exile. About 500 of them settled in Rasuwa, where natural conditions are similar to those in Kyirong. Here they lived scattered in Tamang[2] villages until 1970, when the U.N. High Commission for Refugees together with an already existing organisation of Tibetan refugees decided to erect four refugee settlements in the Rasuwa area. The four settlements are all placed in the immediate vicinity of Tamang villages or hamlets. Most of the actual construction work was done by professional carpenters from among the refugees; the rest of them assisting with the lumbering, carrying stones and doing various odd jobs for the building. Work was completed and followed by an inauguration ritual in April, 1973.

As the refugees in Rasuwa started building their settlements, it was clear from the beginning that their new homes could not be much like their traditional houses. Firstly, the refugees coming over the border had no or few possessions and were thus virtually dependent on the financial aid that was granted them. Secondly, not being Nepalese citizens, the Tibetans were not allowed to buy or possess land. Land for settlements and fields was bought through the Nepalese Red Cross and was put to the disposal of the refugees on a free lease basis. Finally, U.N. aid was granted on the condition that certain architectural standards were reached. So, when discussing architectural changes, we have to distinguish between the aims of the planners and the aims of the residents.

The conditions made by the planners were that a room of specified size should be provided for every family who applied for it;[3] that the houses should be single-storeyed and several rooms combined into one unit, and that they should be tin-roofed and provided with chimneys. The last two items were entirely new to the Tibetans. (As the only means of transportation in Rasuwa is by foot, the tin sheets for the roofs were carried on the backs of men 5 days from the nearest motor road.) Otherwise, the planning was left to the Tibetans themselves. Consequently, the exact location of the houses as well as most of the building methods (dry stone walls with whitewashed interiors, bamboo mats as ceiling), are done in fairly traditional ways.

Let us look at the plan of one of the four settlements (*Thangmujet*, fig. 3). How may we interpret it? The old Tamang hamlet can be seen to the right; to the left the Tibetan settlement, consisting of seven buildings. Each building is sub-divided by partition walls into two, three or four rooms, giving a total of 22 one-room 'flats'. The larger room (top left) is intended as a handicraft workshop. A small shop is attached to another building (bottom left).

Most of the houses are placed around a small central square, with a rice-mortar and a water-tap. This square is the social focus of the settlement (cf. below). No house is assigned any particular position in the settlement—neither central nor in private seclusion. This reflects the egalitarian structure of the community: there are

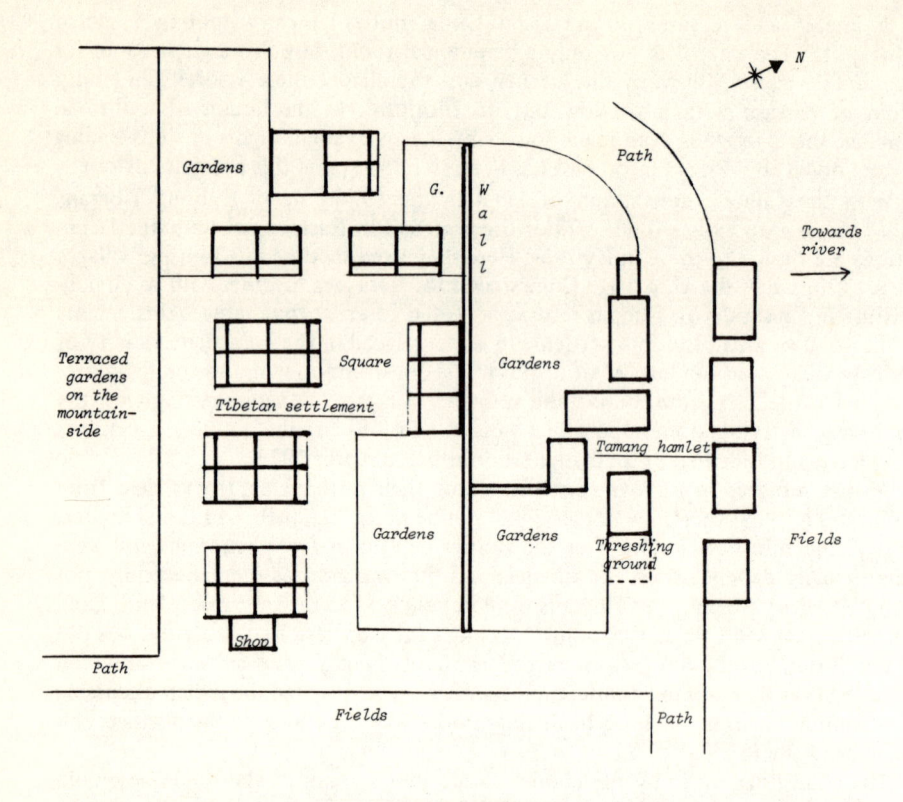

Fig. 3 Thangmujet village.

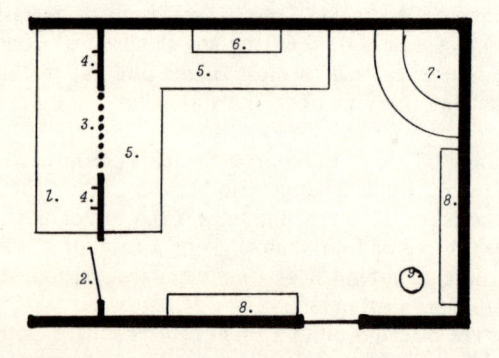

Fig. 4 Plan of a Tibetan refugee house.

1. Verandah with bench
2. Entrance door
3. Latticed window
4. Fastings for ribbon looms
5. Benches
6. House altar
7. Hearth
8. Shelves and lockers
9. Tea churn

no great status differences, and decisions are made by a general assembly and implemented by headmen, whose authority, however, is very limited.

The only significant status difference refers to the village blacksmith. Being in the traditionally 'unclean' endogamous subgroup of *yawa*, his low status is still found among the refugees, and consequently his house is to be found in the Tamang part of the village, not in the Tibetan part, where he does not go except for doing work.

The boundary wall between the Tibetan and Tamang parts of the village in a way reflects a boundary between different ethnic groups, too. Although the Tamang are of supposed Tibetan ancestry, they differ widely in their customs from the present Tibetans. Intermarriage is tabooed, and cooperation is only carried on to a limited extent. In communal works, such as bridge-building, cooperation is expected, but not with Tamang and Tibetans working side by side. Instead, the Tamang arrive one day in numbers to build half the bridge, whereupon the Tibetans by a sort of silent agreement come to complete the work a few days later. But the boundary wall is low and broken by paths transgressing it, and likewise members of the two groups cooperate heartily on a more personal plane, sharecropping, doing trade or tending each other's babies.

Let us then have a look at the interior of the house (fig. 4). (In accordance with Tibetan terminology, I will henceforth call each of the one-room 'flats', a house.) The furniture is made up of a hearth, two or three wooden benches, chests and baskets for food and belongings, and the house altar. The 'chapel' room of the Kyirong house is now reduced to a cardboard box hanging on the wall and containing the ritual paraphernalia. Inside the house you sleep, cook and eat. Practically no work is performed there, as the interior is too cramped, dark and smoky. Also some kinds of work are thought to be disturbing to the house god, who resides in the hearth.

But the house is not simply a sleeping-place. Inside the house, relations are very intimate between the family members, whereas an outsider is received formally. At least as a new visitor you are expected to bring a present, and in any case to accept the obligatory cup of tea. This creates a host-guest relationship, which signifies a boundary between the residents and the visitors. Only by passing the doorstep will you transgress this boundary line. Outside the house other rules of etiquette are applied.

Outside the house there is always a small verandah with an elevated bench. The verandah is used for all sorts of work; primarily for handicraft, which has gained new importance in the refugee situation, as the land is usually quite insufficient to feed the family. On the verandah wall one or more ribbon-looms are fixed, where the women are sitting in their spare time weaving beautifully decorated belts intended for sale. An ordinary loom often stands beside the house under a bamboo-mat roof. The verandah is also the place for informal gatherings, where people "drop-in" for a chat without need to observe the rigorous rules of etiquette inside the house.

The roof has several functions. The refugees grow maize, barley, wheat and buckwheat. This is stored inside the house but is taken out now and then to dry. This is usually done on the roof, where it is safe from animals. Clothes and dyed yarn are dried on the roof. Each roof is fitted with a prayer-flag, which is an integral part of the building, to the Tibetans much more necessary than the chimney.

The buildings are surrounded by small vegetable gardens, fenced by thorny bushes. These gardens are privately managed by each family, contrary to the lands around the settlement, where work is carried out communally and the harvest distributed equally among the residents (on land granted by the Red Cross), or sharecropped for Tamang land-owners. Economic conditions did not permit the erection of a village *gomba*, or sanctuary, in the settlement. Instead, on festival occasions the central square is covered by a large tarpaulin and temporarily converted into a sanctuary by means of an altar, benches, etc. Here the rituals are enacted and people dine and dance together for several days. The square is also the usual meeting place for the village assembly, where every Tibetan man and woman over the age of 15 is entitled to participate. Matters of common interest are discussed and communal works organised at the assembly meetings.

These observations indicate that there are three different spatial areas with different functions inside the settlement: (1) the interior of the house, which is used for sleeping, cooking, eating and for entertaining guests formally; (2) the verandah, the roof and the area close to the house, (the outer boundary is here indicated by piles of firewood and/or vegetable gardens—inside this boundary you will still be 'at home'), which is used for work and for informal intercourse; (3) the square, which is used for rituals, politics and general meetings. To this might, of course, be added a fourth area; (4) the village in general, where relations between Tibetans and Tamang are regulated according to a different code. These distinctions are to a certain extent observed not only in the living area, but also in the production area: the privately managed vegetable gardens, the communal land, and the sharecropped land, which necessitate cooperation on different level: the family, the settlement residents, and the Tamang (fig. 5). Each area (both living and production areas) has its special functions and there are special kinds of knowledge for the handling of these functions. There are even different morals, which are reflected in the various rules of etiquette. You behave in different ways towards a fellow-villager when you visit him in his home, when you assist him in the fields and when you join him in the village assembly.

Finally I would like to give some examples of the ritual dimension of the house. I have mentioned that the house may be regarded as a 'microcosm'—that is, as an integrated part of an ordered universe. This ritual plan of the house includes the hearth with its hearth-god (*thablha*) as a protector of the residents; the entrance door as a boundary with its magical signs to keep out evil influences; the house altar as a point of contact with the universe (every day small ceremonies are performed in front of the altar to enhance the religious merit of the residents); and the prayer-flag on the roof, transmitting its spiritual messages when fluttering in the wind.

During building-time, and even after completion, the house is ritually neutral, and to the Tibetans thus unfit as a human habitation. Only with the inauguration ritual can it acquire the desired ritual status. Before people can move in, a day-long and elaborate ritual is performed by lamas or monks. Sculptures made from butter and dough (*torma*) are 'charged' with evil influences and then thrown away. Sacred water is sprinkled around the room, especially at the hearth, the abode of the house god. Similar ceremonies are performed at the inclusion or exclusion of a household

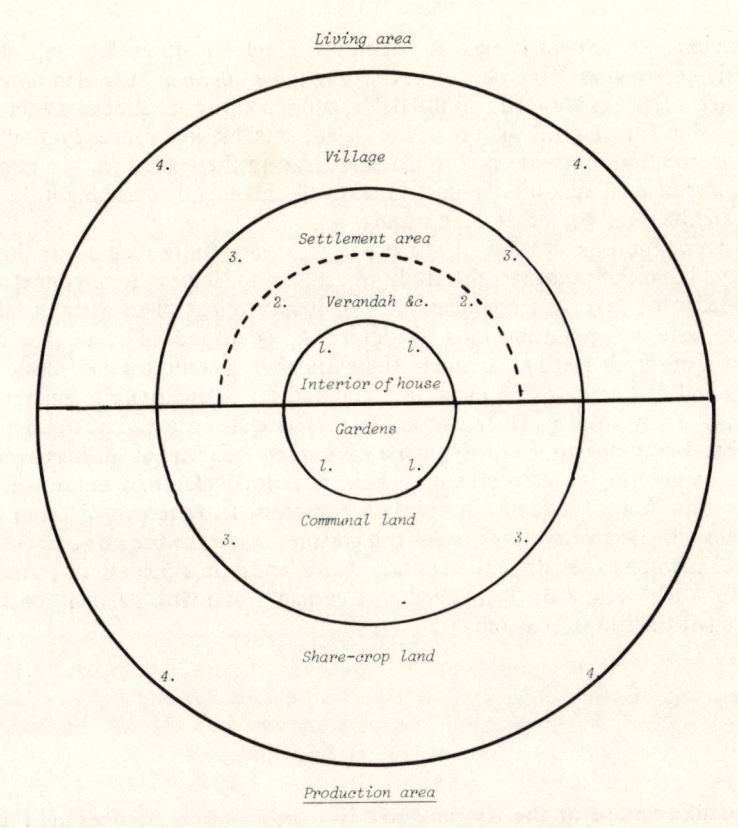

Fig. 5 Organization of space in Thangmujet.

member (i.e. birth or death). At the birth of a baby, the house god is addressed and asked to accept the new member, after which the baby is given a name. At a death, the corpse is addressed: 'Now you are dead. Do not come back but pass on into the existence which is ordained you. Here are other people who can take care of your house and family.' At any time when divination or omens show that bad luck might threaten the house and its residents, it is ritually purified by a lama, who reads from the sacred texts. This is a periodic expense as necessary and as prosaic to the Tibetans as is the electricity bill to us.

In other ritual contexts the settlement rather than the individual home is treated as an entity. At the *mani ronggo* ritual, performed three times a month, one married lady from each house will participate, chanting prayers for a day to gain merit for the settlement and protect it against calamities. Similar features show up at the great yearly ceremonies. For example, at the *drungkhar duchhen* festival in summertime, *tsampa* offerings are made on the fields, and the entire settlement is encircled by a procession carrying the picture of the Dalai Lama. Masked dances symbolizing the Tibetan creation myth are performed, thus placing the settlement in an understandable, traditional spatio-temporal context—all this together making up a kind of 'ritual architecture' or, rather, landscaping.

To sum up, the organization of space is a great deal more than a question of technology. To anthropologists, the study of e.g., South Chinese architecture without knowledge of *feng shui* (geomancy) or of Indian village plans without taking notions of caste and pollution into consideration, would indeed be an absurdity. But, apart from such glaring examples, there are always countless and subtle cultural rules and distinctions that must be accounted for when trying to analyse the architecture of any society. These cultural factors have also proved to be extremely long-lived and continue to shape the house even when technical conditions become entirely different (in the case presented here, the ritual plan of a house will not change as this 'house' suddenly becomes a compressed, overcrowded room in a block of several). Such traditional rules and customs may even become consciously articulated, as when exiles strive to maintain their identity in a polyethnic context—to maintain their feeling of 'belonging' to a certain group with its traditional (or idealized quasi-traditional) customs.

Notes

1. A fuller description of the Kyirong area is to be found in my doctoral thesis: *The Nation in Your Mind. Continuity and Change among Tibetan Refugees in Nepal*. University of Gothenburg, 1975.
2. The Tamang is a Nepalese ethnic group of probable Tibetan ancestry, inhabiting the middle valleys at around 2,000 m altitude. They are the main landowners of Rasuwa district. Cf. e.g. Dor Bahadur Bista, *People of Nepal*. Kathmandu, 1967.
3. The distribution of houses and lands on an unspecified family basis has led to certain consequences as regards household composition. A discussion of these intricacies would however demand too much space in this context. (Cf. my doctoral thesis, see note 1, above.)

The House in Madagascar

Otto Chr. Dahl

Madagascar is generally considered as an African island. The distance from the island to the African coast is about the same as across the North Sea from Scotland to Norway. From a geographic point of view it is therefore as natural to regard Madagascar as a part of Africa as to recognize Scotland as a part of Europe. However, linguistically and culturally Madagascar is not African, but has close affinities to Indonesia. The language belongs to a linguistic subgroup in southeastern Kalimantan (Borneo), and the people are supposed to have emigrated from there about A.D. 400. There are however some features both in language and culture which point to a possibility of an African substratum.

But the Malagasy house is not African. There are no traces in Madagascar of the round African hut. In all parts of the country the house is rectangular and seems to have Indonesian origin, but the house in Madagascar is much simpler than house-types in Indonesia. There is, for instance, no trace of the Indonesian longhouse which seems to be common in Kalimantan.

The Malagasy word for 'house' in general is *trano*, which etymologically is the same as *dangau* in Malay. But the Malayan word means a hut out in the fields and not an ordinary dwelling house. The first Indonesian settlers in Madagascar must have been colonists, and colonists often use simpler dwellings than they did in their homeland. French colonists very often do not say 'ma maison' in speaking of their house, but 'ma case'. I have the impression that the early Indonesian colonists in Madagascar expressed themselves in a similar way, and that perhaps there was real background for it in the house-type.

On the coasts and in other parts of the island where there are forests, the house has a skeleton of wooden posts. Horizontally between them bamboo or rods are bound with bast on the outer and inner side of the posts, and in between them reed or bamboo or palm leaves form the wall. Or clay may be put between the rods, and then it is plastered with a mixture of clay, cows' dung and sand. The roof is thatched with grass, straw, reed or palm leaves. In most parts of the country the floor is only the ground covered with a mat. But in the eastern parts of the island with a humid climate under the trade wind there is a wooden floor one or two feet above the ground (fig. 1).

In the highlands, where wood is scarce, clay is the ordinary material without the wooden skeleton. In old times it was formed into walls with the hands, and one layer left to dry in the sun before another layer could be placed upon it. Nowadays bricks, burnt or sun-dried, are used instead, and the roof is covered with tiles.

In olden times there were wooden houses built with vertical planks even in the forestless highlands. As the wood had to be brought on men's shoulders from far away, these houses were certainly only for the highest part of society. Two royal dwellings in this style from the eighteenth century are still to be seen in Antananarivo (Tananarive) and another old capital. In times when the highlands were still wooded, this has probably been an ordinary type of house. See Coulaud, p.188.

Fig. 1 In the eastern parts of the island floors of houses are often one or two feet above the ground because of the humid climate.

A special house-type has been observed in Ankaratra, the tall mountains in the centre of the island, at an altitude of 2,000 m. This house has no walls, but the floor has been dug half a metre down in the ground, and the grass-thatched roof is based directly on the soil outside the house. The gables have also an inclination. I have seen a very similar house in Japan, at Tsuyama in western Honshu, where a house of this style had been reconstructed on 2,000-year old foundations found on the spot.

For the sake of completeness let me just mention that there are also a few troglodytes in Madagascar, and that a word signifying a big cavern, *zoma*, etymologically is the same as the Malayan word *rumah* and the Javanese *omah*, which mean 'house'. Another tribe of food-gatherers in the forests of the southwest has no houses at all. They make their fire where they happen to stop in the evening, and only if the wind is blowing too hard, do they make a screen of branches as a shelter on the windside.

The traditional house in Madagascar had only one room. Nowadays, however, you often find two rooms, even far from the cultural centres. And where they build in bricks, you also have houses with two floors.

Houses are small. In general they are inhabited by a nuclear family. In the Sakalava tribe on the west coast grown up children sometimes have their own houses even before being married. In this tribe it was an offence to parents if a son built a bigger house than that of his father. Therefore houses became smaller and smaller with the shift of generations. The greater family ordinarily has houses close to each other, sometimes surrounded by a fence. The traditional place of the house of the head of the family is in the northeastern corner of the fence or of the village. The Sakalava have the place for the great sacrifices to the east of this house (fig. 2). We shall see why.

The normal orientation of the house is north-south all over the island, with the door on the west wall near the southern corner. In the Bara tribe in the southern highlands the opening was sometimes cut out of a single piece of wood in this form ( ) and so narrow that you had to enter sideways. Maybe this was for the defence of the inhabitants. An enemy cannot enter sideways. He will be killed before coming in. Still the door had to be sufficiently large for letting a pregnant woman pass.

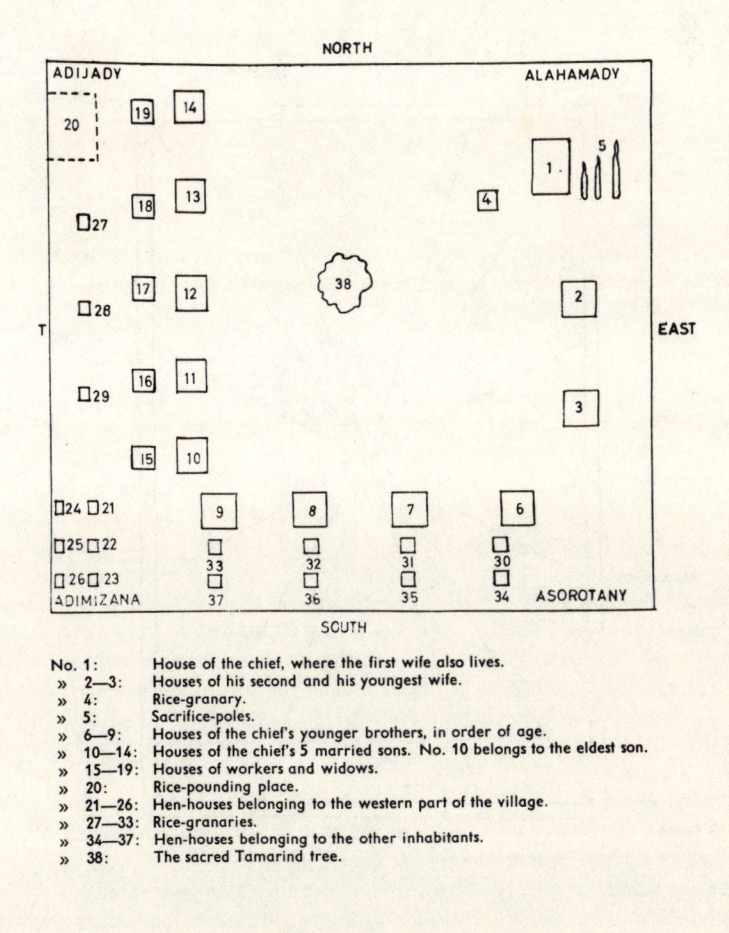

No. 1:	House of the chief, where the first wife also lives.
» 2—3:	Houses of his second and his youngest wife.
» 4:	Rice-granary.
» 5:	Sacrifice-poles.
» 6—9:	Houses of the chief's younger brothers, in order of age.
» 10—14:	Houses of the chief's 5 married sons. No. 10 belongs to the eldest son.
» 15—19:	Houses of workers and widows.
» 20:	Rice-pounding place.
» 21—26:	Hen-houses belonging to the western part of the village.
» 27—33:	Rice-granaries.
» 34—37:	Hen-houses belonging to the other inhabitants.
» 38:	The sacred Tamarind tree.

Fig. 2 Plan of a typical Sakalava village.

In some eastern tribes there is also a door on the east wall near the northern corner. But this door is opened only for carrying out the corpse of a deceased. If the ghost of the defunct comes back, he must follow the same way as that where he was carried out, and as the door is always closed, he cannot enter and become a disturbing revenant within the house. The Sakalava are still more radical. They leave the house where someone has died, and tear it down. If it was a king's house, they cannot tear it down, but put a fence around it and let it fall into decay.

I mentioned the orientation north-south of the house. This is very important for bringing it into the right relationship to the *rohon-tany*, the spirits of the earth. (The word *roho* is borrowed from the Arabic *rūh*, 'spirit, soul'.) If this is not right, it may disturb the destinies of the inhabitants. The reason is that the house is not only a dwelling, but at the same time an astrological calendar. The twelve months of the year and the days of the month have their fixed places along the walls of the house (fig. 3).

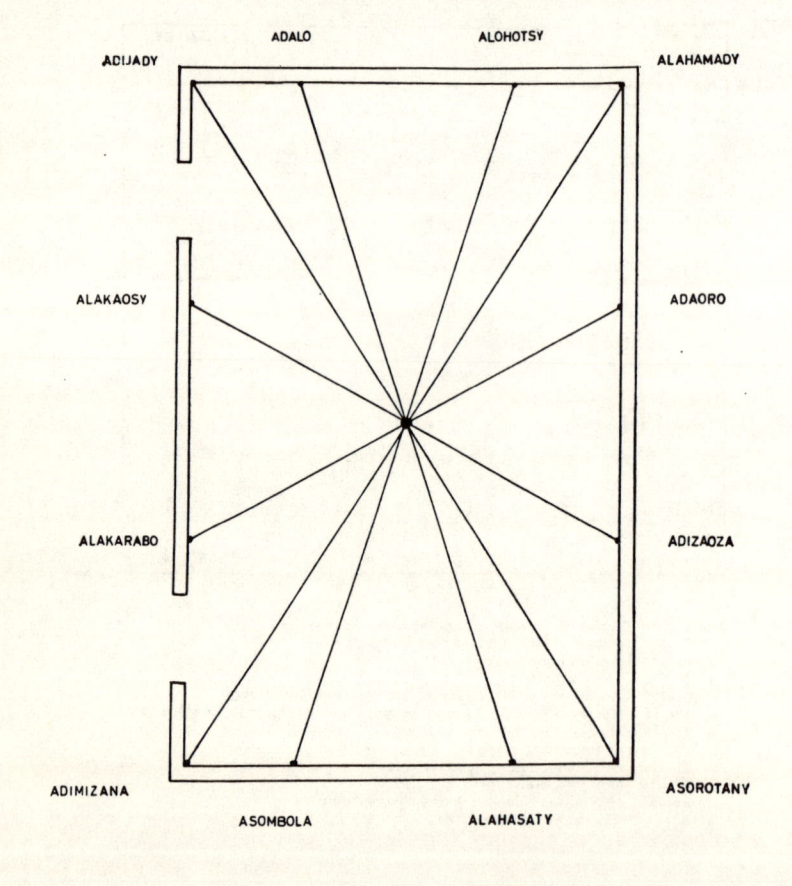

Fig. 3 Opposing destinies in the Malagasy house.

The system is no doubt of Arabic origin. All its terms are borrowed from Arabic. It is a lunar year, a lunar calendar. However, the names of the months are not the ordinary Arabic names of the months, but the names of the constellations of the Zodiac. This shows that originally the calendar has been solar and not lunar and has had an astrological function attached to the stars. It still has for determining the destiny of people, but it has lost its connection with the stars of the sky, of which the Malagasy people have very little knowledge, and it has become a system for calculating destiny directly from the lunar calendar.

The year begins in the northeastern corner of the house. The destiny of this point is called *Alahamady*, which is the Arabic *al-hamal*, 'Aries, the Ram', the first constellation of the Zodiac. One month is placed in each corner of the house, and two on each wall. Thus the twelfth is on the north wall near the northeastern corner, where the next year begins. Not only the months have these names, but also the days of each month. Three days are located in each corner and two in each month-point of the walls. This gives as a total 28 days, but there are 29 or 30 days in a lunar month. Therefore the last day or the last two days of the month have the same name, carry the same destiny, as the month and its first days. When from this point you proceed to the next one, the first day of the next month gets the same name, the same destiny, as the foregoing month. Thus the first two or three days of a month always have the same name, the same destiny, as the month. From these destinies of days and months the fate of the inhabitants is calculated.

It is important that there be no opposition between the destinies of the inhabitants, between husband and wife, between parents and children. There is opposition if a line drawn between their destiny points in the walls passes through the central post of the house (fig. 3). You can not marry a person with an opposite destiny, and if a child is born on a day which is opposed to the parents' destinies, the safest thing to do is to kill the child. The knowledge of the destinies and the system controlling them is a science for specialists. In such questions you have to consult a professional soothsayer. Fortunately he is also sometimes able to change the destiny of the child by exorcisms and by prescribing sacrifices.

We cannot go into more details of destiny here, but we shall have a look at the consequences of the house-calendar for the placing of the furniture in the house (fig.4).

The northeastern corner means the beginning, the origin, and is therefore the corner of the ancestors, the holy place of the house. Here the fetishes of the family are preserved, and here the smaller, the daily sacrifices of food to the ancestors are performed. The holiness of the northeastern corner as the corner of origin explains the reason why the house of the family head is placed in this corner of the village or fence.

At the next destiny at the eastern wall, *Adaoro*, Arabic *aṯ-ṯawr*, 'the Taurus', is the bedplace. This place of the Bull is a strong point and gives strength to the tired couple sleeping there.

The third constellation, Gemini, *Adizaoza*, is called *al-ǧawzā* by the Arabs. The Arabic word does not mean 'twins', but one of its significations is 'irrigation'. Therefore this is the place of the water jug.

The sixth constellation is Virgo, *Asombola*, Arabic *as-sunbula*. The Arabic word

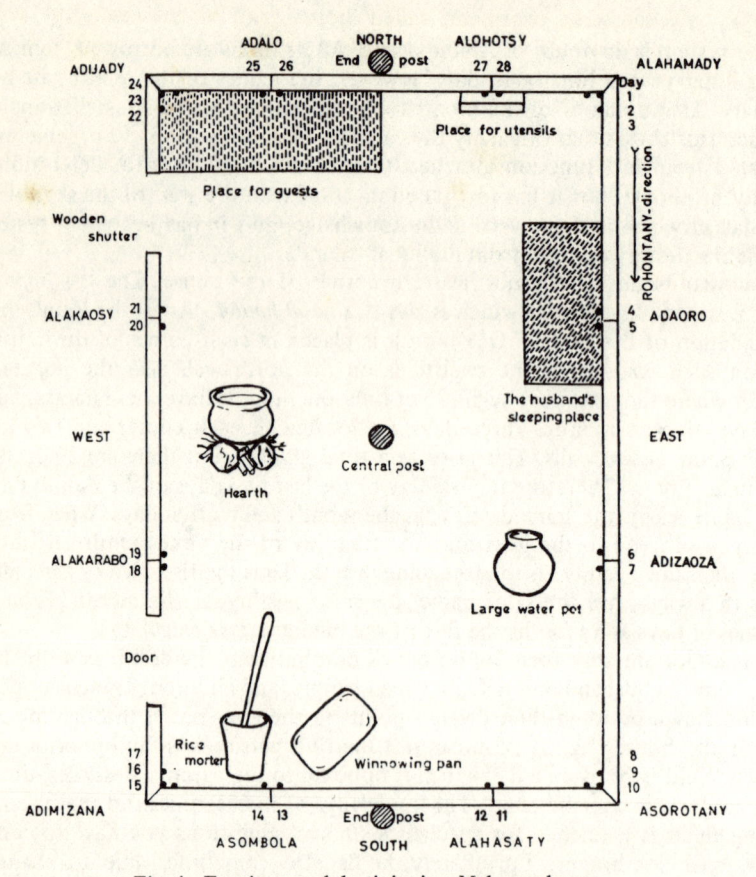

Fig. 4 Furniture and destinies in a Malagasy house.

means 'spike of grain' and is the name of the star, Spica Virginis, which here represents the whole constellation. This is therefore the place of the rice mortar and the winnowing pan.

The seventh is Libra, the Balance, *Adimizana*, Arabic *al-mi zan*, at the southwestern corner. The door moves on its hinges in the same way as the lever of the balance moves over its suspension point. Therefore this is the place of the door, with its hinges near the *Adimizana* corner. We may ask if this is really due to the influence from the Arabic astrology, or if it is much older and has only an incidental relation to the house calendar. The 2,000-year old Japanese house mentioned above had the door at the same point. Is there a cultural affinity between the old Japanese house and the houses in Madagascar or not? I can only ask, not answer.

In Japan I also observed another old feature with a parallel in Madagascar. On the Shinto Shrine in Ise, one of the venerated national sanctuaries of Japan, the gables are surmounted by two rods which form a V. In Madagascar the kings' houses have the same ornament, called 'horns', and on the east coast, where the corpses of the dead are not buried in the earth but put into special houses, these holy burial houses have similar 'horns'.

Other things in the Malagasy house are placed without any observable connection with the meanings of the Zodiac points. The hearth has its normal place to the west of the central post, and the most honourable place in the house is to the north of the hearth. This is given to honoured guests. Here is also often a window. Utensils are placed at the *Alohotsy* point (Arabic *al-hūt* 'pisces') of the northern wall. If fowls and pigs are kept in the house during the night, their place is at the southeastern corner.

Bibliography

Delord, Raymond, Les habitations traditionelles de l'Ankaratra. *Bulletin de l'Academie Malgache*, Vol. 36, Tananarive 1960, pp.307–14.
Ruud, Jorgen, Taboo. *A study of Malagasy customs and beliefs*. Oslo (University Press) 1960. The illustrations above have been taken from this book with the kind permission of the Oslo University Press.
Vig, Lars, *Croyances et moeurs des Malgaches*. Fascicule II. Tananarive (Trano Printy Loterana) 1977.

The Zafimaniry House: A Witness of the Traditional Houses of the Highlands of Madagascar[1]

Daniel Coulaud

It may seem strange in a symposium devoted to 'the house in East and Southeast Asia' to speak about the Malagasy house. The Malagasy, in fact, are a complex mixture of people who came, through different periods of history, from the Malayo-Polynesian world, Indonesia, Southern India, Arabia and the East African coast. The typical features of the civilization of Southeast Asia have been better preserved among the peoples of the highlands who were comparatively late comers (probably around A.D. 1000) and who took a more direct route. The transformation of the environment, the disappearance of the forest—notably on the uplands—has somewhat impaired their original mode of life.

A study of the Zafimaniry is of especial interest from a historical viewpoint: coming from the Highlands, this group sought shelter, in the late eighteenth century, in a wooded area that was rather difficult of access. Whereas on the Highlands swidden agriculture (*tavy*) was superseded by rice-growing and cattle-breeding, and whereas the material and spiritual conditions of life were modified by contact with European influences, the Zafimaniry, enjoying the protection of the forest, have retained much of their original civilization.

The Zafimaniry country (about 700 km^2) stretches on top of the eastern escarpment of Madagascar, east of Ambositra, 200 km to the south-southeast of Tananarive (fig. 1). Its altitude (1,000 to 1,700 m), its coolness, the unusually deep and narrow valleys, the thick vegetation of the forest, the almost perpetual mists and heavy rainfalls (2,000 to 3,000 mm in 250 days a year) due to the southeast trade winds, make it a rugged region which provides excellent shelter. Even today, the only way to go to the country is to walk along difficult paths connecting the 96 villages whose total population amounts to approximately 15,000. The scenic grandeur of the country and the beauty of the villages and houses are most striking.

The house itself cannot be studied independently of its historical and geographical background. It is the tangible result of the visible and invisible worlds. Its aspect, the materials used, its particular disposition, are the expression of the mode of life, economy, social relationships and history of the group. As Professor K. G. Izikowitz has clearly demonstrated, it is a 'microcosm of society', 'the dress of the people'.

The village

Of varying importance, comprising from 5 to 70 houses, the villages usually stand proudly on top of steep hills—a defensive position (fig. 2). The houses are huddled together on hilltops or granite ridges. As building techniques require flat surfaces, men have occupied the summits after levelling and widening them by means of supporting walls. In Faliarivo, 43 houses stand within a 40 x 8 m rectangle, even though it is cluttered with huge granite boulders (fig. 3). Narrow terraces had subse-

THE ZAFIMANIRY HOUSE

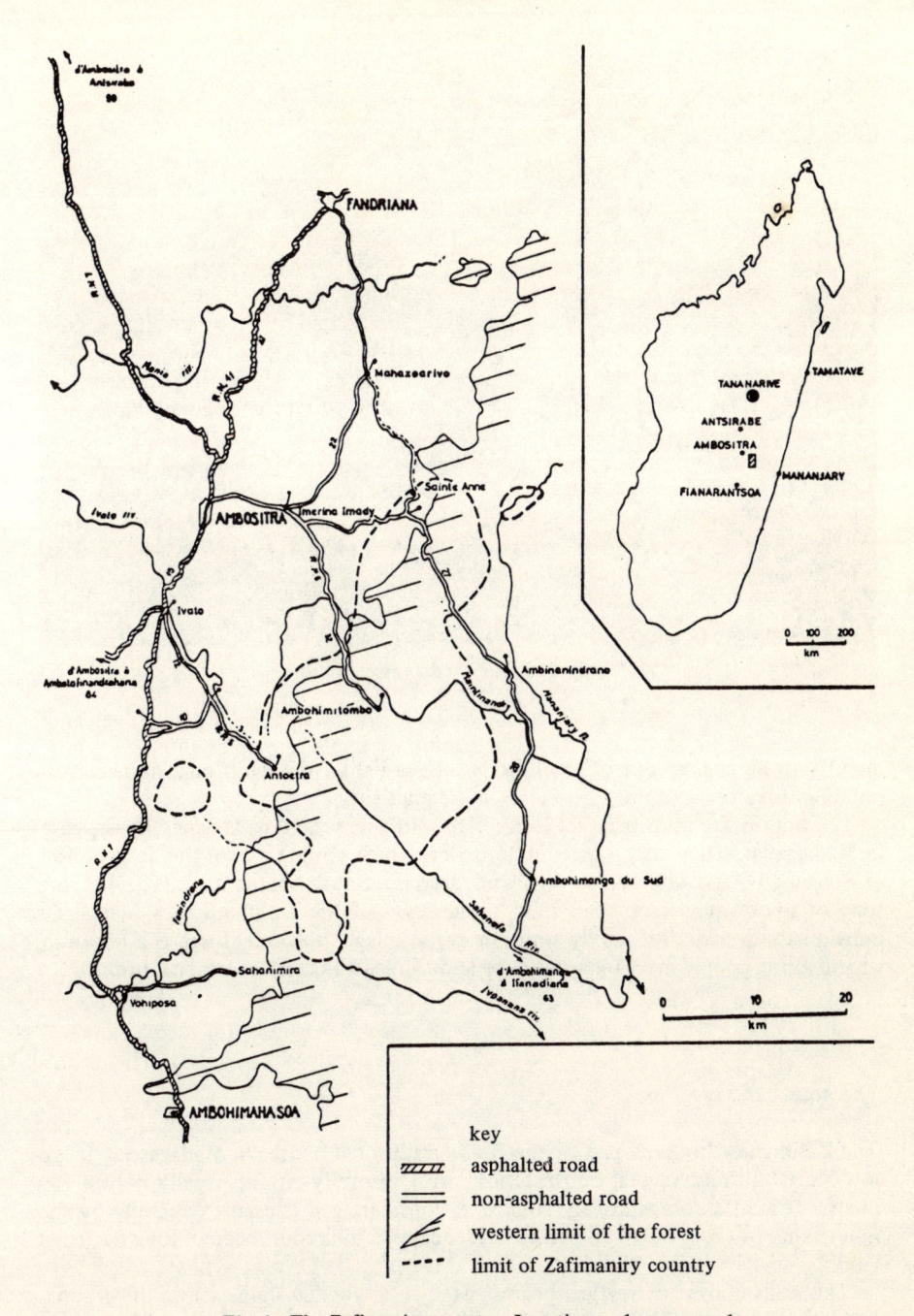

Fig. 1 The Zafimaniry country. Location and access roads.

Fig. 2   Faliarivo – a defensive position.

quently to be cleared out of the hillsides. Thus Faliarivo is built on a slope corresponding to 12 contour lines with a 15 metre gradient.

The houses are invaribaly set in a north-south direction, as is generally the case in Madagascar. They are arranged in long tiers which remind one of the 'long house' of Southeast Asia: Philippines, Thailand, Borneo, South Vietnam . . .(fig. 4). This type of house may have been split, in the case of the Zafimaniry, by increasing individualisation of the family unit. In every village, however, there is a house in which young people meet by age-groups and can lead a partly communal life.

The house: the exterior

The Zafimaniry house is one of the finest traditional houses in Madagascar. It is a low-lying, entirely vegetal construction, with carefully fitted, usually carved elements. It is of a comparatively large size, considering it is used exclusively by the inner family (4 x 5 m on an average). It is capped by a roof made of long flattened bamboo stalks.

The walls consist of vertical beams fitted to a wooden frame set on the ground. Insulation is ensured by means of a small plank resting on the grooves of the beams.

THE ZAFIMANIRY HOUSE

FALIARIVO (1970)
Plan au 1/1000°

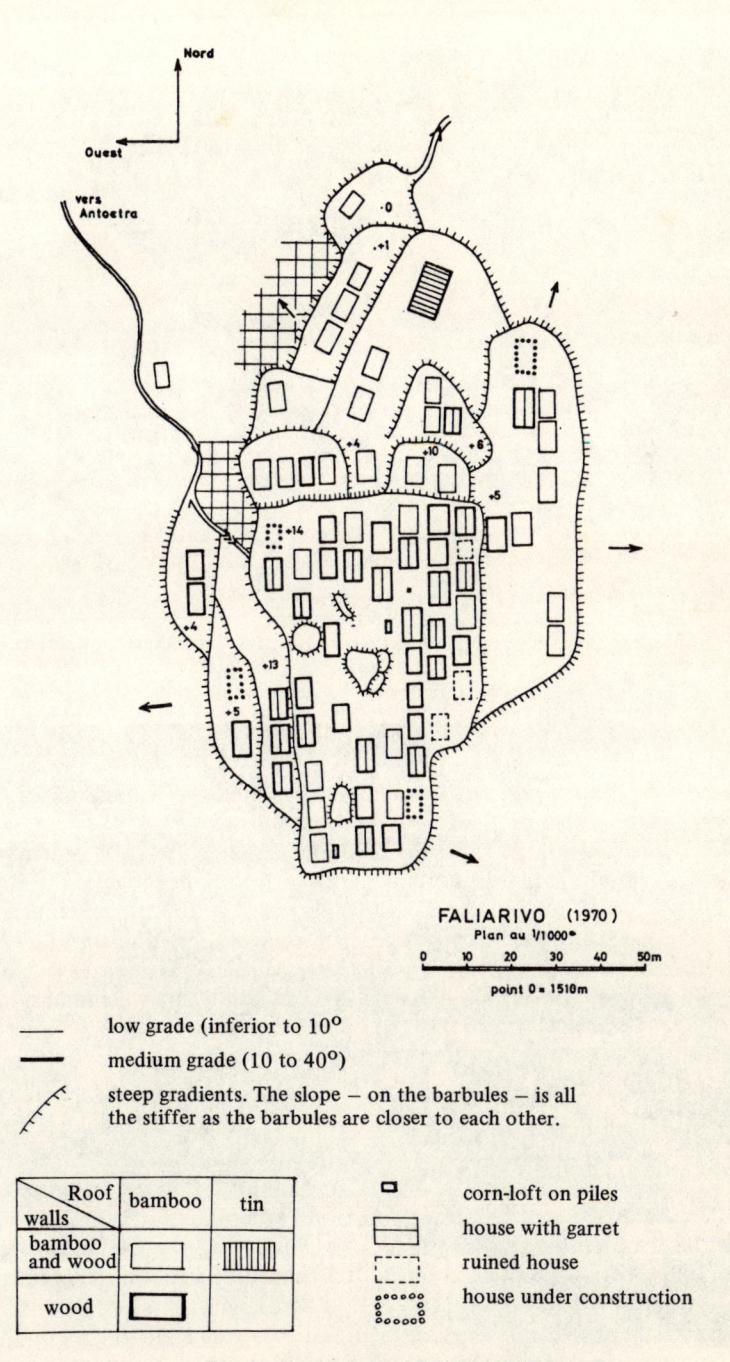

0 10 20 30 40 50m

point 0 = 1510m

— low grade (inferior to 10°)

━ medium grade (10 to 40°)

⟋ steep gradients. The slope — on the barbules — is all the stiffer as the barbules are closer to each other.

Roof\walls	bamboo	tin
bamboo and wood	▭	▦
wood	▭	

▫ corn-loft on piles
▬ house with garret
⌐⌐ ruined house
⁖⁖ house under construction

Fig. 3 Sketch map of Faliarivo (1970).

Fig. 4 Long tiers which remind one irresistibly of the 'long house' of Southeast Asia.

Fig. 6 The triangular gable made of braided bamboo and engraved beams.

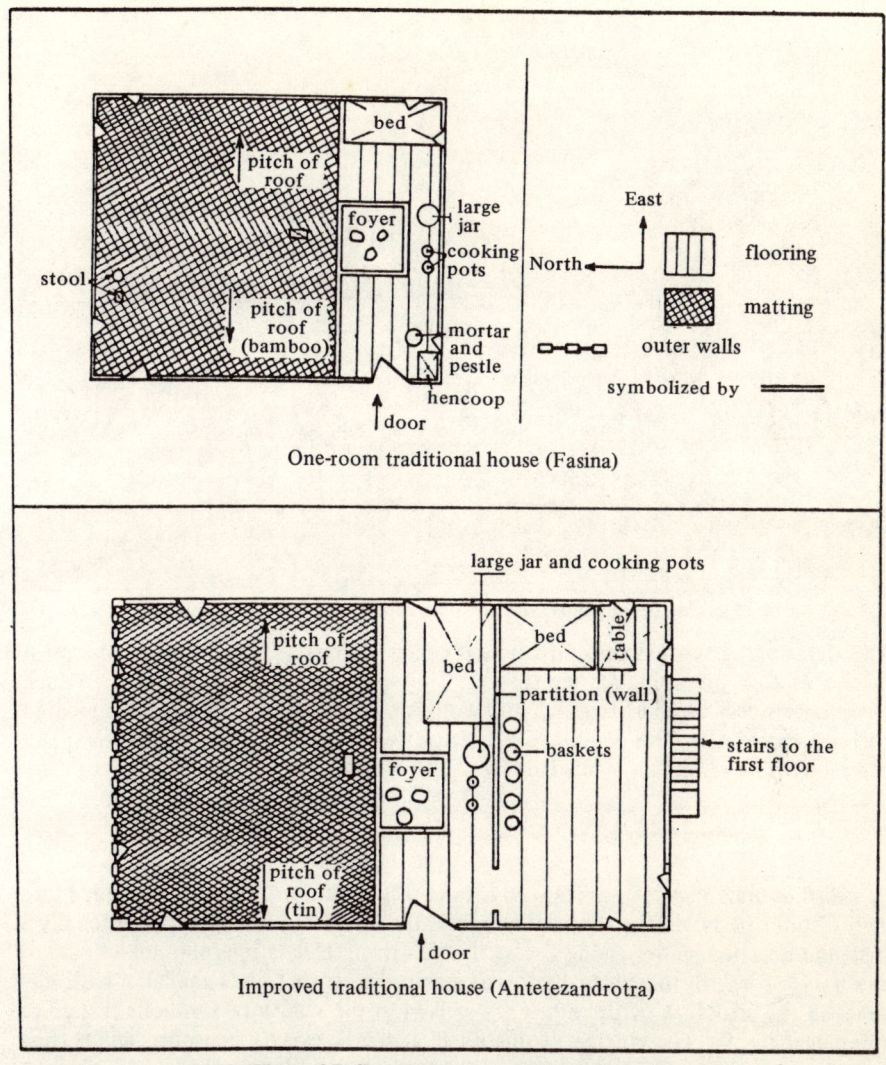

Fig. 5 Plans of Zafimaniry houses. Approximate scale 1/65.

The triangular gable is generally made of braided bamboo (fig. 6). The walls have eight openings (seven windows and one door on the west side). The massive door shutters are ornamented with geometrical motifs which, though of no certain origin, are indisputably very close to Indonesian art. The beams, small planks, the whole surface of the house is engraved with designs forming a herringbone pattern.

This house, although heavy, strong and comfortable, can very easily be taken to pieces, and its transport is a current practice. It is adapted to both the rough climate and the periodic movements necessitated by an economy based on the *tavy*.

Fig. 7 The elements of the house are assembled in a single day by the villagers.

The transport, as well as the construction of a new house, is facilitated by the spirit of cooperation prevailing among villages. This spirit also enables the family, which has progressively brought together the elements of the house, to be accommodated within a single day. The planning of activities would hardly allow a man to spend several weeks working at it unaided (fig. 7).

The house: the interior

A raised doorstep leads up to the only room of the house. This room is divided into two distinct parts: to the south, the hearth, the kitchen, a hen roost, occasionally a bed, the notched ladder giving access to the garret. This is the 'non-noble' part of the house, formerly occupied by the slaves. In the centre stands a pillar, a basic element in the structure of the house, as well as in the residents' symbolic system of reference (fig. 9). The cutting of this pillar in the forest, its transport, and setting into place, are attended by ceremonies—a purely Indonesian feature—in which a pig is sacrificed. North of the pillar is the 'noble' part, where one can receive guests, sitting on three-legged, nicely carved low stools. It is also the part where one eats and sleeps on mats on the ground. An unobtrusive altar is sometimes to be found in the northeast corner, as in most of Madagascar's traditional houses.

The ceiling is high enough to accommodate the corn crop: the cobs tied two by two by their leaves, gradually take on a fine jet-black colour, exposed as they are to the smoke which is a permanent feature of the draught-proof houses. This house is particularly well adapted to the climate (wood is very good insulating material), to the forest environment, to the *tavy* economy (since it is portable), and to social life

Fig. 8 Specimens of shutters. From P. Verin, Les Zafimaniry et leur art. *Revue de Madagascar*, No. 27, 1964, pp. 1–16.

Fig. 9 The interior of a house. To the right (the south) of the central pillar is the 'non-noble' part of the house.

(mutual aid, family quarters). Any modification of these conditions inevitably results in a modification of the house itself.

The Zafimaniry house: the last surviving neo-Indonesian type of house in Madagascar

Ancient texts and archaeological evidence as well as a few relics of earlier buildings lead one to believe that the house still built today by the Zafimaniry was once to be found all over the Malagasy Highlands: in the Imerina and Betsileo regions, but also in the Sihanaka and Betsimisaraka regions on the eastern escarpment.

As the wood supply had to be sought farther and farther away, the wooden house, by the early nineteenth century, became reserved for the chief dignitaries of the kingdom. Some of these houses have come down to us in Imerina and Betsileo country. So wood was replaced very early by pisé and brick, but the oldest prints of Tananarive could still be made of the Zafimaniry type of house, which is characterized by the same overall structure.

The forced migrations caused by the upheavals around the turn of the nineteenth century were followed by voluntary migrations for economic purposes under the firm administration of the Merina dynasty—which ruled Malagasy during most of the nineteenth century—and again under French colonial rule. The slow but general movement towards the southeast made it possible to carry on the most productive form of agricultural exploitation: that of the *tavy*. The border of the Highlands with its vulnerable forest was very soon swept over. As, in the region they now occupy, forest regrowth is easier on a younger soil, under a damper climate, a fairly steady number of Zafimaniry have been able up to now to grow maize and beans on the *tavy*.

More often than not, the wooden house was preceded by a lighter, less comfortable construction made of braided bamboo and gradually replaced, as months passed, by the final construction. Today, the bamboo house tends to become a permanent fixture. The timber is of inferior quality, less attention is paid to careful building, carvings are becoming a rarity. On the edge of the forest, the vegetal elements are being replaced by pisé, brick or cob, so that the houses become less and less distinguishable from present-day Highland constructions.

The causes are manifold. The most obvious one is the disappearance of the forest: a whole phase of the history of the Highlands is now unfolding under our eyes. Permanent cultures (the rice-fields of the flats) are gradually superseding the exhausted *tavy*. Yet this degradation has a different origin: the vulnerability of the forest on the uplands, the demographic upheaval in Zafimaniry country. The peasants have enlarged their *tavy*, accelerated the rhythm of crop rotation, but they are simultaneously kept from moving father west, both by the escarpment and by the Tanala peoples who occupy the lowland which is itself almost entirely deforested.

The search for food and the attendant need of money incite the Zafimaniry to sell the wood which used to go into house-building. The country itself is deserted for the greater part of the year by the men for whom there is a great demand throughout Madagascar owing to their reputation as hard working woodcutters.

The housing problem is receiving individual solutions, such as the search for fresh money (sale of sculptures for the tourists). The rich—for a distinction must now be made between rich and poor—have tin-roofed houses. Some leave the old village and show a growing tendency to live in houses close to the rice fields they have dug out for themselves to replace exhausted *tavy*. In villages on the edge of the forest, some wooden houses still stand among the heterogeneous constructions made of pisé, brick and cob, with or without a second storey, with tin or thatch roofs. The typical layout of the Zafimaniry village is soon lost sight of in what now looks like a shantytown.

Thus we are observing the process by which a people, the last witness of the Highlands' past, is losing its identity. The house bears vivid testimony to the damage suffered: the wooded country can already be regarded as a fossil. Of course this change does not involve only the house, but also the mode of life which becomes less and less agricultural, and increasingly based on the procuring of ready money. Nothing but a radical transformation (already begun in a few villages), such as the change from itinerant swidden agriculture to permanent agriculture, will enable this society to overcome the trauma inflicted by the population boom. Complete extinction of the Zafimaniry villages with their fine wooden houses seems unavoidable. Let us hope it will lead to a new equilibrium in the mode of life of the Zafimaniry.

Note

1. Translated by P. Tibi.